PLOTINUS
A Visionary Recital

MARY CASEY

PLOTINUS

A Visionary Recital

Foreword by
Therese Schroeder-Sheker

After the kingfisher's wing
Has answered light to light, and is silent, the light is still
At the still point of the turning world.
— T. S. Eliot

In thankfulness to
Stephen Mackenna

ANGELICO PRESS
SOPHIA PERENNIS

Angelico Press / Sophia Perennis
Supplemented, retitled edition © 2017
Foreword © Therese Schroeder-Sheker 2017
Second edition 2005
First edition, Rigby & Lewis, 1987
as *Kingfisher's Wing*

For information, address:
Angelico Press
4709 Briar Knoll Dr.
Kettering, OH 45429
angelicopress.com

Series Editor: James R. Wetmore

ISBN 978 1 62138 237 9 (pbk)
ISBN 978 1 62138 238 6 (cloth)

Cover Design: Michael Schrauzer

For
Lucy Amelia Penny

Threnos

'*Beauty, truth and rarity*
Grace in all simplicity...

Death is now the Phoenix' nest,
And the Turtle's loyal breast,
To eternity doth rest...

§

Mary Casey was born in Hampshire in 1915 and died in Dorset at midnight January 30/31, 1980. The Enitharmon Press published two collections of selections from her poems under the titles *Full Circle* and *Christophoros* in 1981; Rigby & Lewis published another selection, *The Clear Shadow*, in 1992; and a selection of journal entries, *A Net in Water*, was published by The Powys Society in 1994. Mary completed three historical novels, of which *Plotinus: A Visionary Recital* is the only one to be published.

Gratitude

to

Louise

&

*"For no greater gift can the gods grant
to a man than this:
a friend who has an understanding heart"*

CONTENTS

Mary Casey's
Plotinus: A Visionary Recital

Generations of Jewish, Christian, and Islamic philosophers and theologians have expressed immeasurable indebtedness to Plotinus (AD 204–270), for whom the Cosmos is a living being, the Eternal is apprehended as Beauty, silence shared is a double freedom, and the supreme aim of human spirituality is union with "the One." Many English-speaking readers have, and treasure, the MacKenna or Armstrong translations of the *Enneads*, and are understandably content to contain their meditations therein. The British writer and Kenyan farmer Mary Casey (1915–1980) loved MacKenna's translation also, and yet took things into a different form. She *lived* into the heart and soul of Plotinian life, death, thought, work, solitude, and creativity. Years later she emerged with what has been called a *visionary recital* of the life of the Neo-Platonic master. Having inhabited an unusually close, insightful, imaginative, and soulful reading of his *Enneads*, she placed as an epigram on the title page a central and timeless image in the T. S. Eliot poem *Burnt Norton*.

> *"After the kingfisher's wing*
> *Has answered light to light, and is silent, the light is still*
> *At the still point of the turning world."*

Mary Casey's recital is illumined with an innate understanding of divergent worlds, schools of thought, cultural perspectives, human interiority, and interiority's redemptive acts and conscious choices. For Plotinus and in the reader, Casey movingly reconciles the Plotinian sense of the microcosmic and macrocosmic, Plato and Origin, Greek and Christian, Alexandria and Egypt, classroom and altar, prayer and thought. She continues with these seeming antimonies and reconciles philosophy and theology, tensile strength and dogmatic rigidity, expansion and contraction, wakefulness and rest, nature and spirit, self-knowledge and avoidance, recollection and Lethe, Gaia and Cosmos, humility and dignity, binding and loosening, and ultimately, life and death.

Casey does so with hermetic and alchemical insight, poetic nuance, and startling authority, and thus she has accomplished things for Plotinus what previous scholars have not, however much we appreciate and revere them. Having treasured this volume as a hidden companion during twenty years of airports, my own Rigby & Lewis first edition [published then as *The Kingfisher's Wing*] is dog-eared and glossed. When I heard that Angelico Press was publishing a new edition, I was overjoyed. There are times when the literary world lauds a work of historical fiction, but I cannot truthfully situate Mary Casey's *Plotinus* in that genre, even though others will. There is something about *Plotinus: A Visionary Recital* that is more epiphany than fiction, more remembrance than reportage, more heartbreaking jolt than comfy read, and more intelligent than smart. The maw of distraction recedes a bit each time we reawaken to an exemplar of disarmament, and Plotinus is just that. Casey's canticle is both haunting and healing, and very warmly recommended.

THERESE SCHROEDER-SHEKER
The Chalice of Repose Project

PREFACE

Miss Kathleen Raine has granted permission for the following passage, from one of her letters to Mary Casey, to be used as a preface to *The Kingfisher's Wing*.

'I want to thank you for the searching self-examination to which *The Kingfisher's Wing* subjected me. The key situations and inter-changes at the level of pure intellectuality reflect the self-searching of my own life as it does of an increasingly great number of our contemporaries: for our time presents us with problems closely parallel to the times of Plotinus.

'You search out the key issues with a subtle insight and serious-ness that is like a conscience speaking from your pages . . . for Plotinus was something far other, and far more, than a philosopher in the diminished modern sense of the term. He was a true "lover of wisdom" – of the spiritual knowledge that has been virtually forgotten in the secular world of the modern west. What you have written is timely, for more and more thoughtful people in our time are deeply dissatisfied with a view of the world reflecting a science only slowly becoming aware of its limitations.

'You have shown what Plotinus was – and that, in the words of Socrates, "the unexamined life is not liveable to man".'

★ ★ ★

'AT THE STILL POINT OF THE TURNING WORLD'

Fullness is All
From Fullness Fullness Flows
Take All from All
Fullness abides
Om
Shantih Shantih Shantih

1.

In all this, all beings, all worlds
dwells the Lord
all that moves in the movement
is His garment
rejoice
rejoice in all this
but beware
beware lest you seek to bend it
to selfish end

2.

rejoice in the world
work in it, accept it
though you live a hundred years
know no fear
do not fear to act
true action does not soil a man

3.

but untrue action
is the killer of the soul
he who acts untruly
moves on to sunless worlds
worlds blind in the darkness

4.

but One there is
swifter than all thought
the Gods cannot touch it
it flies ever beyond them
it is still

in its stillness swifter than all else
in that the Lord of all lives
moves in the waters

5.   He, the Lord, it is that moves
yet moves not
moves not from His stillness
He is outside all movement
inside all movement
in His nearness He is far
in His farness He is near

6.   do not withdraw from the world
He is in all
all is in Him

7.   seeing Him – the Perfect
what grief can touch you?
what illusion deceive you?

8.   He it is that is moving
shining, pure, unpierced by evil
scatheless scarless
all-knowing, never-failing
He orders all in perfection

9.   into worlds of darkness
they plunge who do not know Him
into worlds of greater darkness
they fall who would reduce Him
to their knowing

10.   beyond all our knowing
beyond all our unknowing
He abides
in His stillness
in His swiftness

11.   he who knows Him
in his knowing
and in his unknowing

by his unknowing passes beyond death
and in his knowing reaches the Eternal

12.   into darkness they enter
who are not born again
into greater darkness they
who do not pass beyond birth

13.   He is other than that
which birth brings forth
other than that unborn
that which becomes never

14.   he who knows Him
in the born
and in the unborn
shall reach the Eternal

15.   a cloud, golden and shining
covers His Face
O scatter that cloud
that I may see Thy Face

16.   Thou art the Source
Lord of all creatures
He that sees all
the all-upholder
let me see Thy Form
in the Formless
ingathered in Thy Shining
eternally Blessed

17.   body to ashes
O life return to the Eternal
O Spirit remember
we have striven
remember our strivings
remember remember

18.   O Light Eternal
Holiness unchanging

Shine on our way
let us not stray
along devious ways
for this we pray
ever and ever

Fullness is All
From Fullness Fullness Flows
Take All from All
Fullness abides
Om
Shantih Shantih Shantih

NOTE:
All translation – especially of Sacred Scriptures – is in the nature
of an interpretation. The author of this translation of the *Isha
Upanishad* offers it to all readers of the original as a personal version
in which he has sought to emphasise nuances of meaning that seem
to him especially important and valuable. He would in no way
wish to claim he has rendered adequately the subtle and complex
movements of thought so characteristic of this great Scripture – and
is very aware that to other readers other interpretative emphases
would be more congenial.

G.C.

A PRELIMINARY NOTE ON PLOTINUS

Plotinus, the last of the great philosophers in the classical Greek tradition, was born in Egypt in the year 204 AD. He was about twenty-eight years of age when he conceived a passion for philosophy and before long he discovered, and became a student at, the school of Ammonius Saccas at Alexandria. Of Ammonius we know little but it is certain that the man who was accepted as guide and teacher in philosophy by both Origen and Plotinus must have been a proficient in spiritual knowledge in no ordinary degree. Origen was to achieve a masterly synthesis between his Christian faith and Greek philosophy and exerted an enormous influence on the development of Christian theology. Plotinus – one of the supreme thinkers of the world – was to be a source of creative power and intellectual insight for the deepest streams of Christian, Islamic and Jewish thought throughout the Middle Ages. And today he remains as one of the most potent factors working towards slow but incalculably deep transmutations of western thought.

What we know of the life of Plotinus we owe to his close friend and disciple Porphyry who left a brief account as an introduction to his edition of the writings of his master known as the *Enneads*. Porphyry tells us that Plotinus became interested in Persian and Indian thought – with which he must have become acquainted in Alexandria. Alexandria was at that time the great intellectual and cultural centre of the Roman Empire and to it came students and thinkers and religious seekers from all over the ancient world to exchange ideas and insights. In the face of all these influences Plotinus was intensely receptive and, as need arose, critical. His interest in eastern thought was such that after eleven years with Ammonius he joined an expedition of the Emperor Gordian to Persia in an attempt to reach India. The expedition however was a failure and after Gordian was killed by his own soldiers in Mesopotamia, Plotinus was forced to return as a fugitive to Antioch. From there at the age of forty he went on to Rome where he spent the rest of his life teaching philosophy to all who sought his wisdom. He died in 270 AD in the presence of his friend and physician Eustochius to whom he said shortly before his death: 'I am giving back the Divine in myself to the Divine in the All.'

In some short comments on his personal characteristics Porphyry remarks that Plotinus seemed ashamed of being in the body. 'The body is doomed to fail of its joys and perish.' He would not sit with a painter or sculptor for a portrait as he said he did not wish to leave behind him an image of an image.

He took a close and kindly interest in all who approached him. He became a guardian of many orphan children entrusted to him and fulfilled all the duties of such a trust lovingly and conscientiously. Yet, says Porphyry, he at no time unless in deep sleep relaxed from 'his interior attention, his unbroken concentration . . . his intention towards the Supreme.'

Such was Plotinus the man.

★ ★ ★

Let us now look at some aspects of his vision of 'the architecture of the intelligible universe', to accept a description of his thought used by the foremost Plotinian scholar of our time in England: A. H. Armstrong.

He achieved a synthesis of the metaphysical insights of Plato and Aristotle ethically conditioned by all that was noblest in Stoicism and deepened by his awareness of the spiritual problems stressed by two centuries of the rapidly spreading Christian religion.

For Plotinus the supreme aim of man's spiritual striving is union with 'the One': the timeless source of All – a union which in strict truth already exists yet needs to be consciously realised as existing by man as man. This realisation is achieved by an intuitive intellection on man's part. Such an intellection is possible because the intellectual centre in man is essentially one with the One. However – in order to help the aspirant achieve the necessary spiritual predisposition and intellectual insights effective for realisation Plotinus evolves a metaphysical doctrine as a support to the approach, and in this his doctrine of the Divine is central.

The Divine is, in itself, conceived as a Triad in Unity. The Divine Triad is distinguished intellectually as:

1. The One: the absolute unconditioned ground and source of all.
2. The Divine Mind: the first emanation and intelligible Image of the One.
3. The Divine Soul: the Living Image of the Divine Mind which is the second emanation of the One and which is reflected in the Cosmos.

It must never be forgotten however that these intellectual distinctions are conceived only as practical supports for the finite mind and that the Divine Truth is essentially a Unity.

xviii

The Divine gives birth in its infinite creative outflow to the Cosmos as its temporal Image or Shadow. The Cosmos exists in ceaseless contemplation of, and aspiration of return to, its Divine Source: the One. The Cosmos is a living Being reflecting the Divine Triad back to itself in the One. All modes and manifestations of life in the Cosmos share in their degree in the Divine Life. The Soul of Man is in its essence, the image of the Divine Triad particularised in the space-time life of man in the Cosmos. By realising this Divine Image within his individual soul it is possible for man to effect return to the unconditioned freedom of the Divine. This possibility man shares with all phases of existence which all participate in the Divine outflow and return. It is man's spiritual task to realise this possibility which, in so far as it involves return to the freedom of the Divine, can only be freely undertaken. All manifestation – with its attendant conflict of division and suffering – is conceived as necessitated by the infinite creative outflow of the Divine to the realisation of all possibilities. Yet all suffering is redeemed in that all modes of existence remain centred in the freedom and bliss of their source and return to it. To this absolute source or ground – the Eternal – we say 'all returns' though in truth there can be nothing outside it and therefore 'the return' consists only in realising the truth. But how are we to understand this? In Plotinus' own words: 'It must be at once something in the nature of a unity and yet a motion compact of diversity . . . considering this multifarious power, we declare it to be Essence or Being in so far as it is in some sense a subject or substratum: where we see life we think of it as movement; where all is unvaried self-identity, we call it repose; we know it as, at once, difference and identity when we recognise all is unity in variety.

'Then we reconstruct: we sum all into a collected unity once more, a sole Life in the Supreme; we concentrate diversity and all the endless productions of act: thus we know a life never varying, not becoming what previously it was not, the thing immutably itself, broken by no interval, and knowing this we know Eternity.'

In Plotinus the aspect of the Eternal apprehended as Beauty receives extraordinary emphasis. All finite beauties participate in the One Supreme Beauty which is their source. This Beauty is uttered as Splendour: an eternal shining-forth of the Divine Essence.

But, warns Plotinus, ' . . . to any vision must be brought an eye adapted to what is to be seen and having some likeness to it. Never did eye see the sun less it had first become sun-like, and never can the soul have vision of the Divine Beauty unless it itself be beautiful . . . the Primal Good and the Primal Beauty have one dwelling-place . . . the Fatherland is to us There whence we have come, and There is the Father . . . but what are we to do?

'How lies the path? This is not a journey for the feet; feet bring us only from land to land; nor need you think of coach or ship to carry you; all this order of things you must set aside . . . you must close the eyes and call up another vision which is to be awakened within you; a vision, the birthright of all, which few turn to use . . .'

The thought of Plotinus bears evidence of an infusion of eastern metaphysical doctrines – probably assimilated through contacts established in his Alexandrian years. This makes it of especial interest and value in our time when the deeper religious minds of both east and west are seeking an understanding that has not been readily attainable in the past. It is fascinating to recall that in India during the lifetime of Plotinus there lived another man of supreme metaphysical insight and power. At that time Nagarjuna was initiating the spread of the great Mahayana school of Buddhism in which the *Prajna paramita* doctrines in many respects spring from intuitions essentially at one with those of Plotinus. This is especially noticeable in the use of radical negations when either of these two great minds attempts to articulate in some sense their doctrine of the transcendent Supreme. Nagarjuna's Void and Plotinus' One are indistinguishable once the necessary allowances for different initiating perspectives and philosophical terms have been made. And for Nagarjuna, all beings, all ways have the Void for their Refuge. While for Plotinus all things return to the One: in its fullness we live and move and have our being.

One cannot doubt that Plotinus would have felt at one with those crystallisations of the wisdom of ancient India known as the *Upanishads* (one of which we print as an epigraph to this book) and with the modes of thought that were to flow from them to culminate a thousand years later in the Vedanta. Here we have another example of the profound reciprocities in the mysterious undertides of world-vision that so strike historians of thought. In the approach and emphases of Ramanuja we find a metaphysical perspective deeply congenial to Christian theology as it was to evolve through the Middle Ages in Europe to come to its term in Eckhart, the most Plotinian of Christian thinkers and mystics. Indeed Plotinus remains a key-figure in the deeper understanding of all these movements of thought.

Plotinus' consummate articulation in terms of Greek philosophy of a doctrine that intuits the essential identity of pure metaphysic under the diversity of forms it cannot but assume in history is an achievement of supreme consequence for western man in his attempts to understand himself. In this doctrine the cosmos is seen as metaphysically transparent and the whole of nature becomes a symbol of transcendent realities. Today when, as in the age of Plotinus, we see 'world-views in collision' there is an urgent necessity we arrive at such an understanding: an urgency significantly recognised in the calling of the international conference on Plotinus at Amsterdam in 1984.

But, as is fit, let our last words rest with Plotinus himself: words that sum up all – pointing to a truth that lies at once both within and without the circles of this world:

'Let us hold through our own centre to the centre of all centres as the centres of the great circles of a sphere coincide with that of the sphere to which all belong . . . thus the Supreme as containing no otherness is ever present with us . . . we are always before it but we do not always look . . . when we look our Term is attained; effectively before Him, we lift a choral song full of God . . .'

G.C.

Note: Passages from the *Enneads* quoted above are from Stephen Mackenna's translation.

Thir'd Century A.D. portrait of a philosopher, found at Ostia and thought to be that of Plotinus.

'The truest life is the life of thought.'
Plotinus. Ennead. III.viii.

CHAPTER I

The Festival of Lamps

A faint wind moved through the rushes, they swayed, forgetting the stillness which had held them through the night frozen and silent. The boy in the boat opening his eyes at that whisper saw the river-pool imaging the stars had a different illumination now. The whole surface reflected an obscure radiance from its own deeps, summoned to meet the dawn. Suppose this gleam and this whispering hush of the rushes were to be like this for ever, that this is eternity shining forth from the water? Who says the sun will rise? What is the author of that certainty?

This his thought, purified by sleep or trance, told him, is the hour of contemplation, when there is neither night nor day, the time when the mind's life-stuff is most tensely wrought and free of tension and flaw. It is the gift of the river-god and of the soul of the Sirius star. The energy flashing from Sirius that the river answers, flooding the summer sands.

Parting and pulling the stalks he edged his skiff in among the papyrus wanting a refuge from day, remembering Moses beginning his life of prophecy and law-giving in a rocking basket on the Nile. Then he lay still and flat, his hands at his sides, his fingers sipping the water that stirred in the bed of the boat.

Light of the day returned him to land. He left his boat aslant on the slime that shone like water under the huge heaven, colourless, cloudless, starless, and moved up from the sacred river sinking step by step till he came to firmer ground. A shadow was beside him now but he would not look at the sun. For this day his flight of thought was ended. But he knew now he would not question again, he had prepared in the night on the Nile, and proved his will in the dayspring, from this time his work was not in doubt, it was not of the body but of the mind: to know the highest good. In the bulrushes he had left his limber body, it was a simulacrum of that, unsolid as the dim shadow, passing now over the ridged and cultivated soil, prepared so carefully for the inundation. The sandy alluvium had hardened between his toes when he entered the school-

1

room built of shallow bricks of the same matter, an open room with walls about four feet high and roof above of reeds.

The master who was a Jew, and the best teacher in Lycopolis, taught all the boys who had sharp wits whatever their origin or the religion of their parents. Those who were not eager for learning he drove away, so there were no idlers or dullards among his pupils. They learnt to read and write Greek and Latin in the intervals between the impassioned lectures he gave them on the Septuagint, on Philo, on Plato, on astronomy and music, and on the nature of the soul. The boys with their dark heads, tawny limbs and white tunics were gathered round him. The discourse of the day had not yet begun. In fact there rarely was a formal beginning, the teaching flowed out of the man's thoughts. Often he would begin to share with them his reading of the previous night when the cicadas sang unheard and the moths came from far to his lamp that fostered its flame till day.

Plotinus stood in shadow moving his feet on the sandy floor, watching a sunbeam with motes awirl in the yellow bar, until the master missing his response of mind and wordless understanding waved to him, a command of the hand that could not be denied, although his whispy beard still jerked to his talk, his gray curls swinging out under the small dome of his skullcap. The boy obeyed, the others smiling at his river-stained garb drew him in among them. But today the kindling phrases and half-questions did not touch him. Aloof and life-weary he stood among the rest until the master sensing his absence said suddenly:

'Your daemon has another task for you this morning, dear child. Obey. Go where you will. Yet without you our lesson will win no heartbeats, no flashing glances. Shall we call it a holiday, lads?'

They all denied him this. 'Where shall we go? If he has a daemon we have not. Only your words give life, little master.'

'That is not good,' he waved his thin hands with their golden rings. 'You must think for yourselves, not use what I say as a pleasant drug, or an empty excitement. Perhaps I talk overmuch, but it is all to one end, in my mind if not in yours, it is to awaken your souls; that is, what is divine in every wanderer under the sun. We are made from dust as are these ants busy among our feet, we shall be dust again, but that is not all. We have the gift of recollection, we are one with all those who lived before us and those who come after. They have bequeathed to us, those forefathers, their thought. Now it is our turn. My children, while we breathe, while we know that energy of spirit which is immortal, let us think; then, when we are lost again in the sands as if we had never been – and how can that be? you cry to me, with your sturdy cool limbs and brains afire, your eyes so clear and full of youthful reproaches – then the power of your thought will be of the very woof of human minds, of the substance of the intelligible world which is for ever.'

'Teach us to think, little master,' a Jewish boy said, tossing back his black locks. 'We are not all as this one who does it by nature. See, he looks mildly on us, would give willingly a grave reply, but it is his own thought that he hears. Teach us to think before we go away from Lycopolis, from desert, river, black soil and blank sky. I have heard it is in the desert men learn to think, not in Rome . . . You shake your head. You have taught us to reverence the sages of long ago, to pray to one God, to believe our souls are divine. Now, now, before we go hence into the world of men, teach us to think.'

'O, my beloved children, how can I do that when I in a long life given to the writings of the wise, which are the true temples of meditative reason, have not learnt to do more than praise, assent and wonder at their words? By patience, discipline, discussion, by spiritual devotion, we have tried to make our minds attentive. I can say only, my children: Keep each one for himself a solitude where he may watch and, as the Psalm says, wait on the Lord. Then it may be in this solitude his intellect will turn to the truth, and, if the strength be given, live the truth among men.'

'To think is to know truth with nothing between.'

'Sin?'

The teacher answered quietly: 'After sin comes repentance, acknowledge this as best you may by submission of will. Remember, with the Jews repentance is not grief, it is the act of turning to a new life.'

The sun had left the schoolroom that was built like a lyre. The aged preceptor was bowed over his meditation, the boys moved apart, drifting towards the doorway, to their usual places on the benches, to the shelf where lay stacks of narrow papyri. Not one wanted in his heart to leave that air where poetry and learning mingled, and the freshness and immaturity of their own minds were at once overshadowed and challenged by timeless wisdom. Their other haunts and playgrounds: the streets of the town; the leaden waters of the great river; the hills of limestone honeycombed with tombs in which they would seek for paintings, alien carvings and inscriptions whose hieroglyphs were ever an enchantment to their

3

eyes; these now were as the memory of them might be when the youths were old men.

One after another turned to Plotinus, without speaking, but deciding that it was he who had given the common air another, a sharper texture. As if, one thought, something from the colder regions far to the north they had heard of had entered there, where already the heat was growing heavy with the approach of noon, and touched things with the magic sparkle of hoar-frost. He had had a revelation denied to them, well, no matter for that, for all were embarked together in the same vessel of life. The light one has seen shines for all. The younger boys and those whose souls responded less eagerly to the discourses of their master had already gone. The ones left felt just then they wanted never to go away, even if by staying they only learnt to repeat the words of men who had long ago departed. With an inward certainty they knew now that Plotinus was one whose mind would give a perceptibly different quality to the thought of philosophers in aftertime, the moulding of that vessel was being changed, or even the substance itself.

They looked at him again and he smiled back. They saw his cheeks, always of a remarkable pallor for that land of the sun, had flushed.

'We are only at the beginning,' he whispered.

'What use,' one said, 'to keep thinking and writing and speaking the same things?'

'Because they never are quite the same. Because the soul lives by thought as the body by food. First by what is taken in from outside; but later on all is found within, as one given to contemplation needs less and less food.'

The master looked from one to another of the few who had chosen to stay and added slowly: 'It is incumbent on each one to think until the world is filled with the knowledge of the Lord as the waters cover the sea.'

No more was said at that time. The little preceptor was soon alone under the thatch that rustled more insistently as the desert wind blew fiercely and day waxed. The Greek boy Peter jostled Plotinus between the doorposts and continued walking up the hill at his side.

They overtook bent women with their usual burdens, food or fuel, or sad-eyed young, whose heads nodded to each tired foot-beat.

4

'What is thought to them?' Peter whispered. 'Yet they as we behold the light of the sun. My dear, it is not enough.'

One very old swayed, the hard-won water dashed from her pot to the dust, her hands fumbled for the wall and she leaned there with sunken head.

'Well, what are you going to do then? Unsling the jar from her back, carry it down to the pit in the sand and refill it? Will you do that for every old one who toils up this hill? Could you?' He added more softly: 'Would she be glad if you did?'

By the ruined temple of the wolf-god, from which the city had won its name from the Greeks, the boys came to a stand. Plotinus said: 'I have made my choice this morning. I am going to think and not to suffer. I cannot do both. You can say, if you like, I am not strong enough. That is what I say now, I may find a master who changes it, or myself, my daemon, may, but I think not. Never mind it any more now, Peter. Are you going home, or shall we go among those forgotten graves where you have made so many of your best verses?'

'To the necropolis,' the younger boy said. 'That is the place to lose time, which one of your beloved "elders" called "a certain dance of the intellect".'

'And to press our foreheads against eternity.'

Among the ancient tombs, fragments and stones fallen in the sands, by the columns of the sanctuary of Anubis, the jackal-headed god who presided at the weighing of the hearts of the dead and was still receiving even at that late time, his meed of worship, the boys walked in silence, the best nurse of poetry and philosophy. For, as the master would say at the close of his longest lectures, the force of thought is dissipated in words, dear lads, in silence it comes to white heat, then what you say or write is as though wrought on the anvil. So he would say, and at once go off again on a whole new discussion of dialectic or the art of self-communing aloud. These two pupils understood his praise of both and found for themselves a silence shared was a double freedom, for now and again one would speak something barely intelligible, some mumbled nascent phrase, and the other would leave it unheeded, unless it touched as a spark his own musings, then it might be both minds kindled.

Dogs or jackals skulked in the sandy cemetery, starving, uttering sinister yelps, unalarmed by those two figures so far in thought their human substance carried no threat, though the pariahs fled the lesser boys of the town who came there with the intent to bait them.

'Is the sand alive?' Peter whispered, burying his feet in it, watching how the grains rolled of their own impetus into any scooped hollow, how the shadows of rock profiles changed as the wind shifted the driftage.

'Nothing is without life. That is how we can know things at all, our soul and theirs; they understand better than our reason.'

'Reason rather separates, distributes, divides, divines, without it we could not live grossly as we do in the flesh nor yet have consciousness god-taught. That is the mystery.'

'O, I want to see, to think for myself, for the first time. The weight of reasoning of the elders, of all those before us on the path, is inescapable. I want to begin anew, to begin, Peter, at the beginning.'

'Well, there are two ways of doing that,' the younger boy said, bending his mind to what the other wanted, 'and you will have to learn them both together. All the time you must regard everything as if the reason so unimaginably hidden inside your skull were entirely alone, free of all outward influences, past, present and to come, as if you were a dweller in the very desert from birth, that child we heard of nourished by a gazelle, you remember, whose only art was to run swifter than the wind. The second way is to learn from every man living or dead, whose mind is akin to your own. Find out how he began to think when his world was new to him, move with him step by step. Love him and doubt him. When you have done this, for how long I cannot tell, you will I believe be at the beginning, at the point from which you soar on your own.'

'That is truth. But how do you know it?'

Peter looked less serious. 'Because being a poet and not a philosopher I take flights every moment, back, forward, alighting on flowers, skimming over a dull waste, shedding tears like the rain we never see, and then forgetting the bitter grief as if it had never been. Now you, I take it, must have a method. The gods will guide you.'

'And the daemon that will not let me . . . See! We are not alone today in the ground of graves.'

A man in a parti-coloured cloth fastened on one shoulder was stalking over sand and stones, and by his long shadow they suddenly knew how the day was spent. The emanation that came from him scared them both, their eyes met. 'This sunset,' Peter whispered, 'is the festival of lights, there will be the torchlight procession and

6

everyone will start their lamp-flames that must burn till dawn. Shall we go back?'

'It is like a dream,' Plotinus responded, 'I cannot lift my feet.'

'The dead below hold them fast.'

'So I believe.'

The wild man, his rags blown back, his shameless shadow beside him, strode up to them, halted where they stood by a sunken sand-serrated rock and held up over them his bare arms and gaunt hands and finger-joints articulate as a skeleton's. They saw then his eyes between those cursing or blessing limbs were merry and kindly, black though they were in red whites.

'My children,' he said, 'the plague is coming to Lycopolis, do you know that? Yes, the plague. A camel caravan entered the gates today loaded with corn. Drivers have been dying all the way up the river. Go away if you can. Do not go home. These fevers love youth. You think now you have long to live in the eye of the sun.'

'Stranger,' Plotinus answered in his quiet voice, 'it does not become philosophers to run away, for we study nothing else than to die. While if the gods would have us live long, well then, we can endure their date.'

'Boy, you do not know what you say, untried as you are, bold boyish words without reason. I tell you, children, the black pestilence is on me even now, the first touch of fire, the fury ringing my brain.'

'If that is so, go on to Lycopolis while you have strength. Ask at the gate for my mother's house, she will not refuse you. Peter, give him your stick.'

The wanderer from the desert stared into the clear pale face of the lad in front of him. He had the sense of gazing into water, no murky Nile but the translucent stream of his youth over whose face he had often hung, seeing now on the perfect surface sky and branch, tree and reeded shore, now by a change of vision at which he was adept, the golden shelving bed with ripple traceries and shadowy shoals of fish that shot downstream and turned again to breathe their liquid air. Gladly his dry fingers gripped the knob of Peter's well-polished stick and he hurried on over the sand.

It was then the boys looked at one another, wordlessly weighing the course of their friendship, not long but heavy with value for themselves as they knew now under this threat of annulment. Long after that wastrel figure had gone from them on his unsteady way they stayed silent as though for the first time, for all their talking

7

and philosophical teaching of the little Jew, they had experienced in themselves that the thread of life could on an instant break. And the world go on just the same? What more or less were they than two sand grains of the Egyptian desert?

Still without speech they began to walk in the opposite direction from that bearer of news, which, whether true or false, had had its import for them, and with their shadows behind them presently began to climb towards the limestone cliffs which were the sole emphasis and elevation in the monotonous flat of the landscape of the Nile. In fact those tomb-hollowed hills were ever a hoving presence in the minds of the boys, and they were apt to find their feet bearing them among the encrusted shelves and ledges without any purpose of mind.

'We come among the graves to seek life.' They had reached now the entrance of their favourite sepulchral cell where someone had in later years cut an abraxas figure by the entrance. Within, the Egyptian reliefs were plain with colouring still fresh and the boys had often pondered over the stylised vital men of long ago attending to their inevitable human tasks, and marvelled at the repose of the simply carved effigy of the dead occupant of the tomb. For all the calm, the erect stature with chiselled limbs and remote countenance gave them a sense of intellectual tension. He who knows does not speak. With this statue behind them like an unexplained power in the back of their minds the two boys sat down outside on a kind of balcony with the town below them, the rectangular strips of worked soil beyond, beyond again the river darker than the sand and with certain surprising patches of green reeds. A row of separate white or rose-tinged cloudlets had appeared in the blank blue sky to mark the end of day.

'Our life or theirs?' They glanced into the darkening cave.

'It is all one.'

A serenity spread over them that they associated with a fullness of unanswered questionings. The high awareness of minds that had ceased to think permeated their unresisting tired bodies as if weariness wrought a harmony of overworked heads with limbs and supple skin. They rested in this trance until the lights appeared everywhere at once as at a signal. With a start they acknowledged night, saluted the first stars, then looked down with quiet spontaneous pleasure at the illuminated town. Every open door and unshuttered window offered a burning lamp to the night, and they could see moving lights drawing from all directions towards the square from which a procession of torch-bearers would pass through the streets to the temple.

'As the gods that are for ever we look down on the festival of lamps. Is this shining intended for us?'

'Light shining, a burning purer than fire, the very oil a sacred gift; to me this is the symbol of eternity.'

'The light the dark received not, of the Gnostics?'

Plotinus did not answer.

Peter stood up and said, 'I am going down.'

His shape was black against sky and lamps of heaven and earth, then he was gone.

When Plotinus followed the sharp-edged path down the hillside there was a whiteness in the east, one by one the festival lamps were going out. They must burn till dawn, he thought, remembering also that belief that a flame once given life must not be extinguished but allowed to die of itself. The streets were deserted and shadowy now, though at intervals he passed a still-gleaming dwelling. One cabin with a faint taper at each window watched him as though with inquisitive eyes below the shaggy fringe of thatch.

The flax wick in the terracotta lamp between the central pillars of his home portico had burnt down but a spark still pricked like a glow-worm in the nozzle. He entered the house, groped for some figs and a morsel of bread, and returned to the porch where his cot of rushes was prepared with a blanket of goats' hair. There after feeling for his scrolls on the shelf at the bed's head he lay down, sleepless but thankful. Slaves began to move about the house not long after, he heard the scrape and shuffle of their bare feet, the hiss of papyrus mats, sounds that restored him to infancy, to the breasts of his nurse, that gave him at length to slumber.

He woke in the noon heat to see his sister Deborah standing near his bed in her white robe girdled with agate beads. Her black hair was loose on her shoulders, the glooming eyes in her small sallow face did not see him. She must have been there for a long time, he thought, and forgotten why she came. What a pair of dreamers we are! No wonder mother despairs of her children. He pulled his camel's hair cloak from the peg and threw it at her. She smiled, slowly gathering and folding it.

'You have no mercy, brother, I came to wake you and knew I could not drive so sweet a sleep from your eyelids, but you broke my vision.'

9

'Your eyes were open,' he retorted, 'and so they should look on me.'

'And how seldom when yours are open do they see anything at all that others do.'

She went along the verandah to the cages where the tame quails lived and scattered millet-grains for the little variegated birds, watching closely to see that each one was anxious to feed.

'Deborah!'

But she did not go back.

Plotinus suddenly remembered that threat of the plague. He rose and went to stand by her and said without knowing why: 'Where is the lamp?'

'I have taken it away. I have put it with my dolls.'

'To dedicate to the goddess?'

'Yes, later on perhaps.'

'So you are no longer a child, *core?*'

'No longer.'

'Did a stranger come here last night? A tall fellow, gaunt, sick perhaps, but merry-eyed?'

She nodded. 'About the time of lamp-lighting. I saw the slave give him wine and barley-cakes, and when I asked, Ariston said the stranger came from you.'

'He did not stay?'

'He did not stay. But they said he could not walk well and fell in the roadway when he'd swallowed but three sips of wine.'

Deborah tilted in her hands the red vessel with incised chevron border, her downcast eyes seeing neither pitcher nor birds.

In an uncommon motion of intimacy Plotinus put his hands over hers: 'My sister, are you a bearer of lustral offerings? These pecking fowl do not need purification.'

'I did not notice,' she responded, barely smiling.

'The gods, or the oracle within, order our acts when our mind is in abeyance. I want to see him again, will you try to keep him if he comes?'

She nodded. 'You did not go to school today?'

'Perhaps I shall not go again. I decided, when I was on the river, I had to begin another work.'

'So I shall be the more alone,' she said without reproach.

'And I also.'

'A girl's loneliness is a cluttered one, all day in the house with scolding mama, slaves, and weaving for garments with no end.'

'It will be more precious because you must strive for it; ay, more than honey-sweet life itself. For today, will you come down to the river with me at sunset? We can talk till who knows whether river or sky is the giver of light.' Feeling a tremor he added: 'Not a farewell. I am not leaving Lycopolis yet.'

The earthenware jar slipped from their hands, rolled over the mat scattering its grains, lay still on its side.

'Unharmed, you see.' He gave it back to her. 'But after all there had to be an offering to the gods.'

Plotinus went back to his shelves and took down his most worn codex.

★ ★ ★

The brother and sister with two slaves behind them walked down to the river in the cool air of evening, cool only that is by comparison with the day's heat. The girl's veil fluttered caressingly, their shadows were long on the dust, now side by side, now merged in one as they moved; her jewelled sandals scintillated. Peasants carrying mattocks on their shoulders, stirring up dust with each footfall, glanced askance at those two who trod as on a firm strand cleansed and levelled by the sea.

'Why are we free?' Deborah asked when they stood on the wharf where men were engaged in fastening the cables of a newly berthed grain ship. She looked up at his face which to her vision had always an astral gleam. 'Even in our grief and our tangled thoughts.'

'That is what I want to discover, *core* mine, is it not well to give a life for that? Tell me what more is in your heart, in your soul which knows an immortal life.'

'No shadows now you see, the sun has gone, we can think better.'

Shipmen singing began swinging up the road towards Lycopolis, others lay down on the deck to guard the ship, others again lit fires, and lanterns to hang at prow and stern. A smell of ooze from the river-bed, from mud troubled and inertly subsiding, filtering through arching nostrils into their brain-cavities excited them, the dankness of life-giving death.

'Shall we go farther, listen to the reeds' rustle beginning the rhythm of night, *euphrone*, gentle thought, the tragic writers called it.'

'And wait the stars, whose purer souls speak to ours if we curve our minds to hearken.'

They moved on past the ferry and the thoroughfares of small craft,

11

on past the humblest fishers' floats, those immemorial transports of Nile, two well-bound bundles of reeds yoked together as a pair of oxen. Long-winged birds kept flying upstream, singly, in parties, leaving a sorrowful clamour, lost to unrecording ears.

'Our father used to say,' she began, and he heard no more as the semblance of the venerable Greek corn merchant rose before his inner eye. To owe your being to another man and know nothing of him seemed a monstrous thing just then to Plotinus. The white-bearded husband of the children's only too constantly present Jewish mother had been used to appear at distant intervals and short-lived, when they were small. One evening he would be there and their animal-alert ears would tell them in the altered pace of the lazy slaves as they crisscrossed the courtyard. A few days later at dawn they would be woken by a seemly bustle among the indoor servants, a raised voice, a whinnying horse, and know, as they drowsed he was away again on his business of buying and transporting grain.

Then on a summer noon when they were playing with the sand village they seldom wearied of building, obliterating and rede-signing, nurse had come and squatted beside them; the time when shadows are shortest and there is a certain mercy in the hush of the sun, the deathless falcon, as poised motionless overhead in dazzling quiver of invisible wings he prepares for his fierce swoop to down-ward dark. Her tired face with its network of lines, so comforting to the nervous boy he had wanted to have it bent over him for ever, his head on her breast, held a warning now in its gravity, in the unwonted question in the slant eyes. He would not ask why she had come from her hut in a remote poor quarter but set his fingers to work on the grass of a rickety roof.

'Little ones, I have to tell you your father has found the end of death.'

'He is dead like your sparrow,' Plotinus said almost roughly, alarmed by his sister's stillness. 'It means he will not come to our house any more and bring us beads and carved toys. You know, do you . . . ?'

Deborah said nothing.

'Where did he die?' the boy asked, standing up and refusing to go near the hand offered, palm upwards.

'At Alexandria.'

'Where the boats go up the great river.'

Plotinus with his eyes on the Nile, as the waste of water received that secret luminosity belonging to dusk and dawn when its diurnal sullenness and sickly gleaming ripples were transformed, and the river became mirror of heaven, could remember nothing else any of them had said that noon. He turned to the girl and sensed her white wavering form in-drawn among the reeds, where innumerable small birds sought shelter twittering amid lisping leaves, so that he whispered harshly:

'Take care of the river-god!' And close after in his usual even utterance: 'What said he?'

'I think it was the last time he came home,' Deborah spoke in reverie as a breeze shifted the restless rooted reeds. 'I was sitting up in bed holding my wooden doll, the one without hair, he sat on the beam the cords go through and leaned towards me stiffly yet rather as if he were falling, recovered, did this several times. At last when he was upright, I asked why he did this. "To attract your attention perhaps. When you were smaller you tried to attract mine. Now it is the other way about." I thought he was smiling but I knew underneath he was very sad with a sadness quite unforgettable by me. "I want to tell you children something. Remember. And that it is for you both. You will know when to say it. You are free. You are not born in human bonds as are other children of men. To you, a girl-child, this is not a mystery. Your brother will give his life to learning this freedom and it may be he will distil it in words, a sacred wisdom for those who come after. The better way is to know in silence, as you do." He was there a little longer in the twilight, for no lamp was lit, but not thinking of me any more. Then he kissed me and went out of the room, and the door shut.'

She trembled. One of the slaves stepped near and spread a dark cloak over her shoulders. 'Why then are we free?' Deborah repeated the words, yet scarcely as a question.

A shudder passed through them both.

'Because we know now. But that, since we have become bodies does not absolve us from the necessity of being in our bodies, experiencing in our own all others, always returning by another way, which is the same, to this, as our feet always guide us to the river.'

'This is our desolation, that we must not be together in this way again. We are children no more.'

Plotinus bowed his head.

They went up from the river hand in hand.

CHAPTER II

The Business of Philosophy

The fever that ran to and fro that season among the inhabitants of
Lycopolis was not a deadly one. Few died but many fell sick and
the lethargy made all spirits sink, the life-tide of the place ebbed,
business dragged. The crescent moon Plotinus and the girl had seen
low over the Nile on the night of their farewell waxed, became a
splendid circle, and dwindled again self-devoured, and still he did
not leave his place on the portico. It was not that he'd taken the
plague but rather as if Nile had been lethean to him: he had
forgotten the past, he had no urge to the future. His eyes were
blurred, so that although the *Odyssey* lay always at hand he could
not read a line, nor would memory advance one. Twice a day Kezia
the ancient Jewess and housekeeper brought him cool water and a
handful of dried fruit. A slow-footed slave came to attend to the
quails, never Deborah.

On a night of starry radiance his eyes opened on a pair of winking
sandals at his bedside bound below two white and narrow feet;
recognising by her perfume his mother, he looked no higher.

'Up my child, tie on your sandals and walk out to see the stars!'

'You command as a goddess, mama. I am too weak.'

'No, no, you are not. You have pleased yourself long enough
lying at ease on your bed. Stand upon your feet.'

'I please myself?'

'That's it. You have been happy there with no thought for a bedfellow. That is why I didn't come. Now, you need a spur.'

'Perhaps you are right.'

'I am very right. What you are doing, I see, is talking instead of
obeying.'

He sat up, reached his camel's hair cloak from the foot of his
couch and wrapped it round his shoulders. He did all else she bid
and at last stood.

'Now we go outside.'

When they had taken three or four turns in front of the house
he admitted: 'You are right.'

'It is the stars,' his mother nodded, 'they shine into your soul,

14

show you the path you have chosen. You know, you must go alone. You and Deborah have parted. It is our turn now.'

'How do you know this, mama?'

'The voice of the Spirit,' she said, with a jerk of her small round head. 'We shall not be thus again, my son.' She looked up at him sealing in memory his head with wide brow and uncut curling hair, shadowy by the fiery Arcturus, but not without a gleam of its own. 'Plotinus.'

He bent over her and her two wild hands seized his head, brought it to her breasts. He felt nail-points in his scalp, and an inward wrench as though her backbone broke. She let go and was gone. He heard her voice ring through the house rating the slaves.

In the morning he called Kezia when she came with his spring water.

'I want to send a message to my friend Peter. Will you ask Ariston to take it, now before he starts his work, before Peter goes forth? Will you tell him, Cassia dear?'

'What shall I tell him my child?'

'I want to see Peter. Ask him to come here to see me.'

'They say he had the plague.'

'He will be better now, Kezia, I know he is better,' Plotinus replied confidently. 'Only send!'

Before he'd finished his raisins he knew the boy's tread. And Peter, wasted by fever, was before him in his linen tunic with the red motif at the hem he always affected. He held three apples.

Plotinus took them, smiling a little: ' "Comfort me with apples for I am sick for love." How did you come so quick, quick as my thought for you?'

'I was on the way when I met your slave.' The Greek boy sat down on a stool with seat of woven papyrus reed and held his head. 'The fever still chimes in my brain-pan.'

After a pause they spoke exactly together: 'What did you want me for?'

Plotinus answered first: 'To see you, to be sure, to look into your eyes which do for stars by day.'

'To tell you our master is sick and those who have seen him say he asks for you, ever and again.'

'I must go to him.'

'You have been ill too?'

'No,' with a shake of the head, 'only suffering from a severance.'

'From what?'

15

'From my body.'

'I wish I could, when it is plague-bitten.'

'Mine is for good.'

The boy-poet considered his older friend curiously: 'Do you know what you are doing in your youth, and untried?'

'I am not doing anything. Psyche has left my limbs.'

'And now dwells in your head alone? Well, at least you are not with the dead. And I can for you, very willingly . . .' And he made a satyrish movement on the stool.

'Can you go with me to our pedagogue?'

'I am fagged enough coming to you.'

'Well, then.'

'I am going to talk to your sister.'

Plotinus whistled for a slave to bind on his sandals and give him a staff, adorned with studs and fitted to his height. He left the house unattended.

The familiar road to the school he had trodden in every phase of his daemonic moods, so that corners, old doorways, sagging roofs, all its hollows and windings, were like a map he could use to recall thoughts that had lit or shaded his consciousness, was now as a scene revisited in dreams, recognisable but different, and with that oppressive indefinable dream sense of something unknown and inimical beyond its broken fringe. His body was sluggish too instead of mercurially winged by his mind, he had to force it on. At length he saw the silent school, sad as a nest deserted by the young birds, forgotten by the food-bearing parents, which yet, weary as he was, summoned him to salute it.

The floor was unswept, ants scurried among broken whisps of sedge, long-legged hornets were building dwellings of earth on the rafters, the work of spiders netted all, the dust-covered benches were all tablets on which one could write. The shade welcomed him; spectre-like scattering neither dust nor insects he sat down on the end of the bench against the wall, the place which had always been his, and knew his soul as an unshining light. Stone statue of the rock tombs was not more still. A snake moving on its belly over the stale unsunned soil, raising now and then a hissing head with pronged tongue darting, ventured near sensing absence and neglect. Over the youth's unfeeling foot it slid and coiled about the ankle.

Voices thin and husky disturbed the marmoreal figure and his cool attendant who glided away through the cracks of the wall. Brown children naked or with ragged loin-cloths peeped round the doorway, entered, began to patter with hard-soled fearless feet about the unused school. The querulous curious cries hushed at the signal of the leading urchin who suddenly caught the motionless but not unseeing eye of Plotinus. Each child checked exactly as he was, as at a signal of the song-master. The morsels of human skin and bone with no more sap than insects, that yet challenged him with ambiguous slant-eyed looks through their elf-locks, touched him, as if the disharmony their intrusion wrought in him suddenly became a new gift of the muses.

Standing by the statue of Atlas, groaning under the ponderous dusty sphere he bore on his shoulder, Plotinus caught up a brass pot as tymbal and tapped out with a small stick a dancing-measure known to all the young of Lycopolis. One by one his infant chorus responded; he began the refrain, they took it up, word and gesture joined in rhythm. When breath was scant under the thin ribs he changed the air; recognising dismissal the children linked hand in hand in a ring round him tossed from mouth to mouth: 'Away, away, go away'; until, as in panic, they broke loose and fled from gloom to outer glare.

Absently pushing with his finger through the dust on the celestial sphere Plotinus recollected the master he was going to see and placing him in an obvious mental niche he returned thought by thought to that certain gathering inwardness of consciousness by which he was used to approach his soul.

The sun was high in the aqueous sheen of heaven when Plotinus left that cool coverture of the school roof and followed the path to the master's house, well-beaten into the soil by many meditative footfalls. The sorrowful habitation with dry cisterns and stunted shade trees made him regretful he had not visited the teacher sooner, and that even now he had lingered on his way. The taut-woven web is such that a pull on one thread is communicated to the whole mysteriously attenuated criss-cross, whether of man's body or of the universe itself. Jeremy the deaf-mute who was the only attendant of the philosopher was bearing a waterpot on his shoulder from the well to the rickety door that leaned open aslant as on hinges of cobweb. He was a long-limbed young man with graceful movements known to Plotinus, who had learnt also the careful system of signals by which master and slave guided their intercourse.

When the jar was safely set on its hollowed stone within, as he knew by the sound, Plotinus entered also and laid his hand on Jeremy's forearm. A gleam crossed the sad features of the servant and his obscure eyes kindled, he caught the visitor's tunic and drew him on. Foul odours hung on the air in the inner room where the little teacher sat unbending as a statue on his cot, his yellow rumpled robe falling from the rake-like shoulders. His gaunt head armed with straggly beard was sunk into the wall where its uneasy turnings had worn a groove.

'I come too late,' Plotinus reproached himself, half aloud.

'You could not come before,' the dry reply, as though uttered by a crevice of the mud wall, reached him with no delay. 'We are both ready now.'

'Yes, ready for . . .'

'Death and life. I to speak and to die. You to hear and prepare . . . to live as that insistent daemon of yours will have you. My mind clears, I can remember again, that means, my dear child, the end.'

'The end of death, as Homer would say,' Plotinus' quiet voice and impassive manner betrayed nothing, but his spirit quailed before this third parting. He grudged death the little preceptor who had given his pupils a certain boldness to approach philosophy. 'Never keep your souls hooded for fear of a strange matter,' he would say, 'reason will dull all, use and train your mind as we try to do here but let them have a winged playmate.'

'No matter. What I must say now, boy, is that I leave you, my best pupil, this little dwelling, a mere shell it is true, but with a sweet kernel for one who has mind bared for thought, my papyri, my codices, the works of men of older time, or younger should I say: nearer I believe to the truth.'

The little Jew was spent, his breath came in long-parted gasps, his body shrank still more seeking to be spared the rending of soul from nerves and bones. But words came again.

'Do not go after teachers wiser than I too soon. You have all you need here for a time. Study alone. So will your spirit grow free, dear son, you will not be confused by the multitude of counsellors.'

'I will stay here.'

'That is well. But you may not find it easy. . . . Solitude must be learnt . . . as well as lived.'

'I will teach also, if the boys of your school . . . will have me.'

A spark flashed as of the hard-won hidden fire of silica, the yellow garb twitched and fluttered. 'I ask no more.'

Plotinus took the insect body beneath its expiring wings and laid it lower in the bed. Then he opened the Septuagint, a rare parchment copied in miraculous faultless script, and began to read aloud from the Book of Job. Embarked on the majestic stream he read on, knowing no better power to bear his soul, until he came to the stones of darkness, the shadow of death. At that his eyes luminous with poetry dazzled on the page. Unwilling he moved them to the little master and knew in that face, shining forth, now present, eternity.

A few of the young men and boys who had been taught by the little master followed his corpse to the Jewish burial-ground outside Asyut. When this was over Plotinus returned to his mother's house telling himself he would collect his books and have the slaves carry them, with what else was needed, to the dwelling of reeds beyond the school. Deborah was feeding the quails, she gave him a silent greeting with unquestioning eyes and would have gone away, but her heart forbade her to leave him in the utter bleakness of mood his face betrayed. Side by side they moved to that corner of the portico which had been his from childhood. The girl took a silver knife and began paring an apple.

'Marcus has arrived,' she said presently, testing her brother's ablation. Though he did not look up she was aware he hearkened. 'He has gone out now, but he will return to see you. He has come on business . . . he wants you to go back with him to Alexandria.'

The words fell as a shower of sparks onto the mind that had seemed so numb, he felt a kindling of quivering flames, dancing over the surface they began to generate a warmth, an illusory glow. He began eating another apple.

'I will wait till he comes back.'

The parchments and codices were packed in a carved and inlaid chest. Another lined with sweet-smelling wood was brought and Kezia folded his blankets and laid over them cloaks and tunics. Returning from the garden-court Plotinus was arrested by the scene, symbol of all departures, leave-taking, farewell: a stance of envious time. The bed bare of coverings, the closed chest, the one open with a cloak hung from its raised lid, aimless sandals pairless over the floor, a snarl of thongs. Routed, distressed, his belongings were, in the absence of the slaves, seeking another order.

'So, you will come with me. That is well, just what I hoped. It is high time you began to earn your livelihood.'

Marcus, short and dark-browed, walked right up to his cousin holding out hands which somehow fell unclasped. He was several years older, the Roman blood all but defeating the Greek in his well-protected veins, yet the affinity was not lost, was still supported by adventures shared in childhood.

'And besides, you will find yourself at home in Alexandria, surely, the port is a hotbed of philosophy, new notions sail in with every ship and the schools sift them all. All beyond me, but high thinking makes a place living.'

Plotinus looked gravely down into the small eyes, all but level with cheek- and brow-bones, admired the friendly features and square skull. 'You tempt me, dear, more, it must be, than you can know; I think I may promise you the time for this will come. But it is not now. I have made a compact . . .'

'Of what kind? With whom?'

'With death. With myself, if you prefer.'

Marcus shook his head. 'You can't want to stay here, where time is reckoned by nothing but Nile, his colours and his floods.'

'That immemorial reckoning suits me well. I am . . . not ready yet for the schools, Marcus, and a Nile backwater is no bad place for solitary study.'

'But how will you live?'

'I am going to teach,' Plotinus said with a grand air. 'I am leaving my mother's roof.'

His cousin stared at the unsmiling lips, at the whole cold head, shuddered as at a piece of chilly sculpture. 'Gone away,' he stated, adding to himself: 'In the name of what?'

'Speculation.'

'What made you choose that, of all things?'

'One doesn't choose . . .'

'O, the daemon. How we used to talk about it!' Marcus gave a boyish laugh. 'Stay here tonight. Who knows if we meet again? I have no immortal god within, when I die I am gone for ever; but this night let us take as a gift from greater gods than your indwelling one!'

Plotinus did smile then, whistled for the slaves, bade them remake his bed and spread another beside it for the guest. They brought a brazier burning perfumed fuel to keep off mosquitoes, glasses and a flagon of wine.

'Shall we ask others?'

'Rather keep for ourselves alone this island interval before our ships sail opposite ways.'

'Alexandria is before me. One day I shall go there.'

'But then, I may not be there.'

20

Their eyes met in silence, Plotinus very slightly shook his head.

After dark they walked long outside, never exceeding a certain measured promenade. The sky above the horizon was uncertainly luminous with a reflection of distant lightnings. Single words, fragments of poetry or talk, unanswerable questions that showed an intimate concern for the other, passed between them at random: fringes of deeper thought brushing the silence of their communion.

'I ask nothing more of life,' Marcus said at last, coming to a halt.

'You understand now the repose of the deathless gods? It is to take leave of oneself on earth with every breath. For mortals, that is to know the life of the soul.'

'So there is no fear of dying. This is freedom. But I shall forget . . .'

'That you will not. Your heart will not. Even your busy mind will be embraced by a sense of this consummation, do what you will, what you must, making offering here of what you have known elsewhere.'

'How do you know this, without initiation?'

'In a sense, only those who already know can receive initiation. You take what I say, it may be because of our love for each other. It is complete, Marcus, but it is also the point from which I set out. I have to prove this by reasoning, as other philosophers do, before I can return to the point which although it is steadfast seems, because of all the different approaches, to move as we move.'

'And those who do not understand? They think, don't they, as little as their shadows which companion them on earth and are as mindless as they themselves soon will be in Hades.'

'Well, they can look after us while we are here,' Plotinus answered with a haughty lift of the head.

Marcus objected: 'If all life is one there can be no separateness.'

'That is true. The same life belongs to plants which grow, we think, to feed asses and skittish goats. Even to stones that lie dumb. But it is our mind and hand that give eloquence to stones by sculpture and building.'

'And so, you would say, we use lesser human minds.'

'Why not? Those that can be used. But what concerns me is for my own to do its task as best it may.' He frowned.

Sadly in the shadow of the house roof Deborah observed them, envying their talk, twisting together her thin fingers. When they come in . . . she thought, and then: But it would be no use, the talk would not be the same if I were with them. She saw how they walked on, paused again; caught tones not words. Softly with bowed head the young girl withdrew to her own room, lay down with hand over hand on her breast. In her narrow bed she remembered how Peter had advised her to compose poems. She felt with her mind for words, brought one to ring against another, asked them to sing.

Awake and with intermittent speech the two rested also side by side on their corded beds, the wine forgotten, the dying brazier giving an odd report now and again as the metal cooled.

'From the little I've heeded you are in for a conflict, a kind of Odysseus' contest or pancratium, when you do let yourself go into that great city. The ferment is in the air; passionate missiles blaze about it like meteorites. Even a numbskull, such as this beside you, that would steer a calm course, can't escape those exalted ones dangling above it in mid-heaven like Socrates in his basket. And there are others abased his foot spurns unwilling. It is all matter in skulls, cousin, there is no balance of broad shaggy chests and stout limbs that you used to declaim of from your most prized scroll, when we'd pushed our boat well in among the reeds.'

'I shall never forsake Homer.'

The words floated across from one couch to the other as in a luminous craft, a boat with a lamp shining on the prow. Silence washed back with waves of solitariness.

'There is a restlessness among them more human than divine.'

'Nothing in human minds is resolved once and for all, the struggle achieves nothing, yet because it is of the creation eternally creating the soul of the universe we, who know this, must allow our life to fulfil itself in thought: contemplation and act in one. It might be said somewhat in this way, Marcus: If the mind and the intellect in living beings can do both the body is forgotten, yet remains a passive strength. Men who live in action draw their force from the intellect that is ceaselessly contemplating without consciousness. How can I say it, delving with difficulty; the unconscious intellect dwelling in truth cannot need in any way man's thought, but his thought comes back from it to other men who unknowing receive this essential succour.'

'How do you, almost untutored, know this that you say, confirming, not questioning?'

'For the most part it is recollection, as my master Plato would have it. A word can put the end of a thread into one's hand, a guide to follow step by step. Into some haunted caverns of the soul too it can take one, where veritably the reason quails and loses the guide.'

22

Marcus did not miss the grimness in the quiet voice, but he made no protest, for it told him Plotinus and his deity were inexorable. He raised his head to have it on a level with that other which he knew had been held high all through their talk, arrogant, suffering nothing but the subtle air to impede its liberties. In that dim outline that was yet not without an obscure lucency Marcus sensed the whole high tragedy of man alone in the starry universe. His own unwontedly whetted awareness was, not without a certain malevolence, bred of the contact of their both brains. Sighing he owned how soon, unsustained, he would sink. He launched then a fiery pinnace that foundered in the dark gulf between them.

'Lethe?'

When he woke dawn had mysteriously, movelessly, begun to drink the blackness of night. The unmistakable limpidity, not yet light, tender and alert with promise, touched bleakly the forgotten shapes near him. Memory was yet covered by the waters of sleep. In a divine serenity Marcus waited the restoring of his submerged mind. Chirrupings, gritty pipings, a reiterated teasing sibilance, a clear flute call once heard, awaited with longing by the echo no other note would wake.

When he could see enough he began to study the face on the other cot. The statuesque features of his companion were unchanged in repose, only the day, before sunrise, revealed a patina which made them less imperious. The composed soul and the daemonic spirit were defined in the physical contour. He heard slaves astir disturbing the dormant air. Black hands laid clean tunics on the two beds. A freshly incandescent brazier committed aromatic vapours to the darkness that rose from the river at this hour. A bowl of fruit appeared with cool and hot gleams on an ivory stand. Marcus sighed; that dish of lapis lazuli spoke to him of the day's duties, of the parting to be. He threw back the soft coverings of his sleep, stood, stretched, stared down at Plotinus.

'Are you awake?'

'My eyes sleep but my heart does not sleep.' The answer came quickly in no drowsy tone.

'I must go down to the ship and talk to the men, see the cargo . . .' Marcus yawned. 'I'll come back to see your mother again before I embark. Will you be here?'

The wistfulness in the last simple phrase caused his cousin to sit up. 'We've had our talk, no profit, I think, in a backwash. Come

23

out with me to see the sun rise, with his charism on us we can take our two ways.' And he himself rose up.

CHAPTER III

The Tower of Saturn

The scrap of a house, made of torn palm-fronds and papyrus with floor of stamped earth and the two end-walls of sun-dried bricks of mud, was well scoured and refreshed by Jeremy, whose devotion to his new youthful master was manifest. When his mother's slaves had brought his own belongings there, dumped them in the middle of the main room and shuffled away, Plotinus signalled to his servant to bring from shelf and box the papyri and rare parchments of the little master. And in these he was silently absorbed for the rest of the day. The ones he needed for his daily bread he set apart, the others he listed scrupulously, making many notes on their subjects and particular virtues beside the titles. He was not aware, until his eyes smarted unendurably, that the sun he and Marcus had hailed together had swept with falcon wings across all heaven and gone down beyond the Nile. At that coming-to, and the remembrance no Marcus would hear him or speak that night, his heart dropped stone-wise. Both were embarked now for their voyage through the dark. Did not the sun sail under earth in a shining vessel? *Vale, vale!*

He went out and found the fisherman's way down to the great river.

Lizards, like cameos here and there on the walls, basked in the lamplight when he returned to the room. A mess of fish and eggs, with fruit, bread and wine, was ready for him, and he blessed the servant who was invisible as well as mute. Surely in this hut his mind would be both composed and enlarged. He laid his hands on the papyri that would be its sustenance, the silent waters and springs of other minds.

Tomorrow he would begin teaching in the school, those fellows of his own whose parents were not doubtful of the youth of the master, and a number of lesser ones. He had no zeal for the task, yet he admitted any work that wrought with the substance mind could avail his philosophy, sharpen with life not knowing reflection his sheer intellect. Children also did not shy away from the abstract as so often their elders did, with them it might be he could share the poetry in his heart, his brain-beat. The little delicate-toed ones on the walls had changed their stations and were again set. Moths made mazy death-dances about the lamp. Plotinus stood up, his eyes denying further study; his spirit, just then oppressed by solitariness, sent him to long-legged pacing.

A sense of interior stillness presently possessed him as he rhythmically and unconsciously crossed and recrossed the hollowed floor. His mind lost its too eager searchings, took rest on the underlying tranquillity of intellect, of pure being which is without striving. And it came to him he must learn to be bountiful to being, to believe in the incommunicable nature of it which fulfils itself in emptiness. What use, without this, of the cerebral gymnastics, acts that only found satisfaction in ever more acts: first, the one act, which is contemplation, and which is also the life of reason. The mind however intensely grappling must never forget this. It must when need be take on a kind of opaqueness to its task-master; and what was that, time, reason, the tutelary genius? Even now he was tracking the quiet. Let be. The tide of unbinding flows over all, fluidity itself has an ultimate tenseness.

The youth and mystic transparency of Plotinus, his beauty that was purely Greek and could belong to no other time than the Homeric when gods moved among men, and spoke and loved, not as visions but as living immortal substance, had its influence on the boys who came day by day to learn under the grass roof of the school, or under the trees whose midget foliage cast dancing dappled shade on their faces, on their earnest hands. His unseeingness dissolved their mischief, their minds caught his passion for scholarship which was communicated to them with an apparent impassiveness that caused their wildness to run off it, their response to run quicksilverly into it. Dormant and dull also were happy under his spell. The smallest, labouring with anguish at their Greek and Latin letters, understood, when they carried their copies to him and looked up to his face and eyes, that merely to scratch in the wax of their tablets the sprightly Greek was giving them entry to another world.

With every lesson it was the same: counting and adding on the abacus; astronomy on the cerulean sphere of Atlas; the intervals of music. They learnt 'rounds' and game-songs and those epigrams written in bright sunshine for poets gone down to Hades. At the end of school each day one of the older boys chose and read a few lines from Homer, which all repeated after him over and over so that they carried home willy-nilly this high music singing in their heads.

Peter and one or two others who had been school-friends came in and out at will, discoursing among the empty benches, reading their own poems and verses or plunging into talk of philosophy.

For determined his own studies should not suffer, Plotinus forbade everyone to visit him in his papyrus lodge, and so those who most wanted him got into the way of catching him before he left the school. And it was always the desire of these age-fellows to start discussions so absorbing that he would forget to go home. Their minds would kindle, the flame leap from one to another until darkness fell and all the ways grew shadowy. Then he would bid them farewell, and still they would follow him to the very threshold of his own door. There with his grave uncommunicative manner he would gently close that frail defence of the lightnings of his brain and stand behind it listening to the high-pitched voices receding, dying in the nothingness of night. When the last echoes had lapsed he undid again the leather latch of the token of his liberty and went out to the stars alone.

One afternoon of feast and fair in the town when every boy had left him early Plotinus began examining a scroll he had found dusty and stained behind a stack of papyri. Even as he carried it the tingling in his finger-tips warned him he had something here of stormy meaning. He stood by the slanting board on which such writings were unrolled and laid open to the searching eye, wondering at the scintillant contact of human hands and lettered wisdom. The polished ivory slid easily through, he secured the two ends, then heard footsteps on the path. A figure passed along by the low wall, head hidden by the sedgy eaves, crossed with no pause the worn threshold of the school. He was a young man fair and pale who walked by the master and halted rather oddly behind him.

With fingers just grazing the frayed edges of the scroll Plotinus half turned to acknowledge the unwanted visitor. The young man's smile was so gay, so uncommitted as he leaned against the palm-pillar, it appeared he came with no purpose of speech. The unrolling scroll crackled. Then there was silence.

Not till the slow darkening of the school caused him to look up, impatiently because the faint lettering was escaping him, was the master reminded by an unwonted sense of his mood being shared, that he was not alone. Yet, was there someone by the quiet post

27

that sustained the ridgepole, or was there not? Was it the sprite of the dryad who had been born with the palm-fibres and now died as they dried?

'I believe now what they say in Asyut, that the new teacher is a sage for all his youth.'

Plotinus thought: He came to see me. He did not speak. I know by the flashes of light, the commerce of no words, his soul lives as mine does in that height which is also a dread deep. But, he continued to himself, unsmiling, but not without the influence of a smile in his thought, I do not want to ask him to go home with me. He stepped backwards and let his hand rest on the same post above the other's shoulder.

'You come to see me?'

No third, not the elemental tree nymph herself, could have told which of those countenances in the Egyptian twilight was the more irradiant. The solemn luminosity of human passions transcended was in them both. They were as two jewels whose differing facets struck one from the other a new brilliance, whose depths were never to mingle. Plotinus was the first to veil the mingling of flashing glances although he did not look away. Only the other had the sense that the man before him was a pool of limpid unreflecting water over which his own fires played unquenched. He answered at once, almost before the other voice was hushed.

'I came to know whether I could sometimes talk to your boys. I am no teacher but . . . but there are things I would like to say to them. Could we form a compact? There may be some among them whose hearts are open to my words . . . as well as to yours.'

'Willingly.'

'You do not ask what I would say?'

'There is only one thing men as you and I are seek to say. To one another we have no need to speak. We stand on one ground, though it may be you face outward, I within.'

'There is conflict as well as love, through these we must find . . .'

'The father and creator of the universe.' Plotinus moved back a step: 'And when he is found, or shall I say the soul approaches to him, it is hard to declare him to all.'

'This may be done by means of symbols.'

'Pure thought which is life has no need of symbols. I know, in both there is danger, but take care my children do not take your shapes in matter for truth.'

'You cannot leave people in darkness who do not think. You can show . . .'

'This is the difference between us, my dear, for I have not before seen *Sophia* so alight in a man's eyes. You believe you can teach others knowledge, I that it can only be known.'

'This difference will be as long as there are men on the earth. But if the wise men of old had not tried to teach their inmost thought to others?'

'We should not have been as we are? But by their words we move into what cannot be taught. That is all.'

'We move on.'

'Ah!'

'We climb.'

'By means of more words which ever say less? There is need of one alone, which was in the beginning.'

'But that one was not alone, being with God.'

'Did I not read also there,' Plotinus moved his hand in the direction of the scroll, 'the Word was God?' He shook his head: 'Is God.'

Darkness was deep now under the roof; they spoke not face to face but to a sensed mass of other human being, to a dim pallor on the air.

'We are both preachers, we shall have to talk to others more able to listen. But indeed, in preaching we address ourselves, in true preaching, which like any other activity of the intellect is a discovering of itself for itself.'

'Yes, it is not wanting to tell these others to agree with what we are trying to say, it is with the hope that one word or another will awaken a soul to . . .'

'Know that which is in all souls.'

'I must go,' the young fair man said, and did not move.

'That is a pity. This night will not be given again. Our thoughts weaving themselves have been softly laid together as two pieces of cloth, of different colours it may be but of kindred texture. Come again, if you will, to my school.'

'Which is like a stable.'

Plotinus smiled in the darkness. 'There is no need even of a stable, for the birth of the word.' He sensed an inward flinch but there was no move to go.

On the roof an owl called: Who, Who, Who.

'The being alone, that too is a support. Why deny it?'

29

'O, I do *not*. But it is the simplest. Why build round it . . . ?'

'Because to live a human, a mortal life . . . there is need of stays for the frail mind.'

'Ship ashore propped, but afloat a godlike freedom. The inward virtue holds planks taut among buffeting waves.'

'You trust to your own virtue . . . too much.'

'That cannot be.' Plotinus moved slightly so that his shoulder and hip touched the other's, then away again. 'The virtue is the infinite, not mine more than any other's.'

'But you cannot know it without grace.'

'If you know it, it is a regression to devote yourself to the means, whatever they may be. Don't you see that?'

'The fishers, the diggers of channels for Father Nile . . .'

Plotinus scowled at him in the darkness. 'They know all. Grace is not helped by words. Go and talk to them if you cannot bear to do nothing.'

'You need to learn . . . a great deal.'

'I agree. And I shall. But at the end I shall know no more than I do now. Than they do.' He heard a sigh. 'Never mind. Come back and talk to the boys.' He went outside. 'Stranger, they are dancing in the town, and singing. Do you hear the flutes?' He walked away, a shadow beside him on the ground.

Leaving the shortest way, he turned down towards the river until he came to some cattle lying apart one from another, heavily slumbrous, but not unaware of that lithe figure. The grass, as his feet told him, was newly sprung after irrigation, the animals were pleasantly satisfied. He heard their grass-sweet breaths puffed out on the night. The denial of human companionship, which was something he knew would be with him all his life, pressed upon him with its emptiness. He had not recognised he was tired but somnolence was in that air lagging over their horned heads. Without taking another step he pulled his cloak close round and lay down a few paces from the polished hoofs.

For a time he thought of his evening's visitor, wondered if he would return, then he looked into the glittering points of stars. Their fires quivered through him, each darting star-ray meeting a strung nerve, until he sighed with the kine in quiet ecstasy. High notes of flutes went and came. Forgetting the festival he believed they drew up from the river, from Pan and his syrinx. No god ever dies, let them say what they will. He called then on Hypnos.

30

He opened his eyes at dawn on the void. Stars, clouds, colour were all absent, yet the remote tenuous air was taut as his thoughtless mind. The two became one with nothing between. When he stood, unaware he had moved, still wholly in sleep's embrace, the ground round showed strewn with odd remnants of the fair: a broken pipe, fragments of gourds, gaudy cloth in torn strips. He saw skins of sucked fruits, nutshells, a stub of burnt-out torch. The grass, coaxed from the arid earth with hard-won water, was bruised and darkened by dancing feet. No cows lay near though he saw their flattened lairs. He stared at the place where one was couchant beside him when he lay down.

Half wondering what had so changed the scene – that it was early for the cattle to be taken up he knew, and what should bring madcap revellers so far from the altars and their usual dancing-floors he could not tell – , he felt his soul gathering itself together for the interior cosmic exploring to which his life on earth was dedicated by his indwelling daemon. It was this reasoned exploring under the guidance of the Greek masters which alone gave a sense of purpose to him at that most intense level of his being which it was his determination constantly to experience. Everything now was to be devoted to this realisation of all the highest soul, enclosing and impregnating a mortal body, could know. Anything might draw him away, not so much down, because he believed he could recognise and spurn such meaner evils and desires, but aside, aslant, causing him as he regarded it, though he had not expressed it in words till now, to be off-centre. And the two most potent of these influences, because they were themselves of the very fabric of his daemon-led or daemon-deluded spirit, were poetry and Aphrodite.

Still standing where he had risen amid the refuse of the festival, and it did cause him a momentary contraction of his midriff to imagine those totty ones performing their whirligigs about him helpless and sleeping – and could *his* sleep, often the shyest of guests, have possibly been proof against them? – he told himself his present task, before he dared the warfare of the schools of philosophy, was to yield himself to these two, the muse and the goddess, to the point, and not a hair's-breadth beyond it, where his own intellectual intensity lost nothing to them and their all but irresistible demands ministered to his soul.

Then, and it was a rare thing with him, he laughed, aloud but on a low intimate note, mocking his seriousness and his mental arrangements which greed of flesh, fires in the blood, and bones

31

wholly dissolved could be instant to overset. Yet there was no denying his mind and spirit had made the resolve; kept or not it had its significance.

He walked away, absently avoiding the offerings, his face dark in that moment of gravity that after the radiance of dawn foretells sunrise. With trumpets of silent glory the light-giver sprang over earth's rim. Plotinus had a shadow. Without intent he glanced back. A small figure was half bending now here now there about the place he had quitted, gathering up the scatterings of the festive night.

In the cool of early morning Jeremy was at work trimming back the herbs he kept growing and watered by the walls of the hut. A frank sharp smell of cut aromatic leaves greeted Plotinus; he watched the blade flash and slash, saw broad toes braced in sand sealed by water, enjoyed a physical awareness of time that did not pass in the presence of the slave, in his careful unpremeditated actions. Because you do not consciously think, try to guide the knife, it works unerring. How much, in the same way, is the cutting edge of mind influenced by what it does not know it is thinking? Is, he continued, reasoning aloud in this reassuring oblivious company, the true quality of a man's mind to be reckoned by what he thinks he knows, in the sense of being able to express it in the ceaseless dialogue with itself of our master Plato; or is it rather by the mute ground which might be said to consist of hieroglyphs, complete unjoined images like the wordless writing of the Egyptians of old? Weary with speculating he checked Jeremy with a chafing movement on his shoulder and went inside. In a few moments he was enduring from a rough towel the friction that set all his skin atingle. This over he splashed face and head with a few handfuls of water and sat down in front of his table with its neat narrow piles of papyri and closely-rolled scrolls. He did not observe the fruit and bread placed exactly before him by Jeremy.

★　★　★

Days went by almost unregarded, he could not have told how many times the Nile had changed from green scumminess of lowest flow, when the river lay like a stinking dead dragon, to the brief terracotta of the first flood. How many times in full might and spread and speed the immense torrent had swept by, when his feet had carried him near the threatened banks, aware of nothing but the tide of his thoughts, he could not say. What made some mark on him was the

32

growth of his pupils, those few among them who from boys had changed to thinking men and companions. His mind without warning rebelled, because as it suddenly seemed to him like a snake ready to slough its skin, it would take no denial and he knew the time had come to quit Asyut. He was sitting at the table in the hut, which was now more decay than structure, when the sensation of necessary expansion became irresistible. He faced it quietly and began to consider how he should provide for the school, gently restoring the manuscript he had been studying to its place in the pile.

★　★　★

The next morning the school was crowded when Plotinus arrived late, dressed in the finest of his three tunics, woven and embroidered by Deborah, and a pair of new sandals she had given him that creaked faintly and had a smell of newly tanned hide which pleased him. He walked between the boys and they swayed aside giving a wide way, and with downcast eyes unobserving until he was standing between Atlas straining with the sphere and the desk with its load of lessons and fair copies of the children's hands. By his manner they knew less whether the morning would begin with silence, with a reading from Homer, or with a discourse by their master, which was always what they hoped most for, because his voice was as life to them and his winged words flew among them warm, aquiver as new-feathered birds. He raised his eyes and they knew by the glint at once veiled again, he was going to speak.

'I have to tell you, my children, I am going away. This is the last time I shall be with you in the morning light before the heat comes to lull and dull our minds, the light that makes sweet our earliest studies. I have to say – farewell and remember. Remember in this pure light, the second dawn that spreads the sun's serene over all the earth after his sanguine rising, as the light of intellect shining through mind, the visions the god has granted us. Now, obeying the god, I have to go into the heat, and I ask you to pray I may there, in the stress and strife of minds, know what I am about and that the will of god may have liberty in me. Now, before I go away, take each one a scrap of papyrus and write for me, in one word or ten, not more, the truth he finds in his own breast. This will be your gift to me of farewell. Not this, not this . . .'

For they were all moving, standing, stirring, tearing up the ordered discipline they had learnt from him. 'In sorrow it is well to

33

have work for the hands. See, while you write for me I will talk to the older ones, hoping someone among them . . .'

But he could not stay them. With faces white as his own but without voices or tears all the boys surged round him, holding out their hands with supplication, with appeal, straining to reach him, some looking to his face, others with troubled heads bent as if they feared to look because soon he would not be there for their eyes to see. Wondering, he moved his own hands towards them, touching hair or shoulder or hot palm, saying at last: 'We can pray to all the gods who hold broad heaven and who, my children, are in the soul of each one of us. For you know, for that is what we have learnt together, it is the god in us who allows us to pray to the gods. And that prayer is made in silence. You know that.'

But they would not pray, they would not be comforted.

Then Plotinus gave his rare laugh and lifting his voice said:

'See, we all live, we have freedom in life and behold the light of the sun. We can part without lamentation but, because we have met, with joy.'

The winged word lit in their hearts. They went back each to his place, while the master keeping near him the oldest boys talked to them of the future of the school. The scrawled scraps were carried to him and he read each one aloud, repeating the best more than once, praising the poets. ' "Old Nilus is full with the tears of the ages, I will add no more." "We are the first to hear this teaching, we shall not forget, nor will the many who come after us." "The truth I know is the god in this man's breast." "When my little brother died I did not have this sorrow." "The sun the rock the shadow." "Thought does not grow old." "The sand runs through the hands, one grain of gold stays." "Long I remember the flight of the white bird." "Who made this school a sure vessel for unknown voyaging." "The shades of the old masters meditate here." "The first throw of a far-shadowing spear." "There is Nemesis for man who makes himself the equal of the gods." ' He read that again, and looked round at the boys with the full blaze of his often veiled eyes, so that many quailed before that gaze.

But he was among them now. There was no ceremony of leave-taking but a word and a quiet look for every boy so that each one felt himself no longer a child in his own mind but as one free in the kingdom of thought. Then when he stood in the doorway and they supposed they must watch him walking out of their lives, taking with him the glory that had shone on them also, there was a hush, as though that day they'd all played truant. But standing by the doorpost, neither under the clear sky nor under the shadowy roof, Plotinus gave his last order to his pupils. He asked them to go home. Obedient, remembering former discipline, they made a file and singly in their smooth tunics went past him into the sunshine, holding up their hands in farewell, saying one word that meant both hail and farewell.

Long after they'd gone he stood there knowing in his heart the sorrow he had denied them, waiting on the unwanted finality into which, like a chasm opened in earth, all had sunk of his past, his well-planned days of teaching and study and abstraction. Then, as at the beginning, he went alone into the building with its dry chaffy smell and motes adance in shafts of light. What he made there was a surrender of his state of schoolmaster, wondering whether with this would go the natural arrogance that one boy had said would summon Nemesis, smiling because he knew it was *hubris* that led him to make the gesture, that he could do nothing without that. His mind, long accustomed to halt unbuttressed by future or past, groped forward for no support, remained as a mote sustained by its own whirl in the sunbeam.

He felt again his mind making that calculated thrust against a too confining skin, and held his head high. The time had come to go to Alexandria. For the first time he let it be said aloud in his consciousness. For the last time he looked round his school, laid his hand on loaded Atlas, took from the desk two miniature scrolls of the length and thickness of his middle finger. On these for his own use he had copied certain sayings of Heraclitus, Homer, and Plato, as well as the introduction to the golden gospel he had discovered and was reading when the Christian visited him; they went wherever he did in a fold of his tunic, stitched for their safe carrying by Jeremy.

He began to consider now which of the works from the library of the little Jew must also go with him and which he would leave for the man who would come after him. This led him to wonder what it would cost to repair the frail hovel and make it welcoming for another tenant. He had little left of the small sums his pupils had irregularly brought him, and there was the passage down to the city of the Greek king. At this his overstrained spirit did give an involuntary bound, at this prospect of a voyage on the ancientest of all traffic-bearers, the river Aegyptus. And there was a second leap when he remembered his journey would end at the streams of Ocean.

Before this: Jeremy, Deborah, a walk to the wharf to find a ship sailing, in two days perhaps, or ten, it did not matter. His daemon would not let him stay longer than that though. He remembered Peter who was busy with trade now between Lycopolis and other towns on the river, who wrote poetry no more. Then for some reason he remembered the man they'd met in the graveyard of Anubis, and never seen again, the man who had told them the plague was coming to Asyut. With that he walked out of the school, after he had pressed his forehead against the palm-pillar and against the two doorposts, and took the way he and Peter took that day to the necropolis.

The sense of mystery inseparable from any ceremonial repetition was with him as his new sandals dipped in the dust. He was alone now with no clear-voiced companion. The limestone hills honey-combed with tombs scowled down on him, because – was it? – he walked living the road on which so many clay cold ones had taken their last earth-faring. Unaware he moved his hands over his supple skin, feeling his soul, that was seldom unburdened, pleasantly released from the preoccupations of the school. Under a slanting slab of rock he snuggled into the warm soil of the cemetery and gave himself to the sensation of meditation.

In that dust which had received the flesh and bones of human centuries beyond mind's reckoning, he experienced an enlargement of his thoughts, a nameless expanding which he partly mistrusted as being a loss of the divine intensity of texture he valued above all else, that intensity which he believed to be his essential nature and whose tautness and glistening was the will of the daemon. This expansion and slackening of the shimmering net was, he presently began to tell himself, a preparation for those studies in philosophy, in the wisdom of all men and all cities, which he expected to embark on in Alexandria. From Plato he had learned that the daemon-kind is a half-way nature between the divine and the human, and it was his daemon, Plotinus now decided, among the graves of the cemetery of Anubis, the deity who weighed souls against a feather, that was compelling him to train his human understanding to know the divine. But, and he pressed dusty palms over eyes and brow, what is it that knows that perfect knowledge is; if within, why the doubt, why this labour of the thinking mind? In approaching the mysteries there are stages, purgation, illumination, intuition; but all are present together, not steps, not a process in time. Intuition is eternal, universal, essential to all beings ensouled. What then? In one day an interchange of mind-states, emptiness and sterility, divine light, knowledge that the divine is. The daemon is the intercommunion, intellect the life of the thinking mind.

Then choice; which would be looked on as a freedom, to follow a way of life, to reject this, to devote oneself to the other. I do not choose, I have never had the illusion of that seeming liberty. Yet there is freedom. How define that? Most of the people I see here live, as far as I can tell, without knowing their hidden thoughts, that then is their freedom. With others, a few, the freedom is to suffer the inward energy which is without sensation.

He could no more. Drawing a flap of his cloak over his eyes he thrust forward his feet in their new sandals and rested unmoving as an effigy fallen from a sarcophagus the sands imperceptibly cover.

A dog licking his stone-cold hand stirred him from his sculptured state. The animal's shadow, a monster with elongated legs on the desert ground, told him night was near, and half he thought to stay there among sharp rocks and cavern tombs and shallow graves until the stars began their shining, those first mild lights. They would soon grow fierce and the wind born of darkness, racing in the void, would tear their brilliant splinters down from heaven. So he stayed under the lambent tongue until there came a whistle. The dog leaped and he rose stiffly, knowing he had lain long enough among the dead. A young man was striding past him with arrogant head and careless swing, an immemorial outline against the sunset, the dog at his side bounding. Plotinus whistled. Involuntarily the two turned. The dog with prancing paws spattering sand circled both men as they came close and their eyes met in a silent look, one pair glooming, the other lit with tiny gold suns.

It was quite clear to Plotinus from the first look, which neither of them could relinquish, that his deity had purposed this encounter, that it was part of his entrance into a new way of life. These two suns . . . 'You must have had enough, I want to see you too.' The stranger was speaking and gently turned Plotinus towards the west. But the sun had set. The young man laughed on a happy unimplicated note that sounded oddly over that ancient place of burial.

'Your eyes took the last sunlight of this day,' Plotinus said, unaware how his own pale countenance shone in the afterglow.

The stranger holding out both hands smiled, saying: 'Well, you know, my name is Heliodorus.'

'Heliodorus.' The word echoed back as though all the dead pledged him.

'A word of good omen for us, for a god-given friendship.'

Plotinus was staring up at the limestone cliff, its mysterious unresolvable whiteness marred by the shadows of its ruggedness, and the dark arched entrance of the many cavernous tombs caused him a sensation of interior anguish that was like a cry. He knew in that moment when splendid broad banners, diagonals of apricot and turquoise, swung wide from the zenith to the horizon that he would never come back to Lycopolis. His life until then filled his cupped hands, strained through his fingers, was lost in the colourless evening sands. His farewell made, he faced Heliodorus.

'Come back with me to my house. I still call it mine although tomorrow I collect my belongings and bequeath the brittle roof that has sheltered my head, though it lets through both sun and moonbeams and the stars, to another tenant, even as it was left me. But where have you come from? Are you going to stay here in . . . Lycopolis?'

They began to walk, the dog joyous at the promise of new adventures, and before the stranger answered he went on involuntarily: 'That voiceless interchange of mind-states has made us friends, has it not, as if we had never not known one the other . . . ?'

'At once clash and connaissance,' Heliodorus agreed. 'No, the ship returns tomorrow and I with it. That is, was, my plan, if I don't lose you by it. I came merely for the voyage down the river after living all my days at the mouth of it. But this is enough desert for me.' He looked round him disdainfully in the dusk. 'The ship sails in the bright dawn.'

'Divine', Plotinus corrected him. 'Then I cannot go with you. I will follow.'

'To Alexandria.'

'Alexandria.' The word echoed sombrely from the statue of Anubis, clad, below his open-jawed jackal head, as a Roman soldier, which stood guarding the way to the graves.

'Then you can share my rooms. I have a lodging in Brucheum not far from the Moon Gate.'

'Is not that rash, until you know . . . ?'

'I know now . . .' the low merry laugh again, 'I Heliodorus know

38

I have found a dear and silent companion, that this night we may for courtesy call first we spend in talk will not be the last.'

Lamplight shone out through the many slits and cracks in Plotinus' frail shell of a dwelling. He went to find Jeremy, and signed to him to heat a bath for the stranger and bring food for them both, suggesting by his gestures that he was hungrier than usual. The poor slave's face was so divided between joy at his master's return and despair because it was almost if not quite the last night when there would be this longed-for coming that Plotinus stayed near him considering, and Jeremy waited too in a beseeching muteness. Wordlessly they conversed. But you would be happier here than in an enormous strange city. And the slave's eyes replied: I look on you as a god. How can I live without you here, where all would be desolate without you? The master shook his head, the servant turned away like an animal refused food.

It was not without a singular thrill of recognition and unexplored confidence in their future being together that Plotinus saw the tawny head of his guest as the man stood at the table holding up a familiar papyrus, one shabby with overmuch handling. The presence of another in his rigorously guarded solitude, with no hint of intrusion, marked for him as distinctly as the farewell in the school had done the end of a period. This would be his last night in the home of the Jewish schoolmaster. But for all that, the snake had not yet cast its slough. He saw what Heliodorus was reading were his own thoughts etched sharply and briefly, often only two or three words, in the margin of the *Timaeus* and this pleased him for this was the best means of introduction, and a test of the temper of Heliodorus' mind, which must have something of the quality of his own if those cantankerous black angles meant anything to it. A test for himself also, Plotinus acknowledged, for this was the first time the tension of his own mind had encountered another stretched not so much by constant communing with thinkers of an earlier age as by the stresses of intellectual conflict among living men in a city whose mental atmosphere was at white heat. The mere nearness of another head as inwardly and magnetically concentrated was a strange experience to him, and that this concentration was directed on something of his own vision caused him a sense of being shouldered by unknown forces. The generations gone and to come, between whom he now drew breath, whose reasoning minds were fused in his, they now made human the eternity that flashed in their glances like the lightning of great Zeus, as the *Timaeus* fell from the hands of Heliodorus.

'Plato has found another poet, I see,' and he rubbed his hand over his lion-coloured hair. 'Will you miss that errant fire in me?'

Plotinus shook his head: 'Neither one nor the other is true.'

His only answer was an unbelieving musical laugh so surely inspired by the muses Plotinus laughed also.

'That is better,' Heliodorus said happily. 'I had a faint fear you could only be grave, although these scratchings should have instructed me better.'

His dog, limp on the floor, stretched and groaned. 'Poor Argus, a philosophising master is a tedium for you.'

He received from Jeremy a red bowl of whey and gave it to the dog continuing to talk to the lapping of the long lean tongue. 'What I found there proves I think we shall be inexhaustible to each other, in the dialectics of our two immortal masters. Learn from each other, it may be, more readily because of our meeting-ground of love, an inevitable but unchosen ground from which can grow more perfect harmonies and more fertile discords than one finds in the schools: Aphrodite giving ardour to Pallas Athene.' He rescued the vessel from the polishing tongue that was driving it over the floor.

'Yours here, the believer in divine knowledge, and my stroller in groves who gave all his life to using his human.' He humorously emphasised the echoing words.

Plotinus said: 'The human lives by the divine in it.'

Heliodorus responded: 'Deny you seek to know the god by using your human reason?'

'It is the will of the god I should use my reason to draw near his sheer knowing.'

'Your reason tells you "to live in beholding the consummate, the supreme beauty" as your master says, but that attained, what do you do with the rest of your days?'

'Don't you understand, nothing is complete in that way in this world, Heliodorus, but my reason whatever work it goes about knows my soul has within it, so to say, perfect partaking of the eternal; only by this knowing which I ceaselessly remember can mind think, discover, if that be the law of its daemon, what belongs to the necessities and curiosities of mortal being alive. That remembering I call contemplation; and I believe it was your master, if you call him so, who defined happiness or the highest good of the spirit as contemplation.'

'Very well.'

'While it was Plato, or Socrates if you prefer, who said man could not live without investigating the life he was, one might say, living in. Not a denial of one or other but recognition and emphasis according to the inborn nature.'

'This is derived from your solitary studies?'

'If you choose to put it that way.'

'You have not talked to philosophers or to Gnostics?'

'I have not discovered them in Asyut.'

'And now?'

'Now I suppose,' Plotinus smiled a little, 'there is need for commerce with other minds, a restlessness. Could there be a danger of one's human conclusions, imperfect as they must be of necessity, becoming obscurely stultifying, satisfied without challenge and contradiction? I think so. Temper and complexion can grow peevish or dull.'

They took their supper in silence with the quiet companionship of thought and the assurance of the same activity of mind sustaining them, which to Plotinus was an unfamiliar experience and one that gave an added sharpness to reason, and, perhaps a deeper serenity to the intellect. The destined self-chosen way to Alexandria was freed of doubt now he had met Heliodorus.

The morning air off the river was unusually clear, there was almost a freshness in its stirring as if the approach to the cloudy waters of Nilus had been over snow instead of desert. As in a vision Plotinus saw flat boundless sands white with blue concavities in their crystalline dazzle. He closed his eyes to interpret the breeze and there was a surging in his ears. He understood. He was going to the divine sea. The two men, with their sudden complete friendship as a god between them, destiny whose hands they held for once carefree, walked along the wharf where the viridescent water lapped. Boatmen were bustling on the black ship which had brought Heliodorus to Asyut and one of them shouted to him not to linger, they were loosing the cables.

'This margin of land and water is the best of all for parting, for every severance of mortals is symbol of death, one left on land, one carried out of sight on an element unknown.'

'You will follow.'

They both sighed.

Stay! Come with me! their eyes spoke silently.

41

Plotinus accepted the denial of his daemon and said softly: 'I will find, now I am here, a vessel leaving in a few days. I have an idea I should make my voyage alone.' He stroked with his long hand the smooth coat of Argus.

The Greek half bent his lion head. 'You know best. I have a good store of reading-matter on board. I am giving some lectures soon . . . on Aristotle.'

He sprang onto the deck, whistled to Argus who showed himself unwilling to leave that hand, raised an arm in farewell and at once moved in among the shipmen with no backward look. Plotinus stood still with his eyes on the proud Homeric skull they saw unseeing.

★　★　★

Towards noon he was walking slowly along the street to his mother's house receiving, as was usual with him in well-used ways, intimations from the buildings themselves as well as emanations from all the feet that had hurried before him or dragged sadly over that trampled hardness. The street as he saw it now, as it was in memory, as it might show sharpened in a dream, what differences between these three? And he knew with an added sense of the mysterious that a record was being kept of much that he was unaware of in the mere physical presences of this habitual background of his youth. It is that unconscious observer, who cannot be recalled at will, who returns to places when the living soul, the immortal, has quitted earth. He could just then have envied the unquestioning passers-by to whom, as far as he could tell, this Asyut street had nothing about it to disturb their thoughts of business or of daily stint. Dogs and the smallest human creatures came after him; with more than one doorstep toddler he exchanged an unambiguous glance, they comprehended as well as the older philosopher that the present reality was dependent on the unremembering soul. There was no time for them when the road had not been or future when it might not be. Conscious memory depends on something it recollects, unconscious memory is recollection itself, the possibility, the reality. And the crawling brown-skinned baby took hold of his ankles because he had stopped. 'This is the last time,' he said aloud, 'and for you too, since one cannot step into the same street twice, I suppose, any more than the same river.'

The low-browed dark verandah was unchanged. His unspread bed with the bookshelf at its head stood where it always had. The

42

quails pecked dejectedly behind their bars. Plotinus had seldom returned to his mother's house since he had slept his last night there with Marcus. He stood there now knowing that she was sick and that he would not come there again. The stones of darkness, the shadow of death, fell upon his heart until he could have uttered a cry as he stood in the doorway, the kind of small woeful cry his nurse made when he tumbled or cut his finger with a sharp knife. And with that interior cry came the sensation of her comforting arms.

'My child, my dear one, you are taking a hard way, stony and lonely. May the god who leads you pity you.'

'Maia!' And that warm ring of his voice no other woman had heard or would ever hear. 'You are here!'

'I am here, my bird. Deborah and old Kezia were fordone with caring for your mother and so I came to them.'

He looked down as they stood, each with a foot on the threshold, into the dry face mapped with wrinkles and on a sudden, knowing her bound with age, that she wanted him near and could not easily in the sharpness of waning strength look up, kneeled. For a long unmeasured moment she looked into the man's face following the mould of bone and lines begun in infancy, undaunted by the brightness of lineaments so dear to her heart. When he saw her fold her hands, that for him had always held healing, on her breast – he stood up.

'You are a blessing to us all, Mai', will you go now and see if I can visit my mother?'

'You are leaving us then.'

She spoke so exactly in the tone Eurycleia must have used when Telemachus announced his departure for sandy Pylos, Plotinus bowed his head at the pure poetry of the recurrence of certain scenes.

'Shall I tell mother this, would she understand?'

The little laugh she had always used to lift his childish musings was unmistakable. 'Tongue and wit are still quick, dearie, no venom lost, alas for us, we who wait on a sick body. Your sister . . .'

'No, no Maia, you see how well I am. You are proud, are you not, of your grown nurslings?'

The little woman shook her head at them both. 'You lend each the other light, my blessings. No one will ever see you shine again as old Mai' does now.'

She scuffled away on her bare feet. Hand in hand the brother and sister went to the shelf where Plotinus had left for her the codices he knew she loved best.

'Show me what you have read, your most often companions of thought,' he said, taking them down.

But sensing that for her just then, because they were together, the voice of the masters, even of the poets, was stilled, he let them be. Walking side by side through the portico, between the quails and his bed, he gently drew her into talk, and until she had solaced her soul by telling of their mother's sickness, by remembering, and proving that he remembered also, certain small events, frolics and solemn exchanges of childhood, he said no more of philosophy. His heart indeed was as troubled as hers from the closeness of the bond between them. So they talked knowing, and knowing the other knew, there could be no return to the intimacies of youth.

When they had satisfied their hearts, not with chill lament but with a quiet communion and a meditative exploring of what had once been their life, Plotinus took from among those fairly copied works the *Odyssey* and read aloud to his sister from the Book of Nausicaa. And he was reading, when the nurse came to say his mother was awake, of her farewell to Odysseus as she stood by the tall pillar in the hall of her father Alcinous. This open parting was for the young girl the renunciation of an intimacy unspoken but recognised in the secret heart as, so he understood it in himself, an involuntary leap of the divine life. The meeting and parting of Odysseus and Nausicaa was always to Plotinus the soul of the poetry of Homer in the *Odyssey*. Because they had not touched with warm flesh, and from the first Odysseus had known he must not even in supplication embrace her knees, there was a consummation of the spirit for ever, beyond the rule of Kronos.

How to find a suitable story on which to base what one wants to say: he remembered the words of Critias in the *Timaeus*, and looking now at his sister he knew he had found the story and she had understood. How, he wondered now, would he find their mother severed as she was by her sickness from all the daily cares and preoccupations and visiting of friends that had been her life on earth.

The little fierce woman lay on her bed in a room empty of other furniture; one or two stools and an amphora, a long green web, finely woven as a veil partly screening the way onto the portico; nothing else. As he entered the curtain lifted slightly and a bright shaft of light, an echo from the brazen sky, dived between them

44

and was veiled by the leaf-green hanging. Plotinus stood at the foot of the bed wondering to see how the Jewish features and the Grecian inherited from her two parents were at variance in the tiny face, sallow, dusky almost as a mummy's, the bonework of the skull incredibly frail, brittle under the skin, he sensed, as a dried leaf.

'This is the way, my son, my dear one, to learn that no one belongs to himself. Well you think mind, the ruler, the orderer, is yourself, the limbs useful things to obey, though it is true they also rebel. When health fails King Mind finds each command disregarded, he grieves, rages maybe; then later on, in a malady such as mine is, he learns he has no more rule even over himself, that what one intends when well one says self, that too was an illusion, a very nothing of nothingness, my sweet.'

The husky voice, pausing for breath, the dark eyes, seeming not to see under a bluish milky film, that yet communicated tenderness to her son, humbled Plotinus. Half bending he brought his head close to her, knowing she would drink in his features for the last time.

'I know it. The soul withdraws, the inanimate matter dissolves, the particular existence, form of being once happy in the mortal frame, fades, as a shadow when sun goes. But it is only the shadow that goes, mother mine, what gives the soul shining tangled in flesh and bones shines eternally.'

Her skinny hand smelling of sickness fluttered over his face, falling from curling flakes of hair over high corrugated brow into the lines gouged between nostrils and lips. Three finger-tips touched lightly his two eyes and his mouth. She could no more. With a shrunk smile she whispered:

'And the daemon?'

'The daemon forbids me to stay.'

'So I guessed. That is well. There is more sense in our parting alive on this strange threshold I dream I have crossed, your hand in mine. I see indeed I have gotten a man of the Lord . . . Go now, my son, go, go, before I forget this. The Spirit grieves because it leaves earth and knows human kinship no more.'

The pea-green hanging filled with the breeze surged towards them, a sun-spear pierced the air and was gone. Plotinus stayed a long time in the room, sometimes prowling between bed and curtain, more often standing statue-like under the arch. His mother did not speak again.

When evening came and the sun set and all the ways grew shadowy he left the house and passed down the emptying street unobserved, as if Athene had caused him to be invisible. When he arrived at the river and the ship Jeremy was standing on the quay with two corded chests, one containing cloaks, tunics, sandals and the beloved camel's hair bedcover of his master; the other, to which Plotinus gave a friendly tap with his stick, books and papyri. Beside them was a bundle wrapped up in striped cotton cloth and secured to the knob of a smooth staff. When he prodded this in its turn and afterwards laid his stick on the slave's shoulder the mute prostrated himself with clasped hands, rose again to his knees, pointed to the chests, himself and his bundle and then to the moored vessel.

Calls and the lilt of a song caught in the glimmering web of aether over the water, coracles of the nocturnal fishers were putting out from shore. Birds, their day's hunting done, fled by close to the liquid surface. The new and sinking moon drew Plotinus' eye and he looked above to discover the birth of the earliest stars. Noisy boatmen chanting and swearing along the wharf brought him back from the infinity of the heavens down the pointer of the mast to the lantern at the prow and the beseeching face in the dusk. It was not the time for denial, he gave a very slight nod and signed also that he wanted a cloak. When he had received the soft garment and the two boxes had been shouldered and taken aboard by the joyful Jeremy, Plotinus moved away along the waterfront without looking back at the figure and bundle outlined on the western sky.

Towards midnight he embarked himself on the craft which though small was fitted with a deck of narrow planks well-cemented with pitch. Jeremy had prepared a lair among coiled ropes where he could lie at length face to face with the majesty of the inextinguishable stars.

CHAPTER IV

Alexandria

The sky was a colourless canopy of light that early morning but the colonnaded street was still in shadow that held a slumberous recollection of night over the facades of the buildings. Stately, indrawn between the rigid pillars, they gave Plotinus, at this first experience of the stonescape of a great city, a sense of numbness. He lifted his face to the sky above breathing clear air, remembering the desert and the river. His mind alive again, knowing the infinite mystical horizon, he stood in the very boss of Alexandria where the two highways of noble colonnades met and crossed, ended and began, the point, as he told himself, which in reality could have no contact with line. The instant alone in the centre of the cross, could not this be a symbol of truth for the whole world, the eternal in time which no one could think without an ecstasy? Begin to think, you no longer know. He moved across to the sacred enclosure of tombs, pondering their massiveness and oppressive adornments. Heliodorus had explained to him that the Macedonian founder of the city had his burial among the mauseleums of the Egyptian Ptolemies, and he sought it out, his sense of strangeness, of standing beside rather than outside the sequence of time, was enhanced as he half bent in salutation to the king who had declared himself to be a god.

After that homage he turned towards the museum with a different, a more personal, response, for this sheltered behind Corinthian pillars and sculptured pediment the library, mightiest hoard of written wisdom on earth. Whatever he would learn from the living lips of men it was to the library that his heart instinctively commended him, for here in liberty and alone he could continue the meditation on intellect and soul through the mediation of ancient philosophers which had led him to this city whose scholars ranged the flaming ramparts of worlds seen and invisible.

The sight of a limbless beggar conveying himself diagonally over the museum steps, the heat increasing and the multitudes of men, reminded him on a sudden that he had left Jeremy and the chests on the quayside, promising with signs he would not desert his

47

speechless slave overlong in the busy docks. The beggar edging his way to the base of one of the columns turned up to Plotinus a small head with clear unmalicious features, as if he were blessing the tall man who stood still as marble above him, rather than asking alms. How could eyes close to and of necessity for the most part fixed on the ground, contain such a gaze of human grandeur? It was for that moment as if the two stood equal on a windy headland of the sea, earth-holders and earth-shakers like the great god Poseidon himself. And then again, and Plotinus never forgot this experience, he felt as if he were the one with bitten-off stumps on the hard steps and the cripple long-legged and free above him. For a moment he saw only sandals and limbs, robes and flirting tunics as all the busy passers-by swirled above his head.

A naked white and beautifully formed foot alighting as a bird on the step beside him raised his vision. The man, who was clean-shaven with black hair closely cut all round his head, supported parchments in the folds of his garment with one hand and with the other placed gently between the helpless one's teeth a small barley-cake, so appetisingly baked it made Plotinus suddenly know he was hungry.

With a gesture and salutation he checked the black-eyed and snowy-skinned stranger before his swift foot flew on and asked for the Moon Gate and even, as he met the keen eye, for Heliodorus himself, speaking the name as a talisman.

'The peripatetic,' he responded as if he were not attending, but it was plain also he knew the man.

'You give a sop to Cerberus before entering the sacred store-house of books.'

At that the dark eyes of the older man lost their pebble-like opacity, his ascetic look suffered an undercurrent of warmth instantly affecting Plotinus' own impassivity.

'You know as I do all life is one. Thought is the difficulty, the thoughts of the different ages of men, their passions roused by different objects of worship. We can agree on life but truth . . .'

The air enkindled about them caused others to look or to pause as they entered its ambience on their way to the library.

'We shall meet again,' the man said, bending his brows. 'This is not the time. You asked me . . . you see, that is the Serapeum, the greatest temple of the city, you will find Cerberus there also at the feet of the idol; if you stand with your back to the sea . . .'

Plotinus smiled gravely at the language of this passionate scholar and murmured with an imperceptible movement of his lips: 'The sea.' With Heliodorus there had been a clash, flashes of light reflected from minds of different metal meeting as it were in mid-air. This his first encounter in Alexandria was another matter, elements, fire and water, yet both of them silently admitting they sprang from one source.

They parted, the gathering giving way to the stranger, who moved as if it were not, and pressing closer about the teacher and preacher who it seemed was on the point of going away from the city. For all his calm Plotinus was mysteriously dissolved by the presence of a living master whose voice and eye had straitly entered his soul. With a sense almost of shrinking he wondered whether anything of what he had considered as his own mind-reality would be left him after he had attended the lectures of the schools, so unlike his solitary readings this new experience promised to be. He reminded himself metal liquified is still metal, that it can flow into a number of moulds before the final tempering. If nothing of the original stuff is left that could mean only it had not been original. The deity within which is contemplation can never become anything else.

The man on the steps had obviously himself made the gesture of turning his back on that image which was the heart of the worship and of the most glorious temple of the gods, as he had heard, in all the world. His private initiation into the city, which had begun with his voyage down the sacred river, continued with his salutation to Egypt and Greece by his visitation of the tombs of the Pharaohs and of Alexander, but his intercourse with the living mind of the megalopolis on the steps of the museum must, something within him insisted, be completed by entering the Serapeum. The keepers of the door let him pass without a glance and he recognised by the crowds and the mountains of offerings, it was a feast day. The first sunshine to penetrate there whirled along a mote-spun beam of gold and incense blue to transform the living fruit, the honey jars with timeless motifs in the mild earthenware. Pans of white milk and baskets of matchless weave in this glory of the true god of Egypt received the celestial light and endowed the sultry atmosphere of the temple with the charism of the fruits of the earth.

Plotinus, with a sense of still floating on the green river, passed the huge reed-adorned amphora of Nile water, the sleepers not yet roused from their incubation, those *katochoi* whose corded robes showed they were bound to the temple until the deity chose to grant them release, and stood before the shrine of Serapis. The god of the dead had no revelation to give to the man who came into the presence of the image in knowledge of the divine stillness. His mind dwelling in the soul of the universe became limpid as water reflecting nothing. While his reason considered the complex of impressions the highly-wrought image of deity brought to it, the essence of his soul was free in a transparent awareness, an invisible light of spirit.

'O ye living upon earth who love life and hate death', the call inscribed on the sepulchre rang as a mocking echo in his ears while he looked unseeing at the figure worshipped by the children of the sun. Too great a love of tangible life leads to an imbalance, a dread of death that is disguised by seeking to avoid the corruption of form in its return to infinite matter. The temple, with its gleam as of sun and moon like the hall of Menelaus, dissolved about him, became as smoke, the posts of the door rocked as trees totter to their fall in a midnight gale. All this Plotinus heeded not as he waited before the hybrid idol for the vision that flaming in his soul seared his senses with a live coal, purifying them from the impact of the object studded with gems that winked like the lidless eyes of serpents.

The snake with head raised by the right knee of the seated Serapis first drew him to consider the symbolism of this Zeus-Osiris statue mighty with the devotion of the soul of the antique land. Yes, it was the ruby eyes of the dragon with their rhythmic flickerings that made him remember, aside as it were from the vision, the dumb fumblings towards understanding the idol represented with his attendant snake and three-headed Cerberus couched at his feet, the sceptre in his hand and the corn measure or hamper for offerings curiously poised on the curvature of the skull. As he stared at the benignant ambiguous features between the classic locks that were wont to distil their ambrosial dews when Zeus bent his head, and the fleece-curled beard, he recognised that the sculptors who had modelled the deity had been compelled by a power greater than themselves which guided them as they with skill guided the tools of their workmanship. But although, as Plotinus decided standing before the seated god, they had in some sense manifested more than they knew, and had presented in Serapis a visible and tangible form of the myth of the inseparableness of life and death, of fate or necessity and judgement, it was the devotion of the multitude of worshippers in the polyglot city for the image itself that gave to it its singular magic power.

Gods invisible, gods in some sense visible in certain mortal men, these he knew and honoured, but what was it within him that remained untouched by the magic of this bejewelled majesty? The answer came to him even as he perceived he was no longer solitary in the procession of those who bore offerings, it was the vision of his soul facing the infinite that is called pure contemplation.

' "Though thou exalt thyself as the eagle, and though thou set thy nest among the stars, thence will I bring thee down, saith the Lord." '

The man of the museum steps with his unearthly pallor and black fluttering almost diaphanous robe was close to him.

'Truth. But if you can say that to me in presence of this image before which all nations bow you show one thing. I do not exalt myself, the god within me lifts me to the stars.'

And Plotinus' calm face bent with compassion upon the other in admiration of his tempest-riven spirit.

'May I be forgiven the blasphemy if I say what I think . . . "That in this place is one greater than the temple." '

'There is a word that, if I am not mistaken, will sever the beams of intellect by which we shine, by which we would illumine the darkness which will not receive it, when shooting from our high minds they would join or transpierce, one light the other. It is a word, stranger, I know not and say not.'

'You have come here to study? Well, I believe we shall meet again. Something in you draws me. You see, I found you again by this graven image, did I not? I am leaving the city today, I would learn your name so that in afterdays when you become known . . . Shall I tell you the name of my master here?'

Plotinus shook his head. They were outside the Serapeum now and standing aloof from the moving crowds looking each at the other's head, on the azure heaven, on the Grecian architecture of the building, experiencing a new liberality.

'This crossing of our path is not without the will of the gods. Shall we, symbolically at least, pour a libation to our true master, him of the broad shoulders, in the name of our faith in the divinity of the soul?'

'And,' Origen quietly added, 'of the life of contemplation, however busy our purposes in the world.' His robe sent a butterfly shadow over the rosy flagstones.

They clasped hands, exchanged a thrusting unburdened look and moved softly apart, content, with downcast eyes.

When Plotinus remembered he was in Alexandria he was standing below a crescent arch, a bow of white limestone. The mole dividing

51

the two harbours ran northwards to the isle of Pharos, he could see at the far end of it the tower of the lighthouse. A saltiness in the air fused with the salt blood in his veins, inwardly aquiver he breathed the air of the immemorial tideless sea, the cradle of gods and poets, above all of Aphrodite.

Walking forward into sunlight on the gleaming stones of the mole from under the arc of the Moon Gate, between the Great Harbour on his right hand and Eunostos, the port of safe-return, on his left, he had a sense of consummation, as though his birth on the bank of the dragon-green river, love for his nurse, sister, mother, years between the papyrus meres, the school and dwelling of his Jewish master, meeting with Heliodorus and farewell to Lycopolis, were all an inevitable prelude to this vision of the divine sea. The city of scholars giving birth to new thought, the Gateway of the Moon, the mole running out to sea, the tall tower designed by Sostratus sky-cleaving and crowned with light-bestowing turrets, composed a single structure in his mind of which the cement was grief. He recognised this but it was not until he had paced half the distance of the Heptastadium seeing the seafaring ships and small craft, the blue water, but more aware of the unawareness of his mood of abstraction, that he knew how to spell and read the sadness that bound all – Origen.

The quality of the man's thought was so akin to his own, he felt as though in that chance-sent god-given crossing of the ways there had been a fusion, as though his own reasoning had advanced into fields not yet explored, by mere contact with another mind of such scholarly dignity and natural sensitivity. It wasn't that this passionate thinker was leaving the city on a swift ship the very day his broad-beamed river-boat had landed him there, although he recognised a new hunger for intercourse face to face in which mute taut consciousness gives spirit to words, and the unsaid wings thoughts, it was something indefinable for him at present that he realised would lead to a sharp if not fatal clash at the highest level of the soul.

Alike guided by the intelligible essence of the universe and by the confluence of their stars they might well meet again. He was all but certain they would, for he had an inkling no other man living had emerged from the crucible of this city of philosophers with a more keenly tempered mind, and while they both beheld the light of the sun there must be a magnetic interplay between them. Meanwhile he praised the god who granted him this meeting in a vestibule of the adytum while with a single gesture he absolved himself from all need for temples and gods made with hands. Not, he told himself, gazing up at the dizzy pillar of the lighthouse, that I deny their sacredness, the intrinsic beauty of shrines, but because for me they may bring about some lessening of that conscious intellect which alone can absorb the rays of the intelligible light of Divinity.

But there was something terrifying in the immense height of this tottering tower in the strong wind rushing down from heaven, ruffling the blue waves outside the harbours and hastening certain swan's-down clouds on their vague uncharted way. It was, he decided, the movement of these harmless puffs of white vaporous substance behind the stupendous lighthouse that gave him the illusion the whole thing was swaying over towards him. Staring up, holding his tunic about himself as if it were his precious enfolding soul, defying the gale from the sea, he waited almost breathless since it was impossible to take in a modest breath from the blast that roared round the tower. How, he kept wondering in the whirl, had the thing ever been built? No one would have believed it could be if it had not been. And then he thought, if an idea be conceived, does that mean it can be achieved in the world of our bodily senses, not at once, not by one man, but by a kind of building up of mind upon mind as the twin giants while still children piled mountain on mountain to capture Olympus, dwelling of the gods that are for ever. If that were so, the busy generations would never cease contriving, there would be no end of new wonders. And would any of these, even the most fabulous, make any difference to what must be the first task to every man born of woman on the grain-bearing earth: by means of his intellect to know God with nothing between.

A party of carefree slaves out for the day came gaily towards the lighthouse, some holding hands, others leaning a hand on the nearest shoulder, their dry soles scraping on the stones. Tones of their idle voices shattered and scattered by the wind came to him and he felt a certain warming of his heart towards these unthinking ephemeras of the town who rated their own lives more cheaply than their owners did and so had a liberty in sun and sea-wind and absence, for an hour, of toil denied men who took life with gravity and had minds oriented to the inexorable approach of death, in whatever perspective they regarded that finality of the temporal. As if he who lived in the intellect had not always one foot at least outside time. So he turned his back on the tower and the humble happy ones together and faced Alexandria with all the triumphant buildings along the shore of the harbour.

The light-hued stones sown with black specks and pitted with the wear of salt air sparkled also with quartz, as if the hidden fires of flint would blaze and lightnings dance along the Heptastadium. Plotinus walked alone to his own rhythm isolated in a hollow wind whose fury was a whirl of freedom from all other presences. As he went he remembered that distant king of Egypt Proteus who dwelt in a palace on Pharos, and he cried the lines from *Helen:* ' "These are the lovely immaculate streams of Nilus which instead of the dews of Zeus water level Egypt with the meltings of white snow." ' And he knew through his reciting why he was reluctant to leave the isle and go back to the sea-girt city. Once he had learnt the house, sent for his boxes and slave, there would be an end of his footfree liberty. He would hear again the denials of his daemon.

From the Moon Gate he looked back along the breakwater, knowing for friend the sea-cleaving wall, seeing himself upon it at all hours between the twin harbours, meeting dawn, watching stars wake in the twilight a thousand times, while lamp-lit water lapped the quayside, and the beacon flashed its burning signals.

He remembered this again when long after midnight, worn with toilsome travel and strangeness and the talk of his friend, he stretched himself on the corded bedstead, and the souls and divinities that fill all things, and above all the great gulf of Ocean, called to him so that he threw down the best purple blanket of Heliodorus, which was too thick a covering for the African night, rose as at the singing of nereids, seized his cloak from the peg at the bed's head and took his way down the shadowy colonnade to the sea.

★　★　★

The inner court of the house was filling with young men come to listen to the lecture of the peripatetic. This small enclosed domain was a mark of the fortune of his friend; the three trees sacred to Osiris, the green grass refreshed daily by water from one of the underground canals, the arcade with semi-circular arches and vine-entwined pillars lent the air a sense of seclusion and a dignity of thoughtfulness that he regarded as Athenian. Almost unobserved he watched the others; their clashes and concomitant influences perceptible through that guarded atmosphere as it began to vibrate and undulate, to tauten and shift in nervous patterns under voices growing bold and clear-ringing. The folds of their garments partook

54

of the animation of their features, vivid feet and hands impelling winged words.

The sea-green robe and sunny head of Heliodorus moved among them with a separate radiance and his assurance of being a master imposed itself for that hour at least on the invisible web of mind-stuff of those who came to hear him. It was soon clear that after the example of his own teacher he was going to speak walking. While some of the young men moved with him as their conversation merged into the monologue of Heliodorus, others stood in groups under the leaves and tendrils attentive but not without an exchange of low-voiced comment. Plotinus knew his own soul was returning to its inward concentration which was for him the most intense form of prayer, that leaning by aspiration towards the Alone.

' "He that dwelleth in the secret place of the most high shall abide under the shadow of the Almighty." ' The words so softly spoken seemed to come from within. But there was a figure at his elbow with sallow skin and inquiring eye that reminded him at once of the schoolmaster whose position he had himself taken at Asyut.

'You do not listen, stranger, I can see that. Tell me why you do not.'

Plotinus answered gently: 'Hoping to hear a desired voice we let all others pass and are alert for the coming at last of that most welcome of sounds. So here we must let the hearings of sense go by, save for sheer necessity, and keep the soul's perceptions bright and quick to the sounds from above.'

'As I thought when I first spoke, using words from above to draw you to me. But you have newly come here, as our lecturer tells me, to study in the many schools of the city. And if you are always as absent as now . . . what will you learn?'

'I have, it is so far true, no need to set myself to learn actively. I have studied the old masters until their reasonings are of the substance of my consciousness. Now, when another man speaks, this consciousness is, I might say, in a state of prepared, of exercised passivity, but my soul's perception will return to it if the desired voice speaks through any man's lips.'

'And it has not yet spoken through Heliodorus's?'

'Let us listen now, shall we?'

A wrinkle or two appeared in the ivory-smooth skin: 'On the instant, if I agreed, you would return to the secret place of the most high. I should be hearkening in solitariness.'

'In so high-souled a company?' Plotinus' lips were tender as a girl's smile.

The black gleamless eyes were averted. 'Our friend bade me to bring you to him. He desires to show you to this noble gathering, to have you stand at his side before them. You are his guest, you will not of your grace let him send in vain, or me who am his messenger be shamed.'

'Who could refuse to be warmed in presence of the sun?'

'Why, one garlanded with starry influences of midnight.'

'You are right, my poetry of dark must learn how to shine in daylight. Thoughts challenged and triumphant may dare be clothed in poetry. I must thrive in the intensity of minds in strange orbits as well as explore the interior of soul.'

'Come then, our friend is offering the herald's staff to whoever would take it.'

The sun was low now, would soon leave the court as a well in darkness. Plotinus perceived the shadows of vine-leaves across his face as he stepped forward with that characteristic walk which at once attracted his new companion, stiff and not to be deflected yet with an incommunicable grace as though he did not part the air or press into it but as if it moved in a caress about him. And there was the same kind of swaying as of ripe corn under a favonian breeze of the young men about Heliodorus so that he and Plotinus stood together now as two statues of gods with unlooking awareness in their carved faces.

'This stranger from Lycopolis, my friends, will, I well believe, introduce a new element into the crucible of our city where thought is wrought and tempered with lectures and dialectic, with the mere coming together of minds vivid and intangible. The torch flaming and smoking of old Athens censes us and I swear, by the spirit of prophecy, when it leaves our courts to kindle another land there will be diamond flashes from Sirius, the star of Isis, unseen by the old masters!'

'An encomium for one untried may be no good omen. I have come among you to learn.'

'No high mind learns without teaching. All is interfluous among us, though some say our crucible is giving birth to a crux of rigorous mould from which all else must hang, nay, hangs already.'

'That symbol my daemon bids me avoid. I must think in eternity with no symbol planted in earth however upward-pointing. But if this crux, this sharp shape of heaven-cleaving earth, before which men bow as before God, which stamps darkness on the azure sky as I see it on the roofs of those buildings of the Gnostics, if this is indeed the chosen sign of the One, of the stain and strain and suffering of all life, my philosophy, as all else, will be drawn to it, to that pure point of the centre. All my thought-building is irrelevant unjoined to the point, the known knowledge. That allowed my being, in as much as it is separate, a fragment of Being, ensouled with a very demiurge daemon-mocker, must go as it will.'

Plotinus spoke quietly, with a gentleness that could have misled some among the philosophically intoxicated youth who stood shadowless now in gloom, but his speech seemed to come from the breadth and height and weight of his brow lightened by his eyes, rather than from his delicately cut lips. Several began to speak, impelled towards him by their challenging minds, but they were stayed by Heliodorus.

'This is the first day. We must not beset our guest at his first word among us. I think I can promise you each will have his turn to say to the stranger all his heart bids him and receive those eye-flashes without being turned; and to ask.' He looked round him laughingly. 'He has come to stay not for a day but until he's sifted all our wisdom and lined his brain with golden grain.'

He caught a glance of amused affection from Plotinus and went to talk to his slaves who were laying a table under the portico with silver mixing-bowl, cups bound with ivy strands, bowls of glazed blue ware and red pottery piled with fruits, and baskets of bread and barley-cakes. The platters of grained olive-wood unstained, the bloom of grapes, the wreaths of flowers and peacock plumes, some conceit of insect wings, Plotinus saw all this as a fresco moved forward a trifle from the wall, tangible but unreal. And without turning his head he knew girls were in the shade of the three trees. Hesitant notes of a flute began to fill the air, the player waking his soul with the final heart-aching strain of a song. What taught this piper to begin with the sharpness of desire unfulfilled, and so of timeless intensity?

'Come and see my chorus,' Heliodorus spoke softly in his ear, but every thread of the cobweb sphere enmeshing him vibrated. 'They are all orphans, waifs of streets and sands.'

When he did look he saw lamps lit in the trees and very young children playing with pipes or dancing on the grass, too youthful for skill, but serious over their games as only the youngest are. Other little Arabs made a fire of crackling thorns, carried wooden vessels of milk in both careful hands, cried when sparks showered their thin skins. Husky dry voices, cicadas singing, with ever recurring the yearning flute.

'You have a master-musician hidden away somewhere, taught by Pan himself, it must be.'

'A tongueless nightingale. I never knew who maimed him; he cannot say. His music is the soul of our philosophy and rises from the ruins of words that are our life and our despair.'

Their eyes met.

'I am going to escape, if you allow it.'

'Ah, no doubt you have discovered the earliest star. You love best things just coming into visible being, or just dissolving.'

'There!'

'Come back. Be with me when they've all gone away.'

What it was just then that made that place a prison Plotinus could not have said. Not that incense smell of the children's fire nor the fumes of wine and brain of his friend's guests, but something was causing a darkening of the flame in his blood he could not tolerate. 'All things have become light never again to set' – whose word was that? While the spider's gossamer glistened all over him, shadows were coursing within. He signed to Jeremy who was serving with the others and the slave in a moment brought him an ivy goblet of well-watered wine just as he always drank it, then with an apple in his hand and a broken barley-cake he moved away unregarded.

He walked east along the docks where lights were few on land though the dim vessels carried warning lanterns that send shimmer-paths over the water, rather it was to his eye as if the ripples were lifting a radiance from below and offering it to the air. Above all and fanned far out to sea gleamed the beam of the great beacon-tower. There was a crescent moon reddish as it sank in the sultry firmament, and towards this he kept turning, halting on the quay-side, until all his thoughts became hushed in silence, losing their sharpness and sting, emptying in that one phrase: 'All things have become light.'

The jutting headland of Lochias, guard of the Great Harbour with the palaces built upon it of kings and emperors, warded his vision now from the sea to the north. The buildings on his right hand as he continued to move eastward were of a massive grandeur that weighed on him, not man-made, caverns of mountain volcano hollowed, adorned, with eruptive but stylised carvings. He had to look above for assurance to the firmament of stars. The temple of blackness of the dark-haired god of the sea was agleam with the mystic shine of night light finds in a crow's wings. The intense concentrated interior shine of the black basalt, or whatever ocean-hewn smooth rock the land-dwelling of the god was reared from brought him to a stand. Poseidon, Plotinus decided under the obscure statue, was the genius of Alexandria.

The experience of standing for the first time by the base supporting this figure of gigantic proportions, with stout well-braced legs and arms outstretched in radiance reflected from stars and salt water, from invisible lamps and torches and the igneous stone of the Poseidonium itself, was something he sensed he had been prepared for and that had been prepared for him with its singular shock and harmony. It was for this encounter with the balanced lord of sea and land grasping the trident poised and aimed that his daemon denied him the symposium. Nothing could have surpassed this midnight vision of the majestic bronze god. Visitations by day, scrupulous study of the features, the hair and beard, the work of the master-hand on torso and limbs lost now in the dark, these would have no part in the completeness of the glory of the god as he was present omnipotent in the consciousness of Plotinus.

Dizzied by the impinging perspectives of Egyptian and Greek art his mind, suddenly stilled, received as a seal the impression of the statue of Poseidon. He did not need to look any more, it was enough to move round the pedestal with the influence of the bronze upon him, to face the pediment of the temple, with the sea-wind singing in his ears. A passing festal procession of acolytes with flares showed up the restless relief of dolphins with arching backs, prancing horses with orbed nostrils, caused a monstrous shadow of the deity to leap from the portico to the roof, to the very heavens where the clouds assumed his form. But for the most part the bypassers were weary; worn-out slaves, beggars, starvelings, a weeping dancing girl in tattered robe, a skull-capped Jew bowed over his insistent stick taps. This beat echoing through the precincts drew him from his trance, across which the others had wavered as voiceless eidola, and an unheeded vehement discussion between two men in dark cloaks swaying together, drawing angrily apart, below the colossus of Poseidon Soter, the earth-holder and earth-shaker, knocked articulately in his brain: 'Your mythology, my friend, is a chaos within chaos. There are already too many myths and symbols in the city that far from saving life for wretched mortals drain from them the life of

59

their very souls. You would create a world of daemons, a Hades of shades made of warm flesh and blood.'

'Flesh and blood we are by an unfortunate necessity, and you say a god clothed in this can save us. Are you not inventing another, a more outrageous myth? How prize this higher than human thought?'

'Because it is one and complete. Knowledge of good, God, knowledge of evil, man, these in One Man born of flesh, so knowing evil but without sin . . .'

'What is sin? Is it not sin to be born in the flesh according to the Christian teaching . . . ?'

'The Divine Mind can assume body without sin . . .'

'The Divine Mind is in all men.'

The two men startled. One of them glanced upwards as though he thought the god of bronze spoke; even, that he might be smitten with the trident. A long peal of thunder reverberated over the city. Plotinus stood before them with his statuesque stillness and gravity of mien in the lull following the clap. The undulant wind from the sea ceased, a strong blast from the desert as if on an errand bore past them. The temple-court was deserted now save for Poseidon above and the three shadows by the plinth.

'Thought must be fearless. Make man the centre and at once thought, all his thought, is overweighted with pain, suffering, evil, summed in your word "sin", to miss the mark. The essence is intellect seeing, contemplating by the light of itself. Intellect is equally all because not in space.'

'Who in pain, in desperate sickness, can think?'

'He cannot reason. Intellect in him as in a stone is secure.'

They searched curiously the features of the one who had joined himself to them.

'Love,' one said musingly.

'The radiance about the star that makes all new for the sad voyager through time.'

'Is it fair to silence argument with poetry, stranger?'

'There would be more truth in silence.'

With that word he moved out of the Poseidonian ambit with no backward glance at god or temple or mortal men. If the Spirit gives a man to know the living light of intellect, then it is that one's purification to devote himself to the light, if he can but deliver from obscurity a single ray, by living inwardly in the silence of that intellectual light. He walked on. There are enough dwellers in time to seek to mitigate suffering which like all else has an exact measure, cannot be more or less. Counter it in one sphere, it counters you in another. For myself, as God would have me, I must turn to use my birthright.

He moved on slowly past ships rocking in the ravelled luminosities their lamps threw on the sea of the Great Harbour, their masts edging small arcs across the sky, their prows dipping fitfully. Black cables slackened, tautened and scraped on the quay. True Greek that he was, the company of seafaring ships hoving, the presence of the sea heaving upon the confines of mind freed his nerves of their edginess. One sea for all the multitude of waves and ripples, the fierce races and irresistible currents, the swell, and those subaqueous gulfs and grottoes, the coral palaces of Poseidon himself eternally bathed by the eddying flood. On the one sea to each vessel a destined way.

CHAPTER V

Easter Sunday

Lamplight, softly beaming across the grass of the trampled court where the air though silent still stirred with the searching voices of the young men who had been eager there, showed Plotinus Heliodorus watched, for they both took sleep briefly and in total darkness. He thanked Jeremy for opening the heavy door with deep mouldings, laying hands on the man's shoulders wordlessly telling him to go to his rest. Then he himself took the ancient loved lamp, which because of a crack was always low in oil, and set it outside his door before he lay down half covered by the fleecy rug. A certain strife had to be endured before he gave himself wholly to sleep; body quiescent, absorbed in its own weariness, left the soul limpid, unilluminated but waiting to reflect, to receive down to the troubled deeps of being, the divine irradiance. While mind strove with that touch of a dread god, he did not deny the luxury of his tired flesh yielding all its nerve-wrought stiffness. His bones melted as though they were formed of gently warmed wax.

The rebellion of his mind was against the schools and masters of Alexandria. Rearing haughtily, it declared it knew all and more than all they could teach, there was nothing it could learn from living lips the dead had not said to it. Rebelling reasonably it muttered it was willing to stay in the house of Heliodorus and study in the great library so long as it could dodge all philosophical and dialectical disputations. But this, the god insisted, was an evasion. His mind must be tried and tempered in conflict with other minds before both its serenity and power of intellect were proved fit to fulfil the will of the deity.

Plotinus groaned in the darkness under the necessity of his destiny; what that was he knew not, only that there was for him no avoidance. And he remembered just then what he'd heard them say of Pyrron the sceptic, that there was no difference between yes and no and this once believed the soul knew peace. Between this, at which his lips curled, and the healing drowsiness of his limbs, his strife abated. Agitated wings folding he slept.

Two visions of the night were with him when he woke, and in

62

the light of day he acknowledged them and prepared himself to meet them, once he had taken cognisance of that necessity which was the centre of his being. There was something else that must be remembered before he left his couch while his mind was still a wave-smoothed strand, the sea at rest under Galene, Serenity, most fair daughter of Nereus.

This nameless skiff on a dream horizon he beckoned near, leaned towards with wordless desire, as in prayer his soul gathered herself towards the divine beginning of consciousness one with the end. But ever the ship sailed on until as her hull sank he understood the signal. The resigned philosopher who lived at ease in Elis knowing an equilibrium perfectly maintained by doubt, had not he, Pyrron, travelled east with Alexander and his army to discover in India this withdrawal from passion, a calm to which the wild senses, the fury of fire in the blood, were willingly subject? One day he too would embark on a swift ship, no Nile lugger, and sail eastward. Thence, it might be, he could bring back the needed element to unite the unstable amalgam of Alexandrian philosophy. The wisdom, worship, religions of Greek, Jew, Gnostic, Egyptian, lay edge to edge, overlapped, but never became one.

' "They",' he said aloud, standing naked waiting for Jeremy to come and administer the usual friction, 'want always a way of living, that could be, whether it is or not, practised. I must give all to thought, that is my destiny.' Under the rough towelling he presently added, still aloud: 'No: ethics, which are, humanly at least, thought out, ready for all who want to use them, will not change in the main through the generations, no – pure intellection. And then, what is beyond the study of metaphysics, from whence the vision of beauty visiting the soul with light . . . ?' And he looked into the dark eyes of his slave.

The two admonitions returned and he considered them in turn, and added a third: that he must write to Deborah. The first was that he must find a means of supporting himself while he stayed and studied in Alexandria, and this he at once decided, while his own philosophy was being shaped and disciplined by the masters of the city, must not be teaching. The second was to find or hear news of his cousin Marcus. Clothed in his tunic for the day, having ascertained Heliodorus still slept, he went to walk on the Heptasta-dium hoping motion would bring good counsel. By the end of that day he had discovered the owner of ships about whose business Marcus was employed, had been added to the company of men who copied manuscripts at the museum, and had decided which lectures he would attend, obeying the advice of his friend.

★ ★ ★

But his rebellion was not quelled. A decade of desert moons had set red crescents, waxed to gold floating orbs, worn frail and green in orange dawns over the city and Plotinus had heard many lectures, spoken now and then in the unwearied, but often to him wearisome, dialectical discussions that followed them. It was a training in arranging his ideas, in couching them in words that other minds could receive. He learnt more of the essential thoughts of men nearer to his own time. But he was happier at his silent transcribing. The rebellion simmered.

One morning when neglecting his work he was searching among the stacks of narrow papyri for a stray leaf of poetry he had once found and read and loved and then hidden deliberately as though he feared the beauty of those threnodies, he was conscious of a man standing on the other side regarding him between the files. Plotinus' nervous hands fell still like a pair of white birds on the board in front of him, he could give no reason to himself but this young man faced him as a messenger of the gods descended from the peaks of many-ridged Olympus.

'I bring you a letter,' the young man said softly. 'I have arrived today from Syria, from Origen. He said I should find you at the museum, and behold!' – he offered the little scroll, finger-long, fastened with green knotted and tasselled silk – 'I find you here in good company.' And he signalled to the sculptured heads and statues life-size of gods and philosophers.

Then after a significant but reserved meeting of the eyes, he added: 'For all that, you are restive. I will, if I may, see you again before I leave the library.'

As he moved back Plotinus felt a light rather than a shadow on the air was receding, he kept his eyes cast down while his finger-tips grew curiously alert at the touch of the letter they curled upon. At the same instant he perceived the age-veined papyrus fragment lying before him, full in his vision, the faded lines of divine poetry miraculously clear. 'You who know royal fulfilment and still paths; how many leaves the earth sends forth in spring, the sands in the ocean and rivers whirled in confusion by the waves and the blasts of the winds.'

He took the two into a niche by a pillar where he often stood concealed, and not without a touch of the breath of Nausicaa he loosed the silk. 'What this is, and how it will be, you well behold, and it is right for you to match yourself with it through wisdom.' So the poem; the letter, superscribed to my most loved son after the Ionic mode was of an essential brevity Plotinus admired, though he acknowledged his heart's cry for more: The spirit of kinship between us cannot be disavowed, the bearer is of the same gender. I beseech you, seek out the porter who was my master, he will guide you to the sovereign initiation. He alone is your peer in intellect. You are in need of trying your full strength. Origenes Adamantius.

Because the man was banished from Alexandria, as he had learnt after the encounter of the day of his own arrival, because of his recollection of him and all he had heard of the temper of his mind, an acute sense of deprivation came upon Plotinus as he stood under the voluted capitals with the scroll in his fallen hand. He recognised just then, though he could not have said how, the solitariness of his destiny. Origen had attained through his Greek thinking to faith that in some mysterious way supported his reason, was the quintessence of it as, and this he did not admit in words, the old gods for all their beauty and their elevating of natural worship could never be. What this revelation demanded of a man who lived for and by intellect alone was, he sensed, a certain complete surrender he himself could never compass. Whether or not intercourse with Origen would have deflected him from his necessity, constricted or given liberality to his thinking, would never be known. As he had renounced his body in the papyrus skiff on the waters of Nilus, so now he renounced something instinct told him could have been a support in his alone life, that strenuous interior life of the mind dedicated to light known by its own irradiance.

The vision inwoven in the texture of his mind was gone and a kind of exulting arrogance succeeded it, almost a contempt for high minds that obeyed forms and ceremonies of prayer and worship, communal observations and ritual where there was need of none of them. Prayer is the inclining of the whole soul to God, in silence.

'Truth for the man who has found the god in his breast. But the others? All whose fate is to suffer and not to think?' Then looking full into the illumined countenance before him the speaker added: 'We cannot distrust the children of the gods even if they give no proof of what they say.'

Plotinus' too sensitive lips responded softly: 'One day perhaps I shall give proof.'

The man who was a stranger to him kept close to his side as he moved away from the companion column, brushing him now and then with cloak or shoulder as if he were trying, Plotinus fancied, to draw from him some divine emanation. Catching sight of the back of Origen's letter-bearer he checked and imperceptibly withdrawing himself, he said:

'Philosophers at their peril seek to avoid being mortal men.'

'Are you warning me . . . or yourself?' the stranger responded, halting also and drawing some closely written parchments from the fold of his tunic.

'I can only know whether I am man by attempting to explore my soul.'

'But,' inquired the other, 'what is it that does the exploring? That well-worn oracle: Know Thyself, how interpret it?'

'The only meaning it can have is – live what you would know, not a building up by argument upon argument, rather a disarming. The self that can know hides more cunningly under abstractions than under pastimes and toil, that is the peril.'

'And danger has grace.'

'So I am a philosopher. But,' with a faint smile, 'not a brave man.' He moved another step back.

'O, O,' cried the young man, 'why are we always in motion, why are you escaping me?' And he made a gesture of despair.

'It is the nature of time, my friend,' Plotinus answered gently, 'and one learns that the mind, after solid and wearisome labour, only takes cognisance as a bird on the wing.'

'Why . . . ?How . . . ?'

'Because it is no longer where it was. Pinion it if you can, you will not have the Reality that is self-living . . .'

'Can anyone "have" that?'

'Perhaps in the sense they can know for an instant that it is.'

The young man raised his eyes. 'That is faith.' Plotinus walked away.

Finding his storm-footed messenger pointing reed pens he said: 'Have you anywhere to stay, just come from Tyre and the sea? You know me since you were sent to me. What is your name?'

'The same. Men call me Origenes. Yes, I have a cabin on the shore of the sounding sea.' He caught the gleam in Plotinus' eyes and went on happily: 'It is theme for an epigram. I made friends with an old fisherman and spent many nights with him in his leaky craft. In return for burial he said he would leave me his boat and shapely oars, his nets and lines, and hut built of the planks of wrecked ships whose seafaring was done.'

'And?'

'I buried him with an oar on either side and the boat for tomb.'

'And the hut?'

'Come and see, if you will.'

'I must be here until evening, come back for me then. Will you?'

Origenes smiled: 'I ask nothing better. Do you want these for your work?' And he held out the neatly pointed pens.

Plotinus went with him to the portico and the broad steps where he had met the older Origen. They stood in the glare of hoar and azure watching kites swoop and rise with a turn of tail-vane, yellow crooked beak against the sky, taunt of yellow eye, and far above, vultures, black circling motes.

'Two thousand years forward or back: birds, sky, dust, shadows, and god the Sun.'

'And ant-men, a tattered flapping medley on their endless food quest. The earth must weary of her trampling brood.'

'She is more weary in the deserts where no man is. You soon know that if you wander far from the Nile.'

'All things are filled with souls and divinities, as Heraclitus says, but souls are more keenly wrought and stretched when they have the eloquence of eyes and lips more god-like.'

'The invisible harmony is better than the manifest,' Plotinus added from the same authority. 'Stars or desert or man. But it must twang as bowstring or lyre so that mind taut likewise can perceive the music.'

'It seems sometimes it's only by discords and disequilibrium, a self-willed choice, we learn there is harmony and unison.'

'All is there as in a seed. He says custom is man's daemon, so . . . most people's divagations are slight, the daemon sees to that. Even among philosophers there are many of this kind. But if one's daemon is . . .'

'Divine?'

With an indescribable glance Plotinus and his shadow retreated into the library.

The sun had swung down to the sea and the facade of palaces along the eastern wall of the Great Harbour was gilt and stained with rose, the carvings oddly triple-cut with jet shadows, when the two men walked down to the waterside. The passers-by shuffled with the weariness of day's end or stepped with a new alacrity because they were chasing their own desires. The evening- and morning-pace of philosophers alone is the same, not uninfluenced by the illuminations of heaven; porous to sun and stars as to the activities and rest of men, they meditate obedient to the presence of an interior rhythm.

'Intellect is truly being, not intellectually perceiving things outside of itself, it possesses all things in itself not as in place . . .'

But Origenes with a musical laugh checked him, even though with a hint of regret: 'I cannot now, my brain is still wave-rocked. If you will, let the hour of torch-lighting talk to us. Perhaps when we have drunk a little wine we can try the temper of our sharp swords. I believe if the gods love us we may have many days and nights together for those contests that whet mind's cutting edge.'

They walked on in silence, Plotinus smiling a little, obeyed, but soon forgetful of the city and heedless of the new promise of coolness in the wafture from the water as it drifted into the dying dryness of the desert air. When his sandals sank in sand and there was a hush of small waves, salt on his lips and the stars of the Bear just beginning to point the sky, he sighed and allowed his thoughts to wash back into formlessness. Origenes pointed out his low shelter, which itself resembled a boat resting keel uppermost, and Plotinus with nod and sign went on down to the edge of the sea.

On the brink of sea and night, fingering the slim epistle of Origen, as if indeed that alone saved him from solitariness in his dedicated life, he listened to the sea. 'All who rightly touch philosophy,' sighed the waves, 'study nothing else than to die and to be dead.' And what then, he wondered, gives so irresistible and daemonic a life to the god liberated by this study of the true philosophers? The answer came clear to him as he walked softly along the strand of the many-voiced deep, and knew himself following in the footsteps of the priest and prophet of Apollo: the spirit of Homer. In the spirit of pure poetry he would approach the inmost shrine, and that meant a leap at the last, after complete study of all the known philosophical approaches that could be realised under the aspect of his chosen master Plato. And he clearly saw just then in the form of a vision of Aphrodite the foam-born, of golden Aphrodite as a fair-tressed comet shooting down from heaven to the little laughter-loving waves, that by the spirit of divine poetry which was kindled in him, alive for evermore in sleepless light, he might discover for all men the soul of man, which is Aphrodite. The vision of the goddess with her long hair streaming faintly gold from the stars her limbs moulded with foam by air and waves, in that one indrawn breath before it was gone, showed him soul in all is one.

The piercing intensity of the vision left his mind bare. The rhythm of the sea, of his own motion, the flicker and sparkle of stars in their eternal and constellated communings one with the other, possessed him. There was nothing else.

He was brought to a standstill at last by men launching a black ship into the divine sea. Scrape of keel and splash of water, gruff voices and the clear-toned ones of lads, beat into his visionary brain, though it was not until his hands met the gunwail and he was straining with the rest of them that he knew he was not living in the *Odyssey*. Amid their heaving the seamen looked askance at him and swiftly away again, resuming their rough chant punctuated by orders from a leader who held a lantern. Suddenly the vessel made a leap of life, another element possessed her, he felt her quiver as she owned the power of the sea. The crew cried triumphant, some began clambering aboard, others standing in the water, stared at Plotinus. He felt their eyes as he bent to wash blood from his hands. With a clear voice he prayed Poseidon to keep the ship strong in the welter of waves and winds, bless her voyaging and bring her again to the haven.

As he splashed back to the dry sand, odd talk drifted to him: 'His face was alight.' 'A flame danced above his brow.' 'An immortal come down from heaven.' The oars rattled and he saw, looking over his shoulder, they'd set up the mast. The ship afloat reminded him of Origenes' fisherman's cabin. Something made him feel for the letter which he meant to keep as a kind of phylactery. It was not there. Lost in the launching of that Grecian coaster, he thought, and turned to go back along the shore.

A beam of light guided him to the opening in the side of the pitch-glued hut, a brazier of charcoal glowed there with fish broiling on an iron grid. Inside the messenger of Origen was unpacking his books and papyri, his lamp-lit profile handsome and absorbed. A boy was spreading a bed in a corner of the hut partly screened off by a draped fishing-net. Plotinus had such a complete sense of looking at a scene in the theatre he could not bring himself to enter but awaited the chorus, fishermen would it be, or young students of the city, or an Aristophanic one of creatures from the deep? He felt unreservedly confident now that his season of rebellion was at an end, that he would be able to plunge into the studies for the sake of which he had come to Alexandria. And while he still enjoyed the scene before him, he began telling himself a story of how, when he had learnt everything the porter could teach him, he would go and visit Origen in Syria. Though I suppose he'd want to make me a Christian, would he not? What matter, I doubt if I shall ever meet another mind as true as his. But I must be content with his more youthful namesake. As he thought this he knew Origenes had discovered him.

Standing in the doorway he said: 'My dear, you have come. You were a long time gone. But I was unpacking. Will you eat with me?'

Plotinus bent his head, looking with affection on the young man who was setting on the table flasks of water and wine, a pair of wooden cups, a basket of bread and salad in a beautiful bowl with winged human figures upon its side. To these the boy added a slim vessel of olive oil and the cooked fish smelling of fire and sea. A wind passed over, rustling the reeds of the roof, carrying the sound of waves and the call of a night-flying bird. The door swung to and opened wide again. The youthful slave propped it open with a billet and taking his flute he sat down cross-legged by the brazier and began to play softly. When he had poured a libation to Hermes the messenger of the gods, the guest said:

'Will you tell me about the School since you come so lately from a master of it?'

'Life is the most important part of study, I have been thinking lately,' the young man said slowly. 'The life of living men is so to say the true mind of learning. You must let all life have full play. The danger of this is that the mind starts making new myths. There are enough of them. They are all made complete from the beginning and can only be retold by men of later time. The danger of not letting life have liberty is that the study of the old masters becomes a ritual. They are beyond criticism. There is dark ground in us all, a dark of not man, not god. Here are the roots of life.'

'What do you mean by not letting life have liberty?'

'One answer: by a denial of the dark. Another: by worshipping the dark as a divine mystery. Life in full liberty faces both dark and light.'

'Contemplation.'

'Is perfect knowledge possible,' Origenes said, not as a question.

'To think so is the unconscious life of our conscious thought seeking liberty in light.' Plotinus looked at him: 'The soul, my dear, is the human ground whether mortal or not in us – the tribes of leaves – and is itself immortal. This is going to be my study.'

'Clement, the master of the school who more than any other man, as all say, was devoted to the Greek philosophers – Athens was his birthplace – came hither because it is here in our time the edge of living mind is most keenly whetted. The Greeks of the early age held sorrows gather thick in certain places, didn't they, and a man entering such a region, of mind or body what matter, was overcome with woe, so now in Alexandria is a clustering of humming honey-gathering worshippers of wisdom not averse either from using their stings.'

'And Clement's work?'

'He taught Origen,' Origenes smiled a little. 'His work, though I have not read largely in it, was to show how our philosophers prepared the way for the Gnostics, that wisdom and faith are one. This is delicate ground. One thing I remember, you will approve, I fancy. He said: "Knowledge of God is inseparable from likeness to Him." '

They fell silent. The boy cleared the table and trimmed Origenes' lamp. Plotinus rose.

'You want to study?'

'I am for sleep now, to forget the tossing. Will you stay with me?'

'To see dawn over the bright sea?'

'To wake by the side of your new companion. There is communion in sleeping and waking.'

Plotinus shook his head. 'Not this night.' Then seeing the other's regret he said: 'Be assured, we are friends. There will be many nights when we shall wake and talk while the sun is carried under the earth sleeping in his golden bowl.'

* * *

Sleep is the contemplation of the body, and the mind knowing without images is in a state of pure being. Reason forgets, is as one might say absent-minded, but symbols, now seeming vain, now lit with inexplicable transitory glory, flit across it. Thought is a mael-strom to the man awake, tearing as well as tautening the web of divine consciousness. Rest may be an opening for impressions rejected in the fury of reasoning, but it must also be allowed in its own way to heal, or the whole texture, which alone can reflect unity, will be damaged. At night in the darkness, sight without act. This

71

is the true vision, the sleepless light the darkness cannot absorb. But my daemon is a poet, a maker that is, I cannot rest without some kind of attenuated act, even in night. As a sleepwalker Plotinus traversed the city with his ambient soul enfolding him as the invisible mist rendering Odysseus invisible, the grace of Athene leading him through the glorious streets of the Phaeacians. Lost too to himself he would have kept to no direction, but he was not hidden from the dogs. These scavenging prowlers were drawn to him, the starved and abject slinking after with tails depressed, the more lively bounding up, caressing his hands with clammy tongues. Until at last he noticed this rough-coated company in the light of torches carried by the slaves of some homeward-bound banqueter, and looking from their wolfish grins to the buildings, considered where he might be.

'What are those curs doing, fawning as if they had a master?'

'Sir,' replied one of the slaves, 'dogs discern spirits.'

A point has position if not dimensions, Plotinus told himself smiling a little. I must be somewhere. And it came to him suddenly that in this new life of city and streets and strand he had lost fellowship with his earliest guide Nile. So he asked the man who had spoken and who was dawdling, rebinding his smoky flare, the way to the river.

'Are you not going there? Keep downhill. You will see the lights of the shambles, the dogs' goal. Beyond lies the saviour of Egypt.'

Soon, as he'd hoped at that word, the pack sloped off, and he was aware of the radiance of a mysterious presence, a fluid resistant luminous darkness that was loosing on the air moist breaths and vapours of life-feeding, life-gulping slime. He heard the familiar susurrent reeds, the deathly monotony of the lapping water of the god, his desert pilgrimage ended, his current widened into a lake as marginless as Ocean. Plover flew up in a scattered flight with unruly clamourings. Here and there an eyot winked with the red star of a fisher's fire. With a singular content in the solitariness, a sense of the alone neither sun nor sea entrusted to him in the same measure, he felt his intellect resting in the world-soul ceaselessly fashioning the universe. His thought alive there need labour no more. He made a lair for sleep in grass precariously rooted in dry sand.

Voices of river-birds calling the dawn roused him. Raising a mound for his head, as a child would a vallum for a crumbling fortress, he looked into the infinite, heaven whitening from source and cause invisible; looked too at the vast dragon whose scales outshone the sky. Egypt entering into his Greek blood and the Jewish strain from his mother gave him then a sense that he was a living symbol of the mingling minds of the scholarly city. Intellect alone is above worship and sacrifice. I will offer sacrifices no more to the gods and the images of the gods, but know intellect in all things, the grass blades, the silent grains of sand. To know intellect is indeed pure worship. This too is being. My mind, this singular complexity in time, must relearn freedom in the light of the eternal, until it knows in consciousness there is nothing between. But everything a man is and does is a realisation of the self, finite and limited, fading, but still a necessity unexplained of time, which is motion. Here, life takes the form of motion upon motion, a ceaseless interplay of related motions . . . these papyrus craft adrift on the eternally gliding Nile.

Why live then – from the lightening sky, the gleaming water, the sand grains and the grass stalks the question edged itself into his skull as through the very sutures of the bones – if the soul alone seeks nothing but to be one with the Divine Soul? What is the imperative to live and suffer; to keep under the body, as that Jew has said, so that soul indwelling or infolding this mysterious structure may be free to contemplate Intellect? Why live and fast and deny sleep for a rare or imperfect freedom in knowing that would, in the body's death, be fulfilled once and for all? There must be an answer to content reason why for a season life must prevail in me.

Far over the water his unseeing eyes ranged as if he were asking the ancient river for an answer; it is the same now as it has been for ever. What makes this expanse of water different now from the water of a thousand or ten thousand centuries ago when men waited and watched for the rising of their god the Sun, for the rising of their god the River at the shining in the east of the Sirius star? The waters are not different, eternally they circle between river and ocean, earth and heaven, the difference is in my soul knowing. The superabundance of the one soul seeks to know itself in its outpouring of itself, in the myriads of reflecting souls that without being separate from it make more perfect the fulfilment of knowledge. No life is possible for me, he thought smiling at the words of Heliodorus' master, but one of striving to be one with the Divine Soul. To be in deepest consciousness always There perceiving the light of God, however I am busied with what is Here, so in this way the realisation in me will never suffer interruption. That I will to live

73

in this way is no answer to my question, but it makes me know I must live, as surely as a carrion-eating crab knows or a sacred ibis. Because, as Parmenides says, to perceive intellectually and to be, which as I am now is to live, are the same thing. But to live evermore intensely in intellect is a strain and a stern tempering of the body; all the radiance binding bones, jointed limbs, flesh lapped in porous, vegetable skin, is drawn to the soul. As athletes train their frames for muscular contests so I must inure my body to suffer the directing of all its energies to the life of the soul. Then it may be the soul will restore something, as a grace refined, to the physical nature.

The growing irradiance of the sky, the Nile assuming a brilliant appearance as if the water were clear instead of turbid with all the gathered sand of its long journey through the desert, warned him the sun was rising above that ruled horizon. He stood with the wonder of all those centuries of sun-worshipping Egyptians upon his soul, knowing man's eyes could behold no greater mystery than the source of seeing. Would the soul could so know eternal light! But even as he looked on the round of dazzling gold still as yet obscured with a certain redness, a trace of the darkness so lately consumed, he had a sense of that energy of intellect which was his life, the life of the imperious god in him, become nought.

Slowly restored to consciousness with eyes blinded by gazing, he knew not how long, on Helios, he covered his face with his hands in dread of nothingness. There could be no memory of it, only he recognised that that Alone which he believed he sought and longed for was a warm companioned state compared to this, which presently offered itself to his bare mind in the form of an illumination, that it was a purification and preparation for receiving mystic knowledge. With a shuddering that was at the same time akin to the phrenic irradiance of his whole body, as if he were wrought of immortal fire, he knew this vision of the sun was one with the touch of dread Persephone.

Plotinus went to gather up his cloak, seeing it lying on the sand, with an impersonal feeling as though it belonged to some other who had let it fall hurriedly before entering a race. There was no sign of his couch or the bolster he had moulded with his hands and the animated folds of his mantle could not have been lain on or covered him when he was recumbent. Its rose colour glowed endearingly as he picked it up and gave it a shake, then letting the garment swing from one shoulder he began to walk along the path towards the quay where the water-craft of the Nile berthed.

The ships that morning were moored in idleness, resting on the water as birds with wings folded, forgetful of flights made and to be. Some were garlanded as for a festival and he wondered at the flowery emblems. Moving forward with his mien of one in a sacred procession carrying a dedicated offering, he saw a shadow of a second solitary and abstracted wayfarer with flapping mantle and short tunic and raised his eyes, even as did the other who also impulsively held out both hands. Plotinus recollected the flaxen youth who had once come to him in the school at Lycopolis and through a veil of unwillingness for any human touch just then allowed his fingers to rest a moment on those eager palms.

'How shining you are!' the young man cried softly. 'You have seen a vision.'

'And you also,' Plotinus responded to the joyousness with that full beaming look few could sustain.

'It is Easter Day.'

A shadowless silence fell between the two men at this.

Plotinus asked gently: 'You go to the School that was Origen's, and where now I believe a philosopher-priest lectures?'

Crispin nodded. 'For the sake of the many Greeks and pagans who come to him as pupils Origen devoted himself to the study of their philosophy; Heraclas, who was his pupil for five years, even more. He never puts off the philosopher's mantle.'

'When you came to me before, I was teaching, now I become myself a pupil in this city of the learned.'

'I also. One is like to be confounded by this many-voiced wisdom.'

'You have chosen your guide . . . Why, it is Marcus!'

Crispin's austere companion was changed before his eyes and he saw the cousins embrace with almost a pang, so evident was the warmth of their fellowship.

'I have been looking for you ever since I came here.'

'I know, I've been away. They told me you'd asked.'

'Are you here to see to the lading of your ships?'

Marcus looked rueful. 'There are too many dam' religious festivals in this place, another today and half the men haven't come.'

Plotinus smiled, with a glance at Crispin: 'Well, let this be our day since the gods have let us meet. Give the other half leave and we will go together . . . wherever you will. They will make up for it tomorrow.'

Marcus hesitated, then said: 'I agree. But they won't, all the same. You don't have to try to make the fellahin work!'

'You remember, we said farewell at sunrise. We have been given another.' As his cousin returned to the ships he went on to the Christian: 'Will you come with us?'

'No, I am going to the Paschal Feast. But I cannot understand why you do not . . .'

'Can you not understand,' Plotinus answered gently, 'that it is by the will of God I am as I am? It is not that I choose to stand away from your religion, from any religion, but God chooses for me. Right and wrong here are not absolute but each man's knowledge of the One. That is absolute for him.'

'Can men live without some share in love, human and divine?'

'You know – "The philosopher studies nothing else than to die and to be dead"? I would say: cut everything away.'

Crispin's naturally joyous look was doomed before that unmoved serenity. 'But you cannot live as if other men were not.'

'I do not seek them, it is true, but I refuse no one who comes to me.'

'But living, life, your own life! the young man cried with his face flushed.

'The utmost intensity of life is in a conscious looking towards the Highest. Through that one is more aware of the beauty of earth-life, not less.'

'I must go. Tell me where I can find you again.'

Plotinus told him of Heliodorus and added: 'I am going to begin attending the lectures of Ammonius. Come there one day, if you will. You have heard of him?'

'I have heard he was a Christian, but I do not think he teaches as they do in the School.'

'If ever you go back to Asyut, visit my sister for me.' He lifted his hand in farewell and went towards Marcus who was returning with irritable foot.

★　★　★

The two cousins idled through the day in the city as truant school-boys. The nature of feckless boy in Marcus released something in Plotinus that he had known even in childhood only when they were together. The scene of indescribable massacres and persecutions where as many slaves were chained to their masters as there were men who lived free lives became a playground for them that Easter Sunday. They swung past synagogues and temples and churches, the wild companies of priests and eunuchs who tore their clothes and slashed their painted bodies to do honour to their portable gods and goddesses, they skirted the processions of flower-bearing girls and sleek boys on their way to the gymnasium; in fact just then the gravity of other citizens' preoccupations, devotions and mirth-making touched them no more than if they'd been a pair of those yellow-billed fish-tailed shit-hawks in the metallic sky above. They did stay to watch the puppy-play of naked brats with made-up eyes round the two obelisks in front of the great Caesareum, and Plotinus enjoyed without comment the way his cousin's laughter echoed and re-echoed along the pigeon-holed arcades of the Columbarium where they came at noon to eat the ripe melons they'd bought, choosing them fastidiously from the paniers slung across the back of a little ass. They bought a third for him but the offering was scorned. When they had walked all round the dove-cote of the dead and saluted the ashes of countless generations, they crossed to the care-fully watered oasis in the midst of the court and sliced their fruit with a knife Marcus carried in a sheath of sweet-smelling leather. The jewels in the hilt flashed in the filtered sun and shade of the palm-fronds while the task was carried out as though the carver were a sculptor. Observing the low determined brow of his companion, Plotinus suddenly felt oppressed by his own high thought-knotted one. With a gesture rare in him he pressed the dense cropped hair of the man at his side.

'Now don't you,' Marcus cautioned, 'go into a trance, wondering what's become of *their* minds,' and he waved his knife-blade round the walls of the Columbarium. 'They are dust and ashes like the rest of them. You know, down below, there is a regular necropolis as big as the city of the living, a maze of caves and catacombs full of pots of dust that once was hungry flesh and blood hot with lust. You needn't smile, it's you that makes me talk in this way.' Their eyes met solemnly. 'It is strange.'

'The wise always seek the fellowship of the dead.'

'I suppose so,' Marcus growled. 'I shouldn't have come here without you.' He scowled at the red cloak and without looking at the owner of it said: 'You know, this is a world where men have to work to live, to eat bread, even to snatch an hour for mirth and dance before the grave, or the pyre which devours them and all that is left is popped into one of these little bird's-nest niches. You look at all you see as if it were a play and do your living inside your head which is stored with dust of dead men's minds; is, in fact, a columbarium of a human skull.'

He looked up and met Plotinus' piercing gaze; neither looked away, there was an instant's fusion of two naked souls. Recovering his separate identity by turning aside, Marcus muttered:

'What was that, life or death?'

'What, did some of that dry dust get in your eyes, my dear?'

'What did I look into?' Marcus said, as if dazed.

'Into the one soul, the one part of us clay creatures that never has been and never will be dust. It is the same for us as for them, for the melon-seller and those castanet-rattlers and cymbal-signallers who bothered us so much racketing along with their ass-borne goddess.'

'And you seek to live in that soul instead of . . . your own?'

'I do not exactly seek, Marcus, I must. I can live in no other way. My daemon sees to that.'

'Not a mere daemon, we all have that if we choose to attend. Some god!'

'Do you understand now?'

'No.'

'Nor I. But tomorrow I am going to a different lecturer, who, I have an idea, will help me to understand.'

'But why is this one soul locked up in us?'

'It isn't.' Plotinus laid his hand on the stone bench, touched the trunk of the palm and tore off a small piece of brown fibrous matter that resembled coarsely woven cloth. 'Everything lives in it, but in men it is more intense because of mind which reflects directly that light we knew when our eyes were light instead of seeing things in light.'

'You make me want to live in eternity, as you do,' Marcus said with a muted laugh.

'We all are in eternity inasmuch as we are at all. But we are also as we are. To know you live is the first thing. Some are good at this who cannot think in the sense of having reasoned thoughts they can share in words, said or written.'

'As when you are in love?'

'That is the best way of knowing you live,' Plotinus agreed quietly, 'as long as it is an intellectual passion. You remember the two Aphrodites in the *Symposium?*'

'But is it quite fair, to transmute bodily desire into a fertilising of your own brain, to give, as it were, a mind-consciousness to your senses?'

'Fair to . . . ?'

78

'To life itself, to the energy that is life, that would fulfil itself in lust.'

'This energising in itself is the life of the *nous*, the divine intellect. The highest act of man is to live in knowledge of the divine, if he fails in this – for whatever cause – the energy spends itself little by little in physical desires that never satisfy; the thirst soon returns.'

'Few can attain to knowledge of this act.'

'You are probably right, Marcus, they can or will not. Those who can, must. It is an imperative. In the same way, in so far as they can, men choose what they will do to make a living with their hands. A fellow is not a carpenter by chance. Also, he is not a fisherman. And the better carpenter he is, the less likely he is to change his occupation. Every skill is limiting and at the expense of some other activity.'

'Except philosophy?'

'That too in the stages of being a human pursuit of wisdom or learning. But it is also a reaching into the limitless, a constant remembering of the eternal Creator. This remembering, or silent inclining of being to God, is a partaking of the act of creation. And I believe, my dear, though you may laugh at me for it if you want to, this constant contemplation of the Highest, the Creator of all life as we know it, in mind and heart and nervous flesh, inasmuch as any man does this, he is doing it for all.'

'Are you trying to teach me? I am too dense for that, too old . . . and cold-minded.'

'Never that. Only trying to explain to myself, and before your eyes, the kind of man I am and what seems to me may be the essence of life. Without seeking this essence, with the utmost intensity of all that I am, I cannot live.'

'It is your power to know this, my dear,' Marcus said slowly, 'to have this sure knowledge in your soul of one source of life to join all your living to, so the everyday mindless meaningless fragments are only as it were refractions, not loose ends with no place in the cosmic order, or tendrils twining into the void, which is how I suppose ordinary men's thoughts go adventuring, if they ever do. It is remarkable how unfirm all these earth things *can* become to a certain mode of mind, how real all intangibles.'

Plotinus smiled at his puzzled countenance. 'Can it be you are to become a philosopher?'

'It cannot!' was the indignant retort. 'I never have any notions of this sort unless I'm near you.'

79

'They are there, as they are more or less in everyone. And they do not escape their own notice if you hide them away from yours.'

'Well, it's my concern to attend to the fitting-out of ships and to the freight they carry, cousin, not to the blue of heaven and ocean of their voyaging.' He fingered the diagonal weave of the scrap of palm-bark. 'I shall be glad to be at work again, but . . . there is something about being with you that sets the dullest brain weaving a tissue of gold that will still shimmer in the tomb.' He stood up.

'From this you will see a reflection on everything. Is our holiday over?'

'I think it may be. I am joining a party of friends for the evening.'

'Now?'

'Now I am going to the baths.'

They walked slowly along one of the shadowy colonnades of the Columbarium and falling into further conversation paced it again, finding a reviving coolness in the silvery mourning stone under their feet.

'Ay, these graceful vases are companions for thought and chill riotous humours!'

'You see another peripatetic come to seek their council in the garb of the philosophers.'

A tall man, not old but book-backed by his studies, with mantle and scrip, and sandals swinging from his side by their thongs, crossed the spaces and was hidden by intervening pillars on the opposite side of the court. Marcus observed him and then gave his cousin a merry look.

'Shall I make you known to him?'

'Why not, since you want to be off? I know you are up to a trick but I am not as scared of that as I used to be. He looks like a philosopher.'

'He is.'

They moved into the sun. 'As if we were stepping clear into his heart of flames. Can you suppose days of such glory can ever end in dark?'

'Very easily.'

'Darkness is best for thought, or its two indeterminate borderlands.'

'That may be.'

Marcus, with a certain assurance of not being regarded as intrusive, bent down and looked into the lowered eyes of the man as he passed them. For an instant they remained unseeing, then in

80

their inmost deeps two tiny flames of reluctant recognition wanly kindled.

'You have found me after too long, my son, and yet in the name of God I would you had not in this interval stolen for silence from the Easter liturgies.'

'It is not I who will keep you, I am in haste. But this day fate has restored me my kinsman and given me also a sight of you. I wish, sir, you to allow me the privilege of bringing together two philosophers; Plotinus, I present you to Heraclas, bishop of this city.' And Marcus was gone.

The pair he left were both so immersed in the Tyrian purple of their own thoughts they neither spoke nor regarded one another but absently recognising the introduction and a certain alliance of temperament, advanced side by side with downcast looks. Plotinus was reconsidering his question of that hour between dawn and sunrise and it was without surprise that he found, when at length he looked about him, he was again in the presence of the great river and not distant from the place where he had spent the night.

'You also are a reader of the Greeks?'

'They have thought and said, as it seems to me, all. Yet, this does not absolve each man of seeking to be a philosopher for his own part, though it may be beyond him to decide where their thought ends and his own . . . insofar as anyone can claim anything for himself in so universal a stuff as mind . . . begins.'

'You are right. But to recognise this may well be the significance of our time and this city. This pouring into one vessel of all streams of thought, and of religions, is going to cause confusion and suffering beyond what we can foresee: persecutions and torments of body and soul. Any man who is led by the Spirit to Alexandria at this time with mind bent Godward must direct all his powers to – how would you put it?'

Plotinus recognised the pause of the lecturer and practised teacher who sought to prove the mind of a younger man. He rested in the silence which nurtured them both and then said with a sense of labour: 'To prepare the soul for knowing that light which is itself the vision.'

'By act or stillness?'

'The stillness is the constant underlying certainty that the possibility is. But when intellect surges with the sense of lifting mind on its sweeping crests, then it is necessary to recognise act as a symbol that Being and Intellect are one.'

81

'You would stand alone, my dear son.'

'So cries the god in me. In all this flux and interplay of thought there is room for one mind – not to be aloof from all the influences of those who think, not that arrogant isolation – to offer to this age, which is engaged in preparing moulds for reasoned thought, the experiences of sheer intellect. The edge is whetted by the Greek masters and by the unborn the rays of the sun will call from the grain-bearing earth.'

Heraclas frowned at the speaker: 'Would you claim with the Gnostics you know more than other men, you have some secret knowledge?'

Plotinus smiled. 'The source of divine knowledge is in all men, all beings. My understanding, sharpened as I have said, is the way life, an independent principle as I believe, approaches this knowledge through the particular form of matter I am. If I did not believe this I should quit it at once.'

'Soul too strong for mortal breast.'

'But this deity will hold it together as long as there is need for my thought.' Then in a different tone: 'I believe you were the master of the School after Origen. Why do you not recall your banished master to Alexandria?'

The bishop evidently suffered under this direct question, he muttered that he would have rather been anything than an ally of 'all the evil winds of Egypt' which had cast him out.

'And yet, it is you who deny his return.'

'I must protect the church from the perils of heresy, already it is too much weakened by division.'

'And you fear for your own authority in the presence of a greater man. Men are strengthened by oppositions. But for myself the differences in the church would be a . . . would demand a diffusion of divine energy that is essential for concentrated thought and attention. My philosophy is not yet established but I know it must grow alone in my own mind, insofar as any mind can be solitary in seeking to know the universal.'

Heraclas looked now with unveiled interest in his complex gaze at the man who was so living and yet oddly bodiless a presence at his side; the head did not appear to him outlined on the deepening blue evening sky, it was that for his vision the heaven had been cut through to show him a profile on the infinity beyond. The singular stillness of features at once rugged and hewn with Grecian symmetry and proportion reminded him of a Pharaoh sculptured in golden sandstone he had seen once as a sun in a firmament of lapis lazuli.

'It is well.' He spoke in a tone of finality that made Plotinus turn to him, and he answered the look as though speaking to himself. 'It is well in this age of ferment and persecution, of men desperately seeking the way of communicating a new revelation with the fullness of truth and with no severance of the ancient mysteries, which are of the substance of human wisdom, to have a mind clear of these embroilments, as free of cloud and dark and knowledge of evil as a desert sun at noon. I know. No man is without his dark half, but yours is that of the Greeks of old. From where I stand I can see that with the great light a night such as our pure philosophers did not face in their awakening is overshadowing the broad-wayed earth; a very groping dark for all who are half blinded by light. The excellence of your mind compels homage.'

The assurance of Heraclas before him gave his companion on the shore of the Nile a sense of closeness to a mortal man who had by means unknown to him experienced reaches he had not, perhaps never would attain to. This was something unfamiliar to Plotinus but it caused no sense of envy or even curiosity. He replied with his accustomed luminous composure: 'Your stand is that of history and you therefore look forward more than back. For myself intellect is, if I may say so, instantaneous, and my reality of living while I am unwillingly earth-hitched is to wait upon this intellect with my reason and my soul.'

'I must go,' the bishop said sadly. 'You shed such a blandness upon me, for all the sternness of your mind's disciplines, that I do not leave you easily for the agape. I think we could talk for ever, as the children say; I have studied the Greeks, as I could but do not say, more devotedly than all the Christian sources. Fortunately for me the people of Alexandria accept a philosopher for bishop, though why I cannot say. And, yes, I know it, this seems to make it worse that I do not try to have Origen recalled. But I know, and you'll have to believe me in this, for the sake of our new-sprung friendship if for nothing else, that the church here in the state it's now in, would not gain from his return. And I know all he has of good to give will not be lost wherever he teaches and preaches. His stream will flow into the main current in time.

'One other word: I should like to make you known to Dionysus the master of the School who has taken my place. He also worships at the shrines of our divine masters. He is writing as well as teaching. You would be friends.'

Retreating on the word Heraclas gave over his shoulder such a glance of whimsical challenging affection Plotinus could not believe this was their first meeting; how many times in other lives their souls must have been together in men walking and talking philosophy.

CHAPTER VI

The Decade

Plotinus stood on the threshold of Ammonius' house between the two sphinxes of sandstone rubbed and damaged by their long presence there, and in part perhaps intentionally by the passing students of the god-instructed philosopher. If some one had asked him whether he was there for the first time or the last he could not have answered, so complete was the circle of those ten years; their very days were as one sun-baked Egyptian day, and the ephemeral moods ardent and despondent by turns, in which he had attended the discourses of this teacher of the human soul were as insignificant as flaws over the deserts of Africa. How many times had he fled between those carved riddlers unseeing, his mind in relentless pursuit of the enigma of itself, or wrestling with the doctrine of his chosen sage. As for the first time he saw these symbolic monsters now defaced, as it seemed to him, not by the touch of time but by the impetus of thought-laden minds. Thought unachieved strangles the thinker. Then he caught from the voiceless inquirers the echo of his own words to Origenes as he was leaving the house after the first lecture of Ammonius he had attended: This is the man I've been looking for.

Well, Plotinus now asked himself as he stood on the hollowed stone doorsill between those lions couchant with human illegible countenances, have I been wise or have I not, in leaving my mind malleable for those ten revolving years to the mind of Ammonius? Am I now a philosopher in my own right, or is all the wool spun and I but twirl an empty spindle from habit? Is there nothing left I can call my own in the basket that seemed overbrimming with fleeces of sea-purple? One by one certain responses formed themselves, overlaid with an imperious call to go down to the divine sea. So he took his final leave by touching with his fingers first one kingly neck and then the other of the speechless guardians and giving his mantle an unpremeditated irritable jerk, a gesture foreign to him. His course was now set eastward, tomorrow or the day after he would embark on one of the benched ships that were carrying the armament of the Emperor Gordian on the campaign against

Persia, and it seemed to him now, before the stern-cables were unloosed, he must consider his mind moulded by the years in Alexandria.

On the familiar road from the house of the philosopher to the sea which in his present mood he might never have trodden before, or never ceased to tread, he answered the questions posed beside the sphinxes: for this decade I had no choice but to hearken to the porter, so to that – wise or not wise – there is nothing to say. I am a philosopher. My intellect has learnt its strength and how to interpret the eternal knowledge of the soul contemplating the divine. This is the demand of my daemon. The spindle is bare and should lie idle. But it will not. I cannot lay it down; not anyhow till I am on the deck of a swift ship. Therefore this is an interval for recollection, for examining from the thin gleam left me what I have learnt from the great luminary.

At first mere snatches of the teaching of Ammonius went and came and withdrew again, mingled with fragments of talks with Origenes and Heliodorus, with whom he had sometimes gone to the Aristotelian School, and occasional interspersions from the bishop Heraclas and the master of the Catechetical School, Dionysus. Their voices rose and fell like strophes and anti-strophes of a teasing chorus of mock sages as he came down to the beach and began to walk, with salt water lapping his sandals and the evening air moving about his brow and temples as pleasantly as if they were myrtle-wreathed. And presently as he walked the motion of it, the rhythm and the light breeze endowed his mind with a kind of vacancy through which in a more orderly measure the highest communings of the last ten years began to pass, his own thoughts quiet, other men's words sounding with authentic speech.

The nothingness of human knowledge compared with divine knowledge, that is the grief of philosophers, because they cannot live without striving to experience the strange soul which is the breath of their own, the one soul uninfluenced by earth, by its apparent division into multitudes. It can only be by means of the One that mind is bound to this thinking and owns its high reason, that is the certainty. But the Necessity, the daemonic imperative to think even under the tasselled aegis of certainty that the One cannot be realised by the wrestling reason of man because it alone is: and is free. Plotinus rested his cheek-bones and sea-cooled brow on the palms of his hands. Thought the clashing rocks crashing upon all, but There without this violence of energy – the ecstasy which is union, motionless energy, which is intellect pure – could not be known by life. 'Knowledge of good is the one knowledge of which it is impossible to make an ill use.' These words were his myrtle wreath.

They told him that knowledge on earth is as all else a multiplicity and must be drawn together by thought, by all means that life has, into the simple knowledge of the Good. And what makes belief in this as a possibility perceptible to the complex of mind; consciousness, an unthought reflection of the simplex. And this consciousness, the Intellectual-Principle resting in self-knowledge, is the life of the soul. I must think of the soul not as looking to knowledge but as living knowledge of the Good.

Then, as it were on a pause of this inward and intellectual tenseness, the gates of his senses were opened wide to the serenity of evening, when from on high over the sea, the first stars looked upon him transparent, as he imagined, to the love and splendour of the perfect celestial sphere beyond, and he walked shadowless on the shore not of time but of the eternal. And with the louder plash of the sea under the darkening wings of night he heard a mingling of voices, of the confraternity as he believed of the poets and philosophers of the past to whom he had most consciously devoted himself, whose far-reaching wisdom Ammonius had never wearied of seeking to reconcile. He almost thought to distinguish the tones of one and another as each emphasised the phrases Plotinus had come to associate with their inmost teaching. He cried aloud the names that would be always immortal on the lips of living men. One by one they held towards him their torches and bright brands and censers wistfully steaming until he had breathed strange vapours and acrid fumes, and his cheeks burnt, seared with flames that lightened through the smoke haze. Then he too held a torch that smouldered as though newly-kindled and at one with a caressing wind the vision was gone, only he still breathed a fragrance of pinewood and wild olive.

The beginning of philosophising is the One, all else can be compared to 'the adornments of the feast', even when these adornments are of the essence and necessity of intellect; for, the moment intellect begins its travail, there is a certain losing of the presence of the ultimate unchanging power which can in its own unity never be diminished, although by using in thought what is of this power in ourselves, by trying to understand what is beyond reason, there is some weakening of the pure awareness of the One. And this awareness, since reason will assert itself, may be defined as the energy of contemplation, invisible light, knowledge. The One is known in man by intuition which is eternal and without memory. I never forget this. I do everything in this presence, even in so far as I am in some sense compelled to look away from it. The looking away with reasoning is Aristotle, the reasoning within the presence of the one is Plato. This is not a matter of choice but of the daemon which I might hold to be, at this point of my mind's discussion with itself, the contact of reasoning power with the Absolute.

Already this is diffusion. The necessity of using reason with the utmost strenuousness in the abstract, which makes man a philosopher, is for him the means of realisation, his mind cleaves to the One in the intensity of thought. Other men, animals, plants are by their mere being passively within it. This passive being, unthinking living, life triumphing in them in their particular concrete mode, is the sustenance no dry mind can do without on the pain of becoming sterile. They may even be likened to the sleep of the thinker.

For myself, since there must be a form of words when the silence and simpleness of knowing need a stay, because of the earth-massiveness of body which is not always rendered of small account by the radiance of being, I will say this for the One, the Godhead of Heraclas, the King Unworking of Numenius, for myself the One is the Solitary 'in which there is neither knowing nor anything unknown'.

The name Heraclas brought into his mind just then the corpus of the Christians, a living presence in Alexandria which no one aware of the essential dynamism of the cosmos could deny. The danger for them he thought, is that suffering and love should take the place of contemplation of the Truth. Is it a suffering God they worship or do they make suffering itself their God: as if suffering, not because of thought but instead of thought, is their supreme offering? It is for this indeed they endure unflinching the constant persecutions. Both the good, pleasure, and the evil, suffering, of the body are used and transcended in the intellect which dwells above them in living knowledge of the Godhead. Has not one of their teachers said: 'Though I give my body to be burned and have not Grace it avails me nothing'? This Grace is the soul in God before the fall, and the knowledge by which, after dwelling in man, it returns to Him. Love and suffering are symbols for reality while we are in the body, but even in the body reality can be known.

The waves washed back with their sound of a musical abundance into his hearing; he experienced again his walking, the god-like motion of man on the earth, when by his own powers his proud head, the godhead of manhood, is held upon heaven and the stars, the stars of whose souls it may be said 'the light is itself the vision'. It seemed to him now the time was for rest, for *anapausis* from thought, the source untroubled, limpid in pure contemplation. But this *eudaimonia*, well-being of spirit, was after all the most intense energy and so as with the One there must be an overflowing. The most divine in the eternal fulfilling of itself in stillness becomes through intellect act available. He remembered the words often repeated by Heliodorus, of his master: 'Action according to its own indwelling power is perfect happiness; and this power is speculative.' Ah, there was the difference between the minds of the writers of the *Ethics* and the *Timaeus*, the very warp and woof – these two – of the mind-substance of man; the speculative power of the one directed always heavenwards, of the other towards the explanation of the world visible. Plotinus sighed from a sense of the cumulative weariness of unending disputes in the lecture-room following the attempts of Ammonius to reconcile those two. Plato, like his constructor of the universe, had his eye on the eternal, and this looking to the First must be first. The idea Ammonius always returned to was that it was by the energising of the intellect that the simple energy of the Good could alone be known. While man was living flesh pure contemplation was unattainable without intellection.

How then does he know that pure contemplation is? Here was the place for the teaching of those men from the east whose countries it was his present purpose to visit. It had happened voyagers on shipboard from the east now and again visited the lecture-room, one in especial who had an easy gift for Greek had spoken willingly among them of the teaching of his countrymen, but always with the emphasis that little of their esoteric wisdom could be imbibed without a long discipleship, a literal sitting at the feet of an acknowledged sage. But after he had hearkened to that soft-voiced talker, who reminded him of what he had never known – a forest, with dark pools, chance gleams of gold, mystery upon mystery obscured by arching branches, leafless twig-patterns on the shadowy air, something of frenzy and whirling Bachanal below the olive skin which because of its dark pigment perhaps preserved an oiled opacity, Plotinus had believed his own clearest thinking had its being on the verge of that perfect union the Indian had spoken of.

Always afterwards he was wont to say at these moments: There is not much between. And whenever thought-weariness overcame him and he was ready to lie down with the dead whose toil was over, the powerless heads of Homer's dead, he knew this could not be until he had attained this oneness while he yet was a living man on the grain-bearing earth.

Of all the schools of thought in the city that which most aroused the desire to master their methods with his own reason, which was for himself the mind's way of knowing contemplation by intuition, was that of the Gnostics. And here he admitted that his dialectic, which he was prepared to define as a habit by which a man was able to reason about everything intelligently and not from opinion, was not yet ready to express all that he regarded as wrong in their doctrine. But what he knew certainly was that their approach to knowledge by means of magic was wrong, and that magic could in no way touch contemplation. Matter was not, as they taught, evil, for how could it then receive the form of beauty in this world which contemplation recognised and knew for a reflection of the ideal beauty? 'Matter is not evil, it is weak.' He spoke this aloud. Nor are the men, whom these advocates of a secret knowledge choose to describe as completely composed of matter, incapable of pure understanding of the Good. It is in all things there, inarticulate it may be, but present, in the sense of being. They are in love with their own opinions and, not being able to bear with necessity, dodge what they do not like by deciding that Providence is not here. 'What sort of piety can make Providence stop short of earthly concerns or set any limit whatsoever to it?'

And suddenly he could have cried there on the shore of the sounding sea as his passion for the beauty of earth rose up like a proud-crested spumescent wave, and not as was usual with him at these moments an intellectual surge but a human longing for love and chill lament and a revolt of all his overruled desires against the barren tract of the decade. The way of thought and spirit's endeavour was a harsh one and there was no turning back, he knew this even through the mute anguish of every nerve quivering with spring in his being.

The vernal love-songs of the Greeks sang in his head, Sappho's ardour was in his blood, his unspoken cry to Aphrodite thrilled over the waves. The way chosen by his daemon and self-chosen seemed but a scrawl, a hateful zig-zag in a mockery of stars. But in torment of denial of his physical manhood he knew a consummation of the soul in its striving for the Highest. And in this plenitude he embraced with all that he was as he stood on that sea-beach, with his feet on the patient sand, his light mantle lifted by the night wind, the whole of the visible cosmos, knowing it not less divine than the unseen energy and potency of intellect. Nature instinct with beauty, ceaselessly working to heal, to transform evil, subject to a relentless worship of the world of ideas that condemns her to destroy all her creations because all are but faulty copies, is yet of all things closest to contemplation. And he swore to himself a great oath, as Homer would say, that while he saw light on the earth he would remember this tree of Nature as symbol of contemplation when his soul returned from ecstasy, when her wings failed and she must needs rest on some form of matter, a tree the most exalted, the spaces between boughs and foliage open to the boundless.

Now after this long wave of feeling, with the saltiness of sea and of all tears, had washed through the arrogancies of his mortal mind he was cooled and cleansed of his passions, bare as the sea-strand that rests tranquil, and not uncompanioned because of the closeness of moving Ocean. The very desire that had risen even to the heights of his primed citadel had itself become an expiation. Humility too can be a liberation. And it came to him no concept, no mould of thought, must be treasured because it seemed to have been created by the utmost intensity of thinking mind. There must be room for the indefinite, for the skyey gulfs among the boughs, for what the schools called Indetermination.

Plotinus walked slowly forward then with a sense of unspeakable weariness while merciful waves of non-desire rose and sank back into a sea without horizon, and his inward being was a level featureless expanse under the breath of the spirit. The breath of the spirit, yes, he knew that, but the word sounding now in the deeps of his soul was one of another power – agony.

This word had dwelt with him unaware since a conversation he had had with Heraclas. Now in this present desert of dryness and unwonted humility, this abeyance of intellectual energy, the full power of the words the bishop had used when Plotinus challenged him to prove how the belief of the Christians was another thing from the religion of the Gnostics, which indeed was before it in time and from which the new faith took, as Heraclas had agreed, both its symbols and sacraments: the necessary means of salvation for those who see rather with the outward than the inward vision. 'But, my son, Christ has revealed to us a new dimension of the human soul in which it can know the agony of spirit. Baptism is initiation into the possibility of this knowledge. I do not say that every one receiving baptism will know this in himself though it is far from me to deny it, but I say he is admitted into the fellowship of those who in full consciousness and without ceasing know the agony that is in the centre of the Creator. I say that this was not known until God became Man and suffered this anguish, living through this before the agony of death. I say that in my experience every man the centre of whose circle of being becomes identical for the instant with the centre of the One, and I am using here your words to me, has broken into Spirit through this agony. This is the revelation of Jesus. Any man who has heard this word, Christ, and turned away does so at the peril of his soul. You cannot with intellect alone face a world filled with the unintellectual and barbarous suffering that is not less, my dear, than the soul's suffering as it seeks the Good. All is redeemed in Christ.'

With the grave detachment of mind that came from his dialectical reasoning Plotinus had listened to Heraclas, and because he loved the man, with his dress and hardihood of the philosophers of old, his intelligence schooled by them and constantly dwelling in their presence; because with all this he did something more, which Plotinus himself could not compass with equal intensity, he looked to the future of men on the earth, of all men who made matter alive not only those born to be thinkers. The bishop's talk now was gathered together from their scattered infrequent discussions in the ten years, and he took the essence of it with an inexplicable sense of refreshment and renewal. This might spring in part from their comparable breadth of mind and different soundings of the spirit. Intercourse was an adventure of the unexpected, shields clashed, flashed, as lightning, long-shadowing spears were hurled, shuddered grimly, waiting the staying hand of the god of war.

Heraclitus was the philosopher they spoke of most, comparing the temper his dark sayings, as of an oracle, gave to their thought: 'His fire touches the soul as the fiery coals of the seraph touched the lips of the prophet Isaiah, the Greek metaphysician and the Hebrew join here. But the words of the spirit are few. The sum of things flows like a stream,' Heraclas repeated after Heraclitus, 'and I as a man on earth live in this stream, my friend, and so I bear him on as his self-seeking thought lives in me. But at intervals in this ceaseless flux, and especially now I think in Alexandria, there is need for a crystallisation of thought, a particular concentration of the dry minds of the past in a cool mode. You understand? A lamp burning without heat and shining into time to come by means of an oil compassed of the sacred essences of the men of former time, of whose glory it is given us to partake by their *logoi*. He said too the sun is new every day, and Aristotle said nay to this, but each instant it is new. That, it may be, is our way of knowing eternity in the motion of time. But,' and Plotinus remembered how the man had smiled to himself just then, 'because our talk is on a plane not in time we have no need of it; here you can deal with it when you begin to give lectures yourself. In so far as we seek in our thought, our dialectical discussions, to realise the Transcendent we are free of time, approaching that Being which can be neither past nor to come. For here I think Aristotle was speaking of our apprehension of the Logos, one as the sun is, our sole giver of light, for the vision of which we learn to wait tranquilly, with attention schooled but without impatience, understanding the attention, the divine in us, is eternal; the discipline something less, necessity of Here not There. These two of which you so often speak, could we not regard them also as Time and Eternity?' The note of question was characteristic of Heraclas who was free of all arrogance, free too as Plotinus had often proved of the rivalries and narrowness that bedevilled some of the schools of philosophy.

He began to be aware that the night was far advanced, it must be after the midmost hour of dark. His counsellors the stars were veiled by thin vapours, only here and there a bright one beamed solitary and severed at that time from the pattern-wheel constellations. He sought to re-enter again the house of Ammonius but he seemed ever to find himself standing in meditation between the two sphinxes and accepted the omen that that door was closed to him. How was it that he had crossed the threshold almost daily for the decade, he suddenly wondered. There must have been constant repetition in the old man's long discourses yet even now in memory he shivered at their undimmed brilliance. But the last word came from Heraclas: They say the porter was a Christian.

The effect this word had on his suddenly daunted intellect was to make him turn his face towards the east, eager now for his voyage. The morning star floating clear of the sparse trails of night cloud shone with emerald splendour in a green and amber sky. Dawn, and to this beauty he could give no answer so suddenly enfeebled he was by the re-experiencing in inward intensity of the ten years. Looking full on Aphrodite, forgetful of all else, he drew himself foot after foot to the fisherman's cabin of Origenes. The brazier was gently glowing by the open door, a lamp burnt wanly on a bracket carved with a pair of angry-tailed open-mouthed lions. There was a half-full drinking-cup on the table and some broken barley-cakes. Plotinus ate and drank until there was nothing left, slowly and with no consciousness of what he was doing.

Without looking to see if his friend was asleep behind the trellis of fishing-nets he lay down on a cot in the other corner where he had often slept after midnight talks. And presently with some vision of the dark-haired god Poseidon beckoning from the waves he slept deeply.

★ ★ ★

' "The Lydian flute for me the Lydian joys of the lyre
The Phrygian pipe and the tough-skinned tympana plays:
Living I love to sing to them and when I come to die
Set ye a flute above my head, beside my feet a lyre.
Flute for me." '

The slave-boy's warble ended but he began to play his pipe with many tremolos and sudden calls as of bird and echo in a mountain forest. Plotinus raised himself on his elbow. The lamp was still alight before the carved lions, the table was set for a meal as on the first evening he had come there, the charcoal glowed, beyond the sea rocked under a twilight sky. Morning, nightfall, an eternal interlude between day and dark, well, he was sufficed with sweet sleep. When he stood up Jeremy was beside him at once holding the prickly towel in his hands ready to give the daily friction. He saw then his two boxes, the box of books and the box of clothing, corded and ready for the journey. What was the day? His cloak and tunic newly washed smelled sweet of sea air. He was tempted to resume again his pacing and meditation but something warned him if he did he would never sail to the east. So he went out only far enough to see the long-reaching light fingers of the fanal. As from nowhere Heliodorus was before him, taking both his hands and embracing him.

'Your gold head of the sun shines among the shades, my friend,' Plotinus said gladly, 'and tells me I am still Here. I woke just now as a stranger on the coasts of light.'

'Yes, you are still here, my dear, though why I do not know when you were to have sailed with the Emperor's troops.'

'When?'

'The day before this. Don't look so puzzled. This is night, not morning!'

'I don't suppose all the ships have gone,' Plotinus responded quietly.

'No, there are two more sailing at dawn.'

'You see?'

'Yes, I see. Your daemon kept you back. Well, now until you go, this time, I shall stay with you. Poor Jeremy was in distress when you didn't come. It was he who found you here. And now you haven't gone I don't want you to. You know. I shall stay now till you are on board,' he repeated.

'What could be better? In this time we can talk of what most is in our hearts.'

'Tell me what you learnt among the shades. I see you have been far since we were last together.'

'And it isn't easy to return. Without you I don't know that I should have. But Aristotle is the man to teach one balance, and you have all his soundness, with feet firm and level head. I think I've gone as far as I can living There; as it were known myself in the One, as well as I may, while I behold the light of this sun. Now I shall be able to turn all my energy of this life to being Here, and keep a full intercourse with men's minds and with the life of the earth I love for its beauty, as you do for its reasonableness. Enough. Do you know if Origenes is returning tonight, or shall we partake of the food?'

'The boy says he is coming soon, if he keeps to his usual custom. No, you mustn't, my dear, go so far again,' and Heliodorus scrutinised the features with their new lines. 'You've returned an old man.'

'I know, and there is no need. All that concerns my living Here is There now. It is for me henceforth to show what I can of Plato's ideal world to this one. That is the task the god lays on me. And as Pindar says, it is gain to bear lightly the yoke taken upon one's neck; and not to kick against the goad.' Seeing his friend smiling he added: 'After all, I'm over forty now, and Alexandria has been my playground for a decade. It is time I did some serious work . . . or there will be no time allowed me for it.'

Heliodorus gave his merry laugh. 'A strenuous playground, but I agree the only one for you. You must give your intellect, or its mortal brain-substance, a holiday on board ship or you will not be able to share your learning. I have a notion nothing you find further east will make more intense the taut bowstring. And that is well. It has I think been strained to the limit.'

'I will sleep on deck under the stars as though rocked in a cunubula. I think I shall not come back, whatever befalls, to Alexandria, my dear. If you hear of my arrival at some other landfall, seek me, if the god wills.'

'If I hear? My house has been yours for as long as you willed. I shall be in it alone now. And are you not going to write?'

'I am ashamed. You will hold me wholly without grace. We shall meet again, though that in itself will bring us to another parting of the ways. I will heed all you say. And remember your sound laughter.' And at hearing of it he went on: 'That was the herald of our friendship begun among the graves.'

'Our first parting on the bank of Nile, now this by the streams of Ocean.'

'You will have the beacon,' Plotinus said, 'and when you want my company you can walk on the Heptastadium. I love pacing as dearly as did Aristotle, you will have me at your side then as well as that true philosopher.'

To Heliodorus it was a singular relief to see his friend ready to jest, the bow of his high brow somewhat unbent as they talked. 'Philosophy, they say, tries to understand rather than to change, but . . .'

'But there cannot not be change,' Plotinus interrupted him, 'for as more is understood so the soul winged with intelligence takes further flights and the understanding is changed in discovering more of its divine nature.'

'Don't, I beseech you, begin again . . .'

'Well,' Plotinus said with an air of innocence, 'surely this time it was you . . .'

Heliodorus caught the flute from the boy's idle fingers and instead of answering began to play a melody which at once was joined by a voice singing:

> ' "I know I am mortal, a thing of the day,
> But whenever the stars I see and I love,
> In their circling courses above
> Then my feet on the earth no longer will stay
> And on high beside Zeus my spirit is filled
> With ambrosial life of the gods." '

Origenes with his mantle trailing in the sand came up to them and let his scrip of manuscript drop on the slave's head. It slipped to the ground scattering parchments. Plotinus caught some of them and waved them in the sea-wind.

'The wings of your soul?' inquired Heliodorus.

'I thought my company was leaving this shore yesterday,' Origenes remarked, also inquiringly. 'Now we are a party of three let us pour libations to the immortals and drink my second-best wine. Salix!'

'You call the boy Willow,' said Heliodorus, surprised.

'Yes, it's the virtue of a slave to be supple.' He went in and prepared to mix the wine.

'Mortal of moment, I know it, but of the stars . . .' Plotinus repeated to himself the first line of the song.

'Ptolemaeus has said all in that for one who has it in him to live as poet, if not to sing. I take that for your farewell to me and to Alexandria.'

CHAPTER VII

Reseana

The light beam of the beacon was still shining out across the sea, Venus as a lamp of green in the amber east, when Plotinus and his two friends and the dog Argus, followed by Jeremy and the flute-boy Salix, who had refused to stay and guard the cabin, stood on the wall of the Great Harbour where the two last ships which were to join the Emperor's expedition were about to set sail. The seamen had already fitted the masts in their holders, and one by one the cables were being loosed and coiled on deck. So often in his dreams Plotinus had embarked on a seafaring ship to be borne swiftly over the waves to some unattainable shore he thought now he would soon awaken. While they waited for Heliodorus' slaves to bring up the two boxes he looked at the beautiful buildings on the headland of Lochias, at the temple of Poseidon on the shores of the sea-girt city. The theatre, the Royal Exchange, all the majestic habitations made for gods and commerce, for sport and for the dead, reared one beyond the other in the lustre of dawn. Suddenly he wondered how he had brought himself to leave the city of the philosophers which had silenced Athens. And then he knew it was not Alexandria of the Greeks and Romans for which he was experiencing this all-powerful yearning. It was for the land and people to which this modern megalopolis was the gateway, for Egypt and the Egyptians.

What was it of the kingdom of the sands and the river that would outlast Rome? Something, he told himself, empires of later time would not dare lose or risk forgetting, though they, no more than he, could say what it was. His mind was hovering now between the two obelisks, slender pyramids with carvings of hieroglyphs on their sides, monuments of the ancient kingdom of the Nile, which stood at the present time before the Caesareum, witnesses of another race of men on the earth than that ruled over by the deified emperors of Rome. The abstract form of the two monoliths, hewn out of sacred rose-red stone and carved by human hands before the time-reckoning of men of today, became for him a more perfect expression of the mysterious and puissant virtue of man than the dominating sphinxes themselves. They were not symbols of things

98

earthly, nor of the gods, they were, in their concrete abstractness, There. As surely, he told himself, as were certain inevitable lines of pure poetry.

'Ah, my dear, am I in time?'

His two hands that were unconsciously balanced in the air as if they had no part in him were caught warmly, Marcus' cherished head appeared beside a single obelisk, and instead of the rose glow and silica fires of the granite the stone was black as midnight, the hieroglyphs mouldering as if scraped in charcoal.

'Certainly,' Plotinus returned the clasp, 'though what time it is beyond me to say.'

'I'm glad to hear you confess something is beyond you. But the sailors are ready. How hateful are farewells! Now for days I shall feel a hole of absence in my heart, of the sort that comes with the discovery some treasured possession is lost.'

'Well, that will save you from boredom.' Plotinus' lips hardly hinted a smile.

'It won't.'

With a gesture the whole of the city was swept away, the sand overspread it and a thin wind sighed through the reedy swamps of the river.

'No, Marcus, it isn't like that, for although countries outlast the greatness of the men they give birth to, earth must have us beholding the light – with all that means – so that we can be restored to her dust.'

'And we, now . . . ?'

'Are free dust.' He put his hand on the dog's head. 'Heliodorus!' The word seemed returned in a double echo from the walls of wood and stone.

Plotinus embraced his three friends without a word and signed to Jeremy to go on board. Then he said, 'I shall not look back. There is no real parting. If you think you will understand this.'

The sun rose and long shadows of buildings, of men and dog lay along the quay. He embarked on the swift ship empty and weightless leaving all his labours and kindred and friends. The universe alive and in motion, a shrine for the eternal gods, the words of the *Timaeus* began to repeat themselves with the soft gliding of the vessel over the glassy waters of the Great Harbour. All was silent as in a vision, the very creak and splash of oars inaudible to Plotinus, the seamen voiceless, the soldiers somnolent lying orderly folded in their cloaks. He made his way among stacked shields, sharp spears and neatly sheathed swords to the prow not without awe at the weapons of war, the life-destroyers, keepers of peace that allowed him to think. The strangeness of life dormant and matter came over his mind on the backwash of his intellectual speculations, with those hands nerveless and limbs slack, and the problem of relation between them and the arms. He knew in his own mind the connection between concepts was a most tricky one, could itself lead to madness, the tired brain had a habit of insisting on relations as though its stability depended on them. But the ship was to be a cradle to him, and the purification of the soul is simply to allow it to be alone: simply?

Water, formless as matter, offered an image of this simplicity to his eyes as they rested on its surface before him, as yet uncleft by the craft that carried him away from Africa. All water partook of the quality of that poured out in libations; its levelness imparted serenity, and as he looked the crested waves of intellectual energy subsided. A centurion came now and leaned at his side on the rails, an elderly man with thin gray face and unharrassed brow, yet with the hardness of a soldier that caused Plotinus' aesthetic austerity to wince. Then forgetting the man, he let the smoothness of the sea spread itself over his mind which, it came to him, as regards the world of appearances, is exposed to a process of double reflection; it is mirrored on the consciousness which can describe in speech and to some degree recollect, and also on the unconscious which is mute but, he was inclined to think just then, far more deeply influenced not by the concrete dimensions, but by light shade, pattern asymmetry, rhythm disequilibrium. The unconscious, for example, knows when the body is disorganised by sickness long before the man says I am ill, knows also when the bow of mind in the intensity of intellectual striving is stretched to a tautness by the god within beyond the endurance of its physical fibres.

'You philosophers are well off,' the officer, who had been observing him for some time, said in a pleasing tone, but one which would not brook contradiction; 'You do not have to travel to reach the sites of your battles, you are never checked, as it were, by victory nor bored by peace. As long as you live you are in the ideal state of ceaseless strife. Wisdom is not born once for all into this world as a child from the woman's womb, nor slain as an enemy by the soldier's sword, she is ceaselessly coming into being in the wrestling minds of men of your kind.'

'What then is the energising of poets?' Plotinus replied, pursuing aloud his own meditations.

'Their work is simple but their art the most difficult of all. Their task is to build bridges from the known to the unknown. Those who are not builders may throw a javelin, shoot an arrow from a well-strung bow, catch a winged thing and let it make its own flight or weave coloured leaves for the winds to chariot. Even a gossamer thread may serve for song as those that ferry autumn spiders when the first frost nips.'

'I think I would say their art is to show the unknown by means of the known, the intangible made concrete. To shoot at the unknown shows indeed you believe it is There, but it doesn't help another man to realise it. Nor can you by any means show you have hit your mark.'

The soldier smiled: 'And you philosophers?'

'Our task is to show that what you call the unknown is Truth; and not a god manifesting himself to the eyes but one filling the soul. Or try another way. The philosopher seeks to know without images. The poet seeks to know by realising in his soul the images he creates.'

'You speak wisely, but I am not a philosopher.'

'Well, it is your turn now to tell me of the land to which our course is set, if you know it. And of the wars we are going to fight. That is your subject.'

'That is true, but I am a man who lives by war, not for war. I have been to most of the confines of the Empire, and as far in this direction as the Euphrates, but not beyond.'

'It is in my mind to go beyond. To India.'

'Alexander,' the soldier gave a little dry laugh. 'But the conquest of the mind is a stiffer matter than the land, and perhaps does not gain by moving over the earth. Well, you will have a comrade in the army which has gone from Rome, it may be. The praefect of the guard and tutor of the Emperor is a man of letters before all else. Maybe he is too wise for a leader of men into battle. You will see.'

'It may be no harm for me to be among men who have both feet on the earth for a little while.'

'And all believing when they turn up their toes there is nothing beyond.'

'You are a believer in the immortality of the soul?'

'Not as something living beyond now,' the man answered with

difficulty and looking along the shimmering sun trail on the waves. 'What makes the soul in a man different goes with that man, but he has also his part in free soul. And what his man-bound soul realises while he lives on earth, that is its part in immortality, which in itself is partless. The men know this though they could not say it. But we all have a certain liking for the pattern of matter that is our body, at least while it is healthy and can find fulfilment in its own activity. That is the puissance in us of the life-giving earth.' He took his head between his hands. 'But the mystery is infinite. The initiations in the mysteries teach no more than a person's own instinct.'

'That is true,' Plotinus agreed, 'but some people need, or want to have their instincts guided and sustained by a company. Wildness and orgies are safe as a part of recognised ceremonies, in solitude they are reckoned madness.'

'And meanwhile we have not advanced very far in our campaign against King Sapor who, I am told, claims dominion over the whole world. Roman arms may alter him, but with her great emperors Rome has lost half her grandeur.'

'The young Gordian?'

The centurion sighed. 'What can a boy of seventeen brought up by his mother's eunuchs do with an army that is a law to itself? He is a sapling of promise but where is the authority? It is a terrible fate for a lonely boy to be held divine. For a little while he is a pet, a plaything deity of the soldiers. If this goes to his head and he thinks he can do anything with them . . . but I speak to a philosopher.'

In that cold tone the word struck Plotinus as a stone. He said very gently: 'I am a native of a noble river. Will you tell a Nile-bred man of another great god that gives life to the desert? My soul leans towards Euphrates.'

But for all this asking he heeded little of the soldier's account of the great river of Asia with its floodings and total and menacing changes of course. He let the talk spread as an inundation over his mind and attended only to certain trees that rose above the water which was too dim to receive their reflections. And no doubt the centurion was presently aware he spoke to one who heard not because when the sun roused him with new heat Plotinus found he was alone by the rail.

★ ★ ★

After the troops from Egypt had joined those from Rome and the

102

whole army was moving painfully over the arid plain between Syria and the river Euphrates, he considered the man must have somehow conveyed into his inattentive ears a view of the country, sharp in outline and impregnated with the genius of the soil, so wholly without strangeness was the impression his passive senses received of the level lowness of the approaches of Mesopotamia. And it was not any similarity with the kingdom of the Nile that made this other, and almost equally arid, territory familiar, it was the differences he seemed to recognise, as if they had always been present. The Persian army, which had been threatening Antioch when they first landed and kept retreating before them, avoiding a battle, drawing them deeper into Asia, seemed to Plotinus an ally in his desire to enter the Orient.

Jeremy proved to have the instincts of a campaigner of long experience, he bought two mules to carry his master and his boxes of books and clothing, a small tent and the meagre supply of food that was all either of them desired. A huge amount of Syrian wine travelled on wains with the army and all, soldiers and followers alike, could draw on this when a halt was made for the night. By the time the main body of troops, with the Emperor and the praetorian guard, was drawing near the river at Zeugma, Plotinus, rather to his surprise, found a marching life to his liking. The regularity of it suited meditative habits; the orders, which he did not have to obey and which yet influenced his own disciplines, gave him a sense of stability and detachment. He felt himself to be part of a moving city whose preoccupied inhabitants demanded nothing of him, and whose actions he could watch as if they were players, for within the army rule, and when the enemy was not in sight, they lived in a kind of natural abandon to every gust of mood. The gravity of the philosopher to some degree left him in this reckless company; he forsook Plato and read Homer instead, as Alexander had done before him.

In the last night in the open before they expected to reach Zeugma, Plotinus was sitting close to a fire of the crackling thorny shrub which grew in abundance and provided, once well alight, a brief and brilliant blaze, and reading the *Iliad*. The Shamal, the unchanging north-west wind, died down at this hour, the faint puffs of smoke from the thorny fuel did not distract him. Presently however something did tap his attention, the only influence that could breach such concentration, another mind aswing on the same rainbow arc of poetry. Precisely because of this interference of his experiencing the magic of Homer between camp-fires and the galaxy he would not look up, although his reading faltered. Then a voice at his ear softly repeated the very line at which he had begun to hesitate: 'And into the sleeping heart of Helen there came remembrance.' It went on to say inquiringly: 'Do you suppose the later poet drew from this his teaching of the dialogues, and especially the *Meno*, that knowledge is recollection? The sleeping soul, the woman in our breasts, has all the knowledge we seek, it may be with too much, too human an energy, to pursue. Intellectual energy is a form of intoxication that may as easily blind as illumine the serene self-fulfilling understanding.'

Plotinus moved his sandalled feet, stirring a trifle the ashes falling from ruins of black twigs. After he had breathed and tasted the aspiring hot ash he leaned aside to regard the man at his shoulder, and seeing not the youth of the voice but one venerable and with the mien of authority he stood and made obeisance.

'Is there need of this, between those who follow a path . . . ?' the man said in an amused tone, with one hand slightly stroking Plotinus' cloak.

'A simple salute, if you prefer, for the masters we study, whose spirits we hail in their writings.'

'Who no doubt led me to you.'

'They are always present in our association with ourselves, so that may well be.'

'You have joined yourself to the Roman army for your own ends?'

'Can the army bear this supernumery, this burden of a man who thinks?'

'If they cannot, the soldiers will destroy him.' Plotinus understood by the tone the man who spoke to him was facing his own end. 'Will you let me introduce you to the Emperor, who is my pupil as well as my son-in-law? It may be his mind will stand in need of yours before this campaign is over. But without peril to his own life no man can approach Gordian.'

'If those whom we see not have done with me I shall return . . . whence I came.'

'They have not. I know that.' There was excitement in his voice. 'My son, if I may so call you, you must go to Rome. Do you understand me? You have not been there? I thought so. That is where you must go to ensure your stream flows into the flux of mind. Speak. You may think I say this because I myself am a rhetor. I know what I say. Men must have a living voice.'

'I live, sir, so within myself, if indeed I live at all in the body; how can I speak to men in the torrent of life?'

'Because it is your necessity. The torrent is foul. There is need of a pure stream. I need say no more. Those who live in you will impel you.' The praefect laid his hand on Homer and leaning to the light of the flame read: ' "Therein the sea and the unwearied sun and the moon at the full and therein all constellations wherewith heaven is crowned, the Pleiades and the Hyades and the mighty Orion and the Bear that men call also the Wain that circleth ever in her place and watcheth Orion and alone hath no part in the baths of Ocean." It befits you who know this to speak of it. Some god must have led me to you tonight, as I think now. What is it in your mind to do once you have crossed Euphrates?'

The fire crackled and hissed through fresh thorns Jeremy was casting onto it. Plotinus did not answer and the tutor of the Emperor made an impatient motion as if to leave him, and then swung back, put a hand on his shoulder: 'What can I do for you?'

The mild voice brought back to Plotinus what had been said; he looked at the man, marvelling at his gentleness with a stranger. It could, he thought, have only one meaning. He would have covered his eyes as if to avoid seeing a vision, but the vision was in his soul. Then he found himself saying a thing he did not know he had thought:

'I will not leave the army, certainly while it is still moving east I will stay with it. If there is a battle with the Persians, why, I will fight in it.' Suddenly they were smiling at each other in the flaring light.

'An alliance is made then, worthy of the ancients?' He moved away again with downcast head, again returned. 'You must come and see the little library I travel with, I shall have it opened in Zeugma. There also I shall introduce you to the Emperor . . .'

'Who, being your pupil . . .'

The praefect smiled. 'Whether or not you pursue your journey to the Orient you will, I allow myself to prophesy, return to Rome.'

And Timestheus was gone with long strides as if, Plotinus thought, he were Achilles marching over the fields of asphodel in the underworld. And this man going, left in Plotinus a sense of loneliness rare enough with him, a very sandy waste of mood that swallowed up just then every mitigating reflection, so that he began to pace unaware of the stars, heedless of the reek and mirth of the camp, in a solitude deprived of its customary meditation on the solitary subsistance of the One.

The civilised attitudes of Zeugma restored Plotinus. The place was more Hellenic than Roman and he walked along the streets in that favourable state when the reflection of the outward harmonies of buildings and forum and arcade fostered his deeper deliberations with himself. The high-flung timber arches of the famous bridge which gave the place its name made a curious twofold impression on his senses and mind as he found himself presently, and with the idea that this had always been his goal, on the embankment of the Euphrates. He had a vision of the first two arches leaping out against sullen current and blue sky as if they were snapped off. The rest of this masterly structure of Roman engineers was not there; and not as if it had been destroyed by the retreating army of the Persians but simply as if it had never been. The more inward half of this experience made the bridge, broken or sound, a symbol of the end of the confines of the known solid imperial world and the Orient, mystery, for him just then, before he had crossed the river; almost There over against Here. Of course, the bridge was undamaged, would soon be loud with the feet of troops and the hoofs of caparisoned horses, but the vision was a sign to him for all that. His mind as a bird glided down stream five hundred Roman miles to Babylon, to the only other bridge spanning the longest river known in Asia. He imagined the life of the soldiers occupying the ports built at long intervals down the western bank of this immense river-march of the Empire, and wondered how these men dealt in their disciplined minds with the inescapable division of the world which must be forced upon them in such isolated outposts, build of sun-burnt bricks on the furthest rampart of the world ruled by Rome.

Before his formal introduction to the Emperor, Plotinus was brought by Timestheus into the council-chamber where he could watch the silent young man who presided perforce over the disputing leaders of his army. It was plain Gordian and his tutor were set on crossing the river, pursuing the Persians and, however far they retreated, bringing them to battle; while Philip the Arabian, the rival of Timestheus in the favour of the troops, preached tarrying, even returning, since Sapor had moved so swiftly before them east of the Euphrates.

The name of the river took Plotinus back to his adventure by the bridge. With his eyes on the boyish Emperor who, disguising his impatience with an expression of apathy, yet contrived to convey to the philosopher an unmistakable tremor of sympathy, he met again the onset of a troop of young flashing-eyed soldiers. He'd just had time to wonder, as they surged round him, whether the reviling the mystics used to be subject to at the bridge of Cephissus was going to be his at Zeugma when they began, first one then another, then in a chorus together, to importune him to impart to them the meaning of his philosophy, the meaning of life itself, life presenting itself to him at that moment clad in such radiant flesh, shooting keen questing glances, that with an instinctive movement he hid his face in his hands. And at that they cried aloud to him as to an oracle, to unveil.

'We know there is a god in you. Tell us! Tell us! What is this life that for many will run red into the sands, dry and blacken and become dust? But the sun will rise again.'

Plotinus looked round on them and they hailed the light of his countenance, pressing away, praying him again to speak. And he said: ' "*Nil igitur mors est ad nos, neque pertinet hilum*", this is the word of soldiers, and in saying this they are free. Only men who know there is one soul in which all life is can say this and be indifferent to death, to what seems loss of youngness and beauty, and, my friends, is not.'

'How is not?' one said angrily.

'Because of the Empire?'

'He doesn't mean that. He isn't a general lashing us to fight for glory, for our fatherland.'

'Don't you see,' and they fell silent under his voice, 'the being we are now is eternal actuality? There is no other reality. There is Here in the instant. The future is no more real for those who survive than for those who die. If you know this you are as the gods.'

The music of the eddying river about the piers of the bridge was the only sound.

'Lethe?'

'All is within eternity, the ideas themselves of separation and division. Looking before and after is life swinging in eternity. I cannot say more. You feel as I do an involuntary love and understanding between us into which we enter of our own free wills. Necessity includes choice.'

'That is hard!' they cried, whirling round him in a leaderless dance. 'Are you coming with us over the bridge?'

'Over the bridge and into battle,' Plotinus said, with downcast eyes and in the small voice no one missed.

107

Suddenly one begged his cloak and without a word he loosed the cord and flung it into the air over their heads and watching faces, and the freed garment seemed oddly to protest, to wave a farewell as it fell among the soldiers.

It was easier, he confessed, to know eternity in that unpremeditated encounter than in the council-room. He looked at the Emperor and received again an unmistakable summons from eyes under lids already weary with the world's weight. To inherit the wealth of the Gordians, to be emperor of continents and islands, is no more than to sigh with dry breath over that hollow land between Rome and Persia. And for Plotinus with the boy Emperor before him and with the vision of the chorus of youths by the river still present, there was no answer to the despair in the heavy-lidded eyes. Only he knew he must speak to Gordian, find some word that would start a sparkle, or his philosophy was vain.

The conference now was becoming an open dispute between the Emperor's tutor and Philip the Arabian, a harsh swarthy fellow with all the ambition to be a leader of men that was lacking in Gordian. Such dark and violent emanations were communicated to Plotinus from this hero of the soldiers that he knew any attempt at resistance would be of no avail; all he could do, while the man spoke, was to wait for the presence of the divine light, the spirit his soul composed received, in silence and emptied of passion. And this was no avoidance of thought or deflecting of evil from himself, for he continued at the same time to listen and to balance the arguments of Philip and Timestheus.

When the vote was taken to cross the river and bring Sapor and his army to battle then, like parted fragments of quicksilver, and under the jealous eye of Philip, the Emperor, his mentor and Plotinus ran together, their minds gleaming and united. And thus it befell that the hard hoofs of the mule well-chosen by Jeremy rattled over the bridge at Zeugma beside the round varnished ones of the imperial horse, and Gordian's spirits rose as they rode together eastward over the plateau of Osroëne. 'Rather,' he said more than once, 'this arid land and the Shamal than the barren talk and gales of greed in Rome. You taught me well, Plotinus makes my studies live.'

'Still your eyelids are laden.'

'The eyes below flashed at that. What do you expect for one who carries in some sense, symbol or figurehead, the load of a corrupt civilisation? You have not been to Rome.'

108

'Is there no way,' Plotinus asked, with a trace of eagerness, 'of founding a city to be governed as Plato suggests in the *Republic?*'

The young man, who five years earlier at the age of thirteen had been presented to the people as their Caesar, shook his head. He even gave a brief uncomfortable laugh as he turned to the man on the mule.

'An ideal city is an *ideal* city,' he said. 'As you value your philosophy, my friend, do not try to establish one Here.' Perceiving that his new companion was experiencing for, it might well be, the first time in his life the discipline of being humbled, he went on: 'There is nothing honourable in my Rome. Do not think you can judge it by Alexandria where, I know it, there is still passion for thought and beauty. Not only the beauty of boys.'

Plotinus flinched.

'You do not know,' Gordian went on with some bitterness, 'the world I grew up in and you never can know it as I did, or need to. Let the whole world go on its sensual way, if you try to stem that you will be lost. That is to say, I think you will lose your divine gift . . .' He smiled. 'We will fly our hawks.'

The weariness as of the dissoluteness of the Empire reflected in a face so young cut Plotinus' heart more than anything had done just in that acute way, since he had parted with his sister Deborah. Gordian saw what he was not intended to, that sudden tearing into sentient transparent shreds of the serene almost formally philosophic brow and pale visage of the man Timestheus had brought to him for a friend. But the serenity was not a mask, it was moulded by true thought, he was aware of that; and that instant's vision of a human face totally ravaged, as it were from within, was a revelation. He knew nothing he could have told in words but he experienced a feeling of clarity and liberation: a direct communion with life unburdened by mortality. Plotinus was saying in his gentle way:

'Philosophy must be lived even to the very quick of our being, earthly as well as divine. Intellect in its mode of soul is of the texture of flesh. Yes, cast your winged hunters, though there may be no quarry for them in this mid-river desert.'

They were riding in a small company apart from the main army which was distinguished by three dust clouds far out over the plateau. Plotinus felt at home in the wilderness, the blue sky meeting an indefinable hazy horizon, the sand eddying in the Shamal, the little thorny plants and hot outcrops of stone gave him a sense of empty content. His thoughts became isolated and free to soar as the solitary bird of prey overhead; or as the gazelle that sprang away from them in high stiff-legged bounds as though the ground threw them up to heaven. Now something not of this savage region was before him, a perdurable work of man as he slowly recognised, broken and crumbling but even so ready to withstand centuries of grinding by the eternal north-west wind with its sand-sharp blasts. These stumps of rounded and chiselled stone, their fallen summits long lost in the undulant dust, brought the three men to a halt: an involuntary and silent gesture of homage to the unknown builders in the desert. Was there water once, an oasis of clear springs, palms and a grove of poplars?

★ ★ ★

At night Plotinus bivouacked apart in some dell in the sand or in the lee of a meagre covert of thorn-bush where Jeremy swiftly kindled a fire, set out simple fare and spread a couch. As the days passed it began to be known throughout the army that the Persians had halted this side of the river on which stood the town of Reseana and were preparing for battle. When this had been confirmed by the heralds and the men had been burnishing armour and whetting swords with din of voices and bronze till long past midnight, the Emperor came to find him. Plotinus, who was lying on his back watching the splendid constellations and frequent falling stars, edged over a little in the hollow that was fitted to his form, and Gordian, without a word, stretched himself at his side.

'Rest, when the body sleeps the soul watches, is sacredness,' Plotinus said after they had remained for some time in silent intercommunion.

'Will you promise to keep out of the battle?'

'You know I will not.'

'If I command it . . .'

'I should not obey, and there would be an end of our friendship.'

'You are in good company,' the Emperor said pettishly. 'Very soon, I think, no one will obey me. Very well, I will send you a sharp sword, a helmet and a shield and . . . intreat you not to use them!'

'Why?'

'Because I know,' the young man said, sitting up and throwing his purple cloak from him, 'you are the thinker men most need in this time.'

'Since the spirit of prophecy is upon you, speak further.'

'I will. Listen, and obey in this if not in other things. Rome is riddled with religious rituals, ceremonies and sacrifices to a multitude of deities who are added to every day. I know, I grew up in the very core of it. Your city is not very different in this, although there the religions have a more spiritual and thoughtful character on the whole, I believe. You do not need them. Keep clear of them one and all, as you are now. Have nothing to do with all the clutter of gods, priests, wizards, magic-mongers, astrologers, diviners and worshippers of hieromancy. Give this Empire, that they call me head of, by your presence, by whatever means else the power of the spirit gives you to use, the clear thought of your intellect. I who as Emperor am your father, who in years and I may well say in love am your son, lay this upon you. Live and let the work of mind be consummated in the world.'

'My son,' Plotinus said very gently, 'I obey.'

Gordian sighed. 'Youths mature swiftly in palaces. I have an odd feeling I've learnt all I can from Timestheus, who saved my mind's manhood from the pampering eunuchs, and that what I bid you teach is beyond my reach . . . reason's not spirit's, my dear. Emperors these days are apt not to last long. I don't mind. Now our – what did you call it? – our tutelary genius has brought us together, I think I was chosen for some purpose.'

'You may win the battle also.'

'In name, perhaps, but that would be still more his doing than this is. There is Here, I believe, a god-given compact. For this hour I can forget my enemies.'

The noise of the preparation for battle was dying down, though the concourse of soldiers hummed with stridulant note like bees bent on swarming and fragments of song jetted starwards. Watchful, Jeremy, sensing the tension had slackened between the two, brought two narrow horn cups of wine and they pledged their agreement in silence and fire gleams.

Plotinus attached himself to the young knights who had hailed him by the river and there was a lively counterpoint of military and metaphysical skills in the bleakness of dawn. Wine, diluted after the Greek custom with water, flowed. The generals had decided thirst was more likely than Persians to unman the Roman soldiers. With wonder Plotinus looked at the faces of the men transformed, made not of clay, in that cold irradiance of glory reflected before the rising of the sun. He marvelled at the strenuousness of their

111

limbs and the beauty of hands eloquent as the wings of birds, not plying their tasks, unconsciously poised as minds grew absorbed, idle, unnerved, at rest, as if already beginning to suffer the withdrawal of form. Of the men who prayed the hands were lifted to perceive the light supernal; others, more heavy birds oppressed with earth, hung dully. Christians, standing apart, held theirs together; the light touch of wrists and finger-tips, the taper spire, communicated to him a singular sense of atonement. Nothing, it seemed to him at that time, was nobler than this devotion of men on earth, their preparation to give and to receive death.

The sun rose. The trumpets were blown. He who bore the imperial eagle strode forward. The ensign-bearers of the legions took their stand and the soldiers fell into their disciplined lines, minds set to the business of battle. The attack of the Persian archers and slingers began at once before the dust, which would soon dominate the conflict, had become dense. The din was so continuous and meaningless that for Plotinus it came to resemble a volcanic or oceanic eruption, a breaking forth of uncontrollable and non-human elements. Again by its very intensity it became a vortex of silence such as he could have imagined beyond the ultimate stars. Certain ringing strokes rebounded from this whirl, voices commanded, encouraged, exhorted, surely in vain, for the whole wing which had been swinging forward, every pinion exultant, was now flagging, falling, fragmenting, strewing fluttering plumes. The air groaned. He was stifled by this substance of suffering. He could breathe no more. But he did not fall, and he kept hold of shield and sword, and his insatiable mind pursuing its reasoning insisted that soul is separable from body but not from the contemplation and intuition of divinity.

The tension of the engagement was stiffening again now; he felt the right wing gathering itself for another powerful thrust. The general shape of the battle was beyond his discernment, but the whole Roman army became for him an eagle with eyes ablaze and blood streaming through sun-gold feathers which were the bright shields of the warriors. The great bird riddled with Persian darts and javelins was yet being manipulated in a masterly fashion so that its wide-spread wings began to encompass the whole opposing army, while beak and claws stabbed and recoiled, stabbed and stabbed again at the heart of the loosely united forces against it.

Kill! Kill! Kill! Kill! the words kept ringing like an incantation in Plotinus' brain, ringing in the din of war. And they were obeyed.

Could a man stand passive in the midst of slaughter? Could a philosopher? The question confronted him at that moment when the Persians were scattering every way at once in the furious dust, still shooting as they fled. He thought of that energy of the soul which never spent itself and yet was the dynamism of all souls, and his arms holding shield and sword – blade nicked and pointless – fell, not, as he thought, from weariness and war-strain but from the exploring energy of intellect.

But even while his mind was debating whether a man who entered a fight by choice might also hold his hand before the day was won, he knew he had been wounded, that from necessity he halted there among the slain and stricken, that soon he would sink among them. Still standing, he felt a kind of exultation because even now he could resume his habitual dialectic.

★ ★ ★

Reseana reminded Plotinus of the Lycopolis of his youth. There was that mingling of the art of the Greeks with the more earthy and fabulous monsters of a different culture; that careless huddle of dwellings of the poor tacked on to the glory of a city. There was a life-giving if minor river; above all there was the waste. The level unfertile land seared and rejected the gaze in every quarter; from where it began biting into the narrow irrigated area to its counterfeit horizons. The very feebleness of his body reminded him of that season when everyone had the plague, and though he had not, he was the more infected by the stricken air of the little town. Reseana also was occupied by men sick of the plague and men who had been wounded in battle. Seldom, he thought, could the aftermath of a Roman victory have been more sombre. The defeated Persians had, it is true, vanished for the present over that mirage of the desert's rim, but the army that had triumphed was restless and divided, and Timestheus who had achieved the victory was sick; rumour said he was dying.

But still the orator turned soldier was determined to continue the pursuit, while Philip the Arabian urged the men to go back from these furthest confines of the Empire which the other Empire of Sapor was bent on thrusting back. This Plotinus learnt from the knights for since the battle he had spoken to neither Gordian nor Timestheus. One day when he returned from his wanderings among the Corinthian pillars, the dragons and chimeras, he found a message calling him to the general's lodging, and with his mind bent on

113

India and the possible ways of continuing his journey he obeyed this call.

'You see,' the man lying on the couch said, 'I am dying. I can do no more. I have entrusted all to the Emperor and prayed him to carry on the campaign. He is young; will you stay, not close to him but where he can find you when he has need?'

The gravity of Plotinus' face and the lines of distress in his high brow at what he said caused the guardian of Gordian to smile: 'Yes, my son,' he answered what had not been said, 'this is not the plague, nor the work of the Persians: another enemy, I think. But that is a common fate of those in high places. I have another word for you. They tell me there is in this town a devoted disciple of the prophet, the last of the prophets as he insists, who is converting all the Persians. Go and see him. You have heard of Mani the prophet of light?'

After a silence the dying Roman beckoned him nearer and Plotinus at once kneeled down close to the couch.

'The Greeks are the lovers of wisdom, I know it, the law is the Romans' part; but, my dear, there are other things too, besides these, besides even "the soul is Aphrodite". Do not forget them in your high and dedicated seriousness.'

It was plain he could say no more. Plotinus remained on his knees until he felt a hand on his shoulder. Gordian was standing above him, he looked as if he'd been weeping and yet his expression just then was so tender and undismayed and lit with valour the philosopher's heart bent before him in love.

Timestheus was so determined the army should go forward that against the will of everyone he resumed the march, himself being carried in a litter. Gordian who rode slowly beside his sick father-in-law was evidently unwell, and dispirited by the divisions among the soldiers. The whole company of men on foot and on horseback dragging like a wounded dragon, as Plotinus fancied, through that unfeeling landscape, might have been a funeral procession; not only for the Emperor and the praefect of the praetorian guard, who led the army towards Oriens, but for the entire Empire. Riding on his mule with the disciple of Mani beside him in immaculate turban and silver-starred robe, Plotinus was aware of forces of physical destruction which for that time were irresistible. He felt his own deepest soul succumbing to them as the Persian sage at his bridle explained to him the desperate division between the material of light

114

and the irremediable dark out of which the princes of evil had constructed man.

The very passion with which the follower of Mani was explaining to him that light, the light they saw now with their eyes, was good, was itself the principle of goodness, and that the evil of the world was brought about by the darkness being intangled in light, was for Plotinus a complete denial of the Spirit which was the sole Good of his own faith and philosophy. A denial also, in its volcanic fervour, of Happiness, the contemplation of the Soul of the cosmos within itself, which wisdom knows but may not explain, because it is not division but Unison. When he brought himself to turn towards the preacher beside him he saw what he had expected, a face so distorted by inhuman wickedness that its contours seemed to be dissolving into chaos, as though they could no longer receive that glory of the Spirit which is the beauty of form in all visible and sensual creation. The whole Greek in him revolted at the amorphous duality the man was describing now as the ultimate triumph of light. The bloodlessness of the whole thing made it bare of meaning for him to such an extent that his mind acknowledged in a single flash what Heraclas had said of the sacrifice of redemption: not without blood.

'The angels forsake the world, which by the works of the unjust has become solid dark, and as it falls in ruins it is devoured by fire black as the evil it is destroying in this hideous cataclysm.'

'And what then is left?' Plotinus asked with simplicity. 'Since your understanding of the universe is a material one, even after this there must be something.'

'What is left then is light, totally and eternally separated from darkness.'

'So that, after this monstrous struggle, the two principles still exist, as distinct as they are now. What of the intellect that recognises the difference?'

'The light is the intellect itself, which is good.'

'And its realisation is to be fully separated from darkness, in some future time, after the end of this world? But if this world is darkness, although created by the powers of light, when it is destroyed in the final conflagration, what remains of the principle of dark? Why did the good spirits, as you say, create the world, if it is destined for nothing but obliteration, and the evil or dark spirits mankind whose destiny it is to liberate the light? Your position to me seems an endless prolongation of an abstract dualism. The soul of every man and animal and plant knows Providence better than that.'

A sense of horror came over Plotinus not at the darkness, which the fellow in the turban was now telling him was to be banished by the virtues of the elect beyond a wall, a real physical erection as it seemed, called the Great Ban, but at the hopelessness of this fanaticism of matter. The man was going on speaking of the churches to be established throughout the world by the apostle of light, churches whose servants would be dedicated not to life which is thought, to approaching by prayer the divine, which is within the power of all men, but to the impossible task of dividing material light from material dark. His mind went to the Gnostics in Alexandria, who were obsessed by the same kind of notion, with their spiritual elect. With an inclining of his whole being he knew that light which can never be confounded with darkness. In this same instant of revelation he knew that it was in all men. But in this very certainty, his mind balanced on the razor's edge, he renounced once and for ever all churches. There was spiritual initiation but it was for freedom of intellect to approach the One.

'Coming as I do from further west', he began, when the disciple of Mani was for a moment at fault for words, 'I think religions are a torment of our age. There are far too many of them, my friend, and they are all in their own eyes, in the eyes of the elect who maintain them, right. There is, of course, safety in numbers in a sense; they may act as correctives on each other, but also they lead to persecution. Churches are built on martyrs.'

'All killing is forbidden by our prophet.'

The glittering triumph in the man's eyes made Plotinus answer in his gentlest voice: 'Mani will not establish a church without some one being sacrificed.'

Since now at least the disciple of the last of the prophets had the look of partaking of the reason and nature of mankind, of being Here instead of in his wholly, as the philosopher regarded it, fantastic and materalistic There, he wondered whether to speak himself. Such men, he thought, will worship anything occult and magical and elaborate, do anything to avoid the point of pure light in the soul by which they know. It is no use telling them to cut everything away. What interests them is not the One but the human means which must always fall short, and not the clear means all men must live by but the most obscure ones they can invent. Intellect knows truth in all that has material being, realises it with no intermediate structure. My daemon would have me desire ceaselessly this truth without a conscious striving with or against darkness which would, for me, be a weakening of the spirit. The same Necessity causes another man to fight evil with all his god-given powers, and to see the symbols as reality. I do not seek to alter the nature of a tree but to see in it the divine, another man may have to saw off branches or make carvings in the wood. All our ideas are determined by all other ideas. I should not think as I do if he was not thinking in his way.

As soon as he recognised he was still obeying his daemon in seeking not to combat evil as it presented itself to him at that time in the belief of his companion, Plotinus found he could turn to him and listen to what he was saying as if it were indeed his own dialectic, but he did not escape, all the same, a sense of weariness as the hopelessness of Mani's teaching was so eagerly demonstrated to him. At the midday halt he invented an imperial summons and escaped from the nodding turban and fluttering veil.

'Drink, my dear!' Gordian said, holding out his own gold wine-cup with an indescribably intimate look. 'What has happened to you?'

Plotinus said over that goblet darkly agleam in sunshine, and not without smiling: 'Why, I've been in company with a preacher of the Persian prophet of light and he has shed darkness on my soul.'

'I believe that, your very looks are dark, their white radiance shadowed. Drink, ascetic as you are, and restore your soul.'

'I believe there is no human being who does not in some sense possess this thing which we hold to constitute happiness, if it is not slain for him by religion. It is not what religion should do, but it is what men using it as a power make it do. They are wrong. Even mourning cannot be – which, as Homer says, it is the right of the dead to receive from the living – unless there is joy as a kind of counter-pressure.'

'I believe,' the Emperor assented, receiving back his wine-cup, 'we shall have to put that to the proof. My father-in-law is close to death, and this guidance of the army is a very burden on my soul. Come and see him.'

Timestheus lay barely conscious in a hastily erected tent. His utter immobility and haggard face made Plotinus believe he beheld a dead man, and yet there was still an emanation of the life-principle, some hint of that intellectual radiance he always physically experienced when he was in the company of men who were thinkers, in that spiritual sense in which he defined the word to himself.

'My most dear son,' the old orator said without unclosing his eyes, 'I leave you with a burden too heavy for your years although the stature of your mind could endure it. I fear it will be your end.' Then he asked: 'Who is there with you?'

'The philosopher Plotinus.'

'Well. Keep him near you.'

The head of the Egyptian physician, outlined on the scarlet wall of the imperial tent, took him back to the tombs in the limestone cliffs above Lycopolis with its rigid and exact outline. He remembered Peter and others of the boys who were with him at the school of the little Jew, at whose death also he had been present. Then Plotinus wondered what it was in Greek and Roman that made them a power the air itself acknowledged. Walking in the streets, the temple-court, by the sea-shore in Alexandria, he had always recognised when one of them was drawing near him. It was something besides a more dynamic intensity of being and force of physical presence. It was, he decided characteristically, a possibility in them of concentrated thought, whether consciously realised and strengthened by temperance (which at that point he defined to himself as 'an inward conversion of the soul to intellect') or simply latent. And this potency of authentic life in the mind, as well as in the dauntless bodily substance of these builders of cities, was always tempered by a sense of the urgency of time in the existence of mortal men. For the Egyptians, and for the people of the Orient also, the flow of time, the inevitable alternations of night and day, were in a sense eternity. For the Greek time was a kind of matter, something on which he could himself work, approaching in some way by action the beauty of the transcendent, which did not originate in time. Time which is a limitation is also essentially liberty to man, because without it he would not be aware of the movement which is life in process, life involved as distinct from the solitary, the alone of the One into which he has now returned. His gaze moved from the head of the Egyptian to the head of the Roman. And he thought, it is a mark of their reckoning time as eternity that they seek to conserve the body, we to destroy it, in the particular form *that* soul has moulded, as swiftly as possible.

There was an interlude. The ceremonies of the funeral of the Emperor's father-in-law and the entertainments provided for the army to mark this event gave Gordian time to make his own decision. His mind was clear when the next council was summoned, and he refused all the suggestions of Philip the Arabian and his faction that the army should forthwith return to the west. The march which followed his decision was disastrous. All the men were mutinous, food began to grow short, and the country provided nothing. Plotinus believed Gordian was doomed; he thought it was partly a kind of despair and partly lack of confidence in his own judgement that made him so determined to carry out the policy of Timestheus to the limit.

'Philip is set on ruining me,' the Emperor said once to the philosopher. 'If I agreed to go back he will do it and if I resist him he will do it. He wants my place and he will have it. That is the point it has come to. Do you not see it in this way? Well, I will agree to nothing. I am going to end keeping to my own will, not because I have yielded to his.'

Plotinus could have wept in his love for the young man, and because of his helplessness. The devoted unreason of the Emperor and the wilful unreason of the army appeared to him not a cause but a clear sign of the disruption of the world of the Romans. The Tower of Saturn was assailed by all that seemed to be not philosophy, and the whole purpose of this journey to the east was vain if it were to discover the wisdom of other men by a man in a structure of thought he believed to be impregnable. The Tower being built of life must, as constantly as life itself, break up and be re-built. And this, the ground prepared, the power without magnitude, the Being of all extended life, achieved best without interference by consciousness. He knew he must neither side with nor against the forces of destruction, which were not evil because they were of the same necessity as the good. All he could do now, for every form of life in the chorus had a part, was to know by intuition, that knowledge by identity that was the centre of philosophy; and, that constant, to be open to life, to let all else build and unbuild about him. In this he could do nothing because he had renounced the senses, but he could be an opening to intuition for those his soul loved.

You can sit too long at the feet of a sage, Ammonius had said to him once towards the end of the decade. It was not for nothing that in search of other sages he had joined himself to an army, Kratos and Bios, Strength and Force, manifest, the violent elements in Necessity, which it was no use pretending were not. When these were under control, their very virtue was the maintenance of order and the protected life; of leisure, art, the opportunity to study the grammar of the universe by entering into the minds of men god-taught in the past as well as by the intercourse of living minds. This virtue being of the substance of force preserved order by means of destruction held back, but ever ready to break forth; was, as he saw it, for ever at war with its self-appointed authority.

Plotinus was fully aware that his own alliance with that authority, in the person of Gordian, exposed him to the enmity of Kratos and Bios, although he never spoke in the assemblies on behalf of the Emperor's strategy or attacked the growing popularity of Philip. As the unwilling army crawled southwards in the direction of Babylon, Sapor's capital, the sheer physical and spiritual hostility of the country increased and more men fell ill. The Persian army was careful to avoid another full-scale battle but their archers were a constant torment on the Roman flanks, soldiers were slain daily and foraging parties rarely returned. On the other hand there were men who sought him out, won him to talk of the philosophers of Alexandria, of his own hope. The inhospitable Mesopotamia was not more friendly to dialectic than to an army of half-hearted invaders, but there was always the night; camp-fires and the stars, that were in close fellowship with his soul, lent him grace to speak to a few who came often to his hearth; and more than he knew drifted into the flickering ring of firelight and wandered away again with the acrid smoke.

In these nocturnal philosophyings he began to feel his way into a mode of discourse that agreed better with his own solitary temperament than the dialogue form of Plato. He was the only speaker and yet he never lectured. With the unspoken aid of his listeners he lifted perplexed questions into the light of intellect, seeking to show that this light which appears splintered in the separate dark of each mind can be recognised, can be known as a pure concentration of eternal radiance. 'As we see in a glass vessel all the sunlight focused in a single brilliant point, so dazzling, it is as if the vessel were this light. From this point or star, the intellect each of us can find lodged in his skull – frangible indeed as a goblet of glass – there is nothing to hinder a man from being one with the Divine Light. In this union, consciousness, our crown here, is no more; the soul then sees before it neither good nor evil nor anything else.'

'But why all this endeavour to know nothing?'

Some began talking, others lowered their gaze or turned away from him in thought.

For the first time in his life Plotinus knew a surge of inward power in relation to the minds of other men. He understood at once that the time of deliberately seeking to learn from others was over. Learning for him would only cease with that end men call death but henceforth it would be inward, intellect discovering itself within by that spontaneity of spirit which must now have freedom. He recognised also, with a certain unwillingness, that when his excursion to Oriens was over and he must go to Rome, the work of his daemon could only be fulfilled among the people who at that time were, and as it were in the midst of their own decay, creating a world in which no cosmic possibility would be denied free play. The very persecutions were a test of the strength not only of those who suffered them. The striving is not towards the good, it is the good itself striving in us.

Recalled by the eyes upon him, unconscious that his countenance was irradiated by thought, he experienced as he returned to them a swift impression that they had looked on him as a god. Someone muttered a word of this and his answer flew back to his strangely stirred audience:

'Only the gods recognise the gods on earth.'

'Timestheus when he read Pindar to me would always begin with a line he said was the glory of all his singing: "Zeus with lightning in both hands." ' The Emperor spoke and a thunder of men enraged went through the camp volley after volley so that each face near him darkened, and no voice could be heard any more.

At once Gordian with the haughtiness of high youth stepped out from the gathering to confront the tempest. Plotinus who had divined his intent was at his shoulder. He saw fires and furious flares ablaze in the midnight waters. In the elbow of the little river where they had bivouacked men were advancing, with torches and lanterns and weapons, upon the imperial pavilion, and he realised with a sense of fatality that the guard had deserted their posts. Caesar was alone with the unarmed philosophers. The soldiers were frenetic, their surging roar of fury denied a single word to the youth they had elected as their leader. Someone gave into his slightly lifted hand a cup flashing with jewels in the deadly glare. With a smile too gentle to be called contemptuous he held it up and poured out the red wine in a libation. Plotinus heard the hiss of it as it dashed into the flaming core of a torch, saw it splash as blood on the foremost sword-blade. Then the weapons tasted blood. But the man still stood erect, held by the swords and spears whose hidden points drank his death.

The roar when he fell broken with many blades made all that had gone before a hush, a sigh of wind in the river-side poplars. Brands and torches whirled and hurled, crashed as the starry host of heaven flung to earth, the water turned to flame. Now the swords slashed zig-zag, crisscross, through the men who had been hearkening to Plotinus. Not one moved except as weapons and weight of bodies forced them down. Thwacks felled Plotinus. When they ceased he lifted himself somewhat from the Emperor's blood into which they had flung him, and saw the soldiers had raised the dead Caesar on their shoulders and were bearing him to their camp. At this singular repetition, a horror came over Plotinus' heart as he held himself dizzily up to see that corpse, with right arm hanging, white ringed hand mysterious and endowed with grace in the torchlight, carried off by those who had slain him. For through this he saw a clearer vision of the thirteen-year-old boy, chosen by the army, invested with the imperial apparel and dignities, raised up by the triumphant guard and taken on their shoulders into the midst of their camp that there they might glorify him.

Now the soldiers were driving the men who were with Gordian at the last with blows of their short swords, pricking them with spear-points, crying they also should be slain. Plotinus, wounded and resenting the foulness of blood upon him still perceived his vision and wondered in his soul at the divinity in man revealed to senses nourished by the substance blood. The dark roar and exultation of the army fed by the Emperor's death was on a sudden pierced by a shrill clamour of horns and trumpets; from all quarters at once, as though every star-ray aimed, arrows shredded the night. To Plotinus it appeared the spirit of the dead Caesar had loosed the power of the Persians on that traitor host. In the consternation of his prodders he sank as though smitten into the watercourse Aboras.

With the cunning of an otter he drifted in where the bank overhung and lay, steadying himself among the stones, where some winter torrent had made a coffer in the crumbly earth. He chafed the stickiness from his hand and felt the flow from his wound staunched by the water gurgling round him. He listened to the tumult of battle, heard once the voice of Philip the Arabian commanding the mutinous soldiers; but in a little while there was only the music of the river in his ears. Then he knew it was time for him to look again on Gordian.

He found the body where they had dropped it in the dust, face downwards, partly covered by the black cloak of many folds the Emperor was used to wear when there was no need of purple for ceremony. The camp was deserted by all and he began to go about collecting lights that he might set them beside the corpse with its many wounds and gashes shamelessly rendered after death. Men on earth demand always human sacrifice, Plotinus thought, as he picked up those abandoned torches under the stars. Because of this the religion Heraclas serves will grow in power, but each man, insofar as by the life he claims as his own he is separated from the Good, knows this sacrifice, of his parted self, his life determined. Once that is let go intellect is free to know itself. He began to talk to Deborah, remembering how in childhood they two had gathered glow-worms to set as lights about a dead bird. He saw as she crouched by her pet her wet cheeks in the steady green gleam and felt his own tears falling although neither made a sound in weeping.

Then he saw a pair of small white hands firmly veiling a narrow moon face with a silver crescent aswing on the brow from a chaplet of pearls. Together the girl and the philosopher turned over the body of the dead man who had been the idol and the sacrifice of the Roman army. Plotinus with his soaked garment cleansed the features from which the trace of a smile was not obliterated. They closed his eyes and folded about him the black mantle.

Feet came charging back to the camp, angry voices rang, so, because to them both sides were hostile, they prepared, with a sense of leaving all, to quit the body of the young man they loved. With a gesture that recalled play with Deborah in infancy the girl gathered dust in cupped palms and cast it upon him. With four hands clasped over his breast they said their *Vivat Imperator*. Then they went separate ways among the shadows.

123

CHAPTER VIII

The Greeks

Plotinus knew his two years of army life had ended with the life of Gordian. With this he made also a final inner surrender of his voyage to Oriens. Walking with characteristic stateliness, as of a statue alive, through the abandoned camp, he recognised the aspects of Necessity offered him with unkind clarity. It was not for him to go on to India alone; it was not for him to acknowledge Philip the Arabian as the immediate successor of the man he had caused to be murdered: and so, whether the soldiers recollected their purpose of destroying those who were round Gordian at the last, or whether after this night attack of the Persians they'd have lost their impulse for cold-blooded slaying, there was no place for Plotinus in the army. This conclusion made, he faced with glinting calm the three hundred Roman miles lying between the elbow of the rivulet Aboras and the shore of the Mediterranean Sea.

By the time he reached the camp it was swiftly refilling with troops who must have beaten off the enemy; there was no mistaking the note of victorious Roman soldiers. The bunch of rustling poplars received him, and for the first moment since the wanton outrage he experienced serenely in their shadow that way of prayer he had believed to be always within his power. The sibilant leaves on their twigs and below his feet hushed the voices for him; he moved past the tethered mules and sleeping slave to the embers dully glowing between three stones, and stared down as though he saw the inward hearth of reality. But there was need of haste. He threw some sticks onto it and stirred up Jeremy. The boxes had not been undone and with the skill of two years' habit they were loaded, the saddle- and pack-mules led out on the far side of the grove, and the bivouac fire – to extinguish the flower of flame, lamp or candle, or its seed in humble gleed, was a thing Plotinus' heart would not allow him to do – was ringed with a bare space of ground. The curly leaves dimly silver and gold he swept away with his hands, praying to the nymphs, daughters of Zeus, the dryads in the heart of the trees; until he knew clamour and clash closing round him with the flicker of angry brands. So he moved softly, forsaking the solace of his last

124

refuge, as he could not help thinking, to face the desert. The word reminded him as he paused by the final poplar, who stood apart from her sisters faintly sighing in the wind, of how men in his youth talked of the Desert of Inmost Libya; that unexplorable wilderness of sand ever corresponding to certain moods of aridity that were not barren of promise. There was always a lift of imagination at the words: *Deserta Libyae Interioris*.

Whether the soldiers tried to follow Plotinus did not know. The night was dark and Jeremy brought the mules down into a bushy hollow, dug out by rain in some forgotten year when torrents eroded the land. When this channel took a bend to the south they forsook it, and Plotinus steered them north-west by the stars, thinking of days of dearth to come, noticing the nag of his wound with his customary unconcern for the body.

Numbed by sorrow and weariness he went forward slowly, stumbling in the dark but unfaltering, and beside him with the closeness and spiritual irradiancy of the newly dead was the presence of Gordian. Now and then Plotinus felt the young hand strike his, again and again he caught the outline of the head proudly poised among the stars. Before his desert wayfaring was over this outward companionship was lost but the essence of the being of the youth was received into his own, so that he knew they would constantly be together in a wakeful recognition. Then he was conscious only of foot after foot meeting the face of the earth. Summoned to look over his shoulder he saw the zodiacal light, and desiring even in this final reach of fatigue to watch dawn and the rising of the sun he made up his mind to halt.

Jeremy hobbled the mules and prepared a couch in the sand towards the eastern horizon and in total stillness and silence Plotinus reclined, smiling a little as he recollected how he and Gordian had talked of the difference between lying up and lying down. Lying up then, to await the dayspring, he felt his skull had become an empty shell washed far up on the shore beyond the wild waves and was aware of nothing but the smooth lustre of the sea-born shell translucent to the lights of all the shining stars.

Endurance beyond what he could have believed possible was given Plotinus for this desert wayfaring. Although himself, his slave and the beasts of burden grew gaunt and weak they found always in their extremity some succour so that they had strength for that day to move on. Before dawn when the morning star called him from sleep and again towards nightfall he realised that transcendency of the contemplative nature, and of God Himself, in a mood of humility rare with him, that made him feel the whole of his silence of thought was composed of beauty. Through the hardships of heat and drought, he perceived beside him constantly as a living yet ghostly companion the young Gordian. Sometimes in the longing of love he sought the youth's face as he had known it living, but most often this was denied by a slight turning away, although the shoulder still moved by his shoulder, and he learnt to be content with this fellowship and the rare revelation of shining spirit when the remembered countenance looked full upon him.

And it came to pass after two days without water or food Plotinus climbed, his body united in its feebleness by a tremulousness of unexplored and grievous strength, a ridge in that bald wilderness whose exposed stones were as the ribs of a long dead monster broken and choked with sand. The early air was undisturbed by the ruthless day wind, no dust rose from the caravan he saw at a distance of a Roman mile from him winding among the dunes. For a while he watched the course of this uncoiling serpent in a mood of despair, a visible hope beyond the reach of himself and his emaciated companion. At the same time he felt himself to be deserted by Gordian.

Then something beyond prediction took place before his eyes. The leaders of the cavalcade came to a halt. The followers as they drew near spread round them in an uneven circle. Someone in the heart of that desolate region had proclaimed an interval of repose.

The aloneness caused by the loss of Gordian remained always with Plotinus, adorned as it were by three memories connected with his joining that caravan of richly-laden camels: the first was the compassionate reception the merchants gave him as if they were glad to take in this addition to the ones already dependent on precious and diminishing resources. Then there was the mule whose life-energy was spent so that it could go no further; the look of the creature standing incapable of moving another step on its hard hoofs, the look of gentle abstraction in its eyes, and the vision he did not see with his own eyes of rusty skin and bones, large cranium and whispy tail, flat on the ground. And the pipkin of water someone gave into his hand; this little chipped crock with its measure of bitter water was ever afterwards in his mind a symbol of life on the earth.

The valley of the Orontes, after two years in the great depression,

126

was overpowering to Plotinus, weak, wayworn, still bearing the wound unhealed he had received among the death-strokes aimed at Gordian. Suddenly there was water everywhere, in carefully shepherded streamlets, in lotus-pools and creviced ferny springs. The opposite mountain-side sparkled with cataracts and cascades among thickets and groves of dusky green. Under the branches of the trees his soul made obeisance, acknowledging the divine influence of their temple growth of verdure and beauty. Down among orchards they trailed until they came to the bank of the eddying river. Plotinus bent to feel the soft grass with his hands while the slave-boys with no delay went into the water.

When the merchants were ready to continue their way they found the stranger senseless in that bed of green grass, his spirit bound at last by the thongs of many hardships, and the strength of his limbs loosed. So it happened he was carried unconscious into Antioch, the Alexandria of Asia.

The romance of the city, as he began to recover and languidly to discover the graces of this capital of the eastern Empire, captured the soul of the philosopher and he yielded to it with a recklessness that did not disown Rome. There was enough of the east in the city to content at that time the longing in his blood for Oriens and all that lay beyond that terrain which for him the word embraced, and at the same time he found here a refined assemblage of all man had achieved in his civilising of the earth. The wildness of nature was present unsubjected in Antioch-by-Daphne. Within the enclosing walls were mountains and torrents and abundant springs. In the beauty of hewn stone among rugged, the defences ran from the height of the Black Mountain down the slope to the river Orontes, leaped across in the glorious arc of a bridge and united with the tower of the gate. Instead of water being hid in underground canals as in Alexandria, it sang and ran sparkling through the streets of Antioch; even the two great intersecting colonnades were not without this music.

The Greek merchant who received Plotinus into his house seemed to look for no return, but to satisfy his guest he suggested he should teach the two children whose mother had not long died. Nothing could have been happier, for the brother and sister began at once to catch their master's passion for Homer, and for philosophical speculation, and in the freshness of their unschooled responses Plotinus himself drank as for the first time full draughts of the source of all true poetry. It was not for nothing the fountain of Daphne was called the Castalian Spring. As he grew stronger he and the merry-eyed brother ransacked the glories of the city; from the two mountain peaks to the measureless palace of Diocletian on an isle in the midst of the river; from the Cherubim brought from the temple of Jerusalem to the oracle of the Pythian Apollo in the sacred precincts of Daphne.

One day when he was among the groves where nature was graced by the beauty and bounty of the sun-god, as it appeared to Plotinus, so crystalline were the streams of living water, gushing from the rocks and forming pools paved with leaves of silvery or gilded brightness he found a cradle where a tree with trunk resembling a cluster of columns drank the water and carried it to heaven to spread a green roof above. And as he rested there wondering at the murmuring rivulet, continuous but not continuously heeded, like the undercurrent of his thoughts, it came to him that his most mystical thinking was in truth independent of the body; so indifferent it was if it moved or was still, was exhilarated or, as at this hour of high noon in the glades of Daphne, overpowered by lassitude. Often his eyes were closed, but now and again he opened them to clear their smart by letting them drink the pools or glide with the glassy flow. With the shifting shafts of Apollo the patterns changed on the floor of the fount and his musing became wordless, his senses dim, as if the stream were Lethe. Or, he half smiling said to himself, the aphrodisiac airs of this grove and sanctuary of unbounded licence were wafting into his usual mood of *sophrosune*.

Pain brought him from the coma into which he had sunk, the sensation of strong hands searching the wound in his side. His eyes opened on a high-browed swarthy face, with eyes dark as the shadowy pools, intent on the sore unhealed in his side. Plotinus flinched. At once the man looked at him reproachfully.

'This wound is poisoned. Without cleansing and care it will kill you. You know that?'

With a lissome movement the young man rose, swung his short madder-dyed mantle across his shoulder and continued: 'Will you allow me to be your physician? Passing, I was drawn by your face in its sickness and beauty. I bent to look closer, such a head had not come my way before, and saw where this evil wound had fouled your tunic.'

'I have no means to reward you whether I live or die. I am a stranger in Antioch and have only my poverty.'

128

'And your philosophy.'

'You have much discernment. I was indeed when you roused me inquiring in "the meadow of truth".'

'I also seek wisdom. I am sprung from the sons of the desert. With the skill in the practice of medicine which is the gift of many of my tribesmen I win enough to supply the slight diet of bread and fruit, the tunic, cloak and sandals which are all a philosopher has need of.'

'Books?'

The young Arab smiled. 'The library here is second only to the one in Alexandria. I have free entry in return for treating the sicknesses of the keepers and scribes. Now, may I dress your wound and take you home? And, if the gods allow, we may share the meditations of our hearts.'

He rinsed his hands in the stream and took salves and linen bands from a wallet lying on the grass. As the scrip fell from the hands of its owner besides the Asclepiad's staff Plotinus saw a snake, slender, silver-grey, slip from below it. The flat head was lifted with flickering tongue, then the portent of the saviour and god of healing with unhurried rippling movement passed into the closeness of grasses. When feebly, and after actually fainting under the treatment, he stood up, the physician wanted to lead him away, but he said:

'First of all I must go to the temple of Apollo and give thanks that this follower of his son has come to bring me healing.'

Zethos mutely held out to him the notched and symbolically carved rod, but when Plotinus demurred he spoke: 'If there lies with me a certain gift of healing the bodies of men, with you there is one of lightning through the clouds of suffering that darken their minds. To think is of more moment than to live.'

The wind went sighing past them through the sacred haunted boughs of the trees of Daphne as they paused with both their hands grasping the staff, the mark of their new friendship. The gilded rays of the sun continually bathed them as they moved side by side into the temple-clearing, unobserved, as though hidden in a nimbus, by the reckless and demented, the man-slayers and law-breakers, the outcasts and satyrs, until they stood before the gleaming statue of the god of the silver bow. And in presence of that figure moulded in the beauty of manhood, the philosopher leaning on the Asclepiad's staff, they exchanged a singularly sunless look.

'We are born too late to know in simplicity the glory of the god, as Homer we know knew; for in his poetry all is transparent to the divine light, and so rightly all men in aftertime name him divine. For us when we stand in the blaze and warmth we are the more aware of the opposite pole, the dark. We dwell in the shadow of matter and through this are forced to seek truth. But . . .' Plotinus looked at the incomparable harmony of the statue of Apollo and then at the sunrays of dying day between the columns of Carystian marble: 'There is such a thing as possessing more powerfully without consciousness than in conscious knowledge.'

'So came Dionysus, to restore us to "the without consciousness".'

'As in honey-wine all the sweetness is due to the honey: this "without consciousness" is the sweetness of Bacchus.'

They turned away from the god and walked doubtingly and in aloofness of thought through the darkling glades.

'What is it now, my friend?' Zethos suddenly asked.

'Pain.'

'Ah, you are using the knowledge of distress to explore its nature?'

'Which insofar as it partakes of pure knowledge, unsullied by consciousness, is free of this bodily suffering.'

'The Arabs of the desert have a saying: The spirit of a man will sustain his infirmity; but a wounded spirit who can bear?'

Plotinus came to a halt with his hand on his side. 'That indeed strikes home. The philosophers, the lovers of wisdom, have not that wounded spirit, cannot I believe in any real sense know it, although they recognise the traces of it in another man; and because his spirit is wounded, and Here a wounded spirit can never be healed, therefore they would seek to shun his company.'

'Yet you suffer inwardly, as much I may say as any man upon whose head my eyes have rested; and many I have looked on in extremity.'

Zethos bent close in the obscurity to the human countenance beside him, where the deep-graven lines of thought were enhanced by the strain of sustaining an injured body, and saw there the shining of one who had closed his eyes to behold the vision of Beauty which is the birthright of all. 'It is not matter for judgement that a man is as he is, no one in my philosophy is condemned; in life, joined to the body, every soul suffers and is tempered according to the nature of its bodily companion. But it does not have to devote itself to all the bodily experiences. "A man does not himself feel all the experiences of the tools with which he is working." '

The Arab physician assented. 'Nevertheless, the experiences of

130

the tools have their effect on him. And if we linger in this place of sacred licence we may pay with our lives. Can you walk back?'

'I rather believe after so thorough a searching of my wound it is beyond me.'

'Well, let us pass black night among the outcasts, or go into the temple of Apollo, for all the gods have healing powers, and this one of the gentle shafts more than all.'

'Do you return to the city, Zethos. You have succoured me, in the morning I shall have new life. Only tell me where I can find you again so that I can honour our friendship.'

'With the next moon I shall be sailing down to Tyre.'

'There is a man in Palestine I would willingly see again. If I may I will go with you.'

The philosopher and the physician stood facing one another while a sea-murmur ran through the rippling leaves and the trees received the presence of night in their majestic branches. The rills sang in the solitudes. Plotinus felt hands holding his with cool eager fingers, saw the white arms and the white grave face of the girl, caught the laughing tones of her brother dying with the breeze through the arches of the grove. It was time to leave the children. But he knew with swift happiness, cold and sweet as spring water, there would always be children in his love.

There was a restlessness upon him so that he could not lie down wrapped in his cloak in these precincts of Apollo, but must move softly through the glades in their nocturnal beauty. With no purpose, his soul diffusing itself in weariness, he went on through the gloom until towards midnight he felt a luminousness in those empty spaces among torn clouds over the treetops, to which often he lifted his face. The old moon rising would enter with level beams the caverns of leaves and lead him to the temple of the god. He was in the clearing before the sanctuary when he knew a companion shadow still beside him and saw at the same time lights of votive-lamps shining forth between the pillars of the portico. But the last strength of his limbs was loosed, he could do nothing but lie down on the hallowed earth and yield to that feeling of the senses in which in exhaustion and pain was yet an ecstasy of spirit.

'As far as it is possible for men to resemble God,' the words which had so often been his meditation enfolded and filled his mind while he lay powerless with his shoulders against a tree, his head grown in the grooves of the bark. Men were streaming through the courts of the temple in a kind of revelry of despair, howling,

131

chanting from the paean of Apollo, falling drunk with wine or starvation, falling locked in the unseemly death of love. The moon had surmounted the tallest trees of this pleasure-ground of Daphne, completed the dispersion of clouds and was shedding the serenity of light reflective over all the earth.

Two men he judged to be thieves or temple-strippers came near him with objects they were carrying under their cloaks; they started a quarrel and their booty fell as they wanted hands free for knives. A gilt cup rolled towards Plotinus and he saw the silver ripple of a chain like a snake through the grass. Then a third figure stood with them, spoke quietly and pointed to the plunder, but they were past reason and both turned their blades on him. Plotinus gave a cry of alarm, the two thieves fled, and the peace-maker bent over him believing he also had been struck by the robbers.

'This is an old wound, but you bleed.'

'Nothing.'

'The temenos of Apollo, these sylvan glades, are a place for meditation, it seems, you are the second philosopher I have met with here.'

The man sat down and began tearing the hem off his worn tunic, Plotinus loved his refined face in the moonlight, knowing he saw one who thought and inquired, fearless of death. They began to talk. After the thieves' scuffle the precincts were deserted, the dedicated clearing was untrodden and the beautiful temple of the god became a conformation of marmoreal contemplation in the midst of high-foliaged trees. Their talk enclosed silences of luminous thought as the leafy branches hedged spaces of vacancy, chasms of light in boundless sky.

' "As far as it is possible for man to resemble God",' the bearded man said after a long interval and while a breeze was lifting the leaves. 'When you say God, what do you mean?'

'The truth I know when I am lifted out of the body into myself; but there is soon again the descent from intellection to reasoning, and the "as far as it is possible" is to keep always within reasoning, as it obeys the impulse to energise, the Act which is pure Contemplation. But the silence before the descent is superior to all knowledge.'

'Yet you must philosophise that is to say, to seek to storm intellect by reason?'

'The Reason-Principles have their own force, which has its meaning for intellect, since they proceed from it and this force or

132

power is an intellectual gift. Reasoning is, I might say, the earth-life of a philosopher in which he finds his toil, as a farmer finds his among his fields and weather. The mind has its rainstorms and long frosts and high gales but the golden grain of Demeter must grow, the life of intellect as bread is of the body.'

'How do you know it is not your own mind you are making God, identifying its highest states with Him?'

'If God is not in man how can he be known?'

'To know that what we find as the highest in ourselves is nothing before God and yet to seek to know Him who is all knowledge by this . . . this is our humility before Him.'

So long a silence succeeded that at last the bearded man leaning towards the face in the tree, white as the moonlight which showed the haggard marks and scars of thought, believed his companion slept.

* * *

Sleeping on the deck of the little ship that was bearing him along the coast to Tyre, Plotinus recovered his strength; raising his head from this repose thought-free to look at sea and land, he longed to watch the changing outline of the hills, to speak to his companion, the Arabian disciple of Asclepius, Zethos. But always wave-rocked he slid back into slumber induced, he began to believe, by some sense-sealing narcotic as well as by the motion of Ocean. A long calm delayed the voyage and the ridges and heights of the Lebanon Mountains were an influence, as it seemed, for many days upon his rest.

They put into Tyre at night. The harbour was merry with lights that formed quincunxes to his sight and starry geometrics along the fortified isle; while those on the vessels shone pensively into their reflections, endlessly breaking and recovering their brightness in the ripples. The ship was a regular trader and had her own pilot on board to steer her course between the city and the Syrian shore. Plotinus stood by the old man half listening to his tales of hazardous landfalls on that storm-lashed seaboard, half thinking of the Phoen-icians putting forth at some forgotten dawn to sail west and found their new city of Carthage. Zethos finding him at the tiller said: 'The Arabs call the city Sur. It is one of the busiest marts of the Mediterranean. All the treasures of the east pass through Tyre. Always the source of purple, they make here also glass and that clinging diaphanous silk loved by Cleopatra.'

133

'I shall remember my entrance by night over these dark waters and the myriad lights.'

'This is the Sidonian harbour, that to the south of the isle is filling with silt, it was called the Egyptian.'

When the ship came to anchor they passed the rest of the night on deck in silence until dawn touched the waves of the sea and light shone from the snows of Libanus. Then Zethos bade his patient sleep and himself went ashore. When he returned he found Plotinus with the *Odyssey* in his hand, but narrowly watching the traffic of small craft and looking over at the island made perfect in beauty.

'I see there is to be a separation.'

'Does my face so betray me? Then I am no true Arab. The man you seek is at Caesarea, another fifty miles down the coast. I have found a place for you on another vessel.' Zethos looking at the philosopher added: 'We shall meet again in Rome.'

'I know it,' Plotinus agreed, 'you have healed me. More, you are a man dear to my heart.'

'Well, remember to eat!' the other said, not knowing how to go away.

'The sorrows of parting are always thick about harbours, but the sea is one. I am glad to have seen Tyre in your companionship.'

Tossing in his little boat Plotinus once more found himself absolved of thought, his spray-washed creaking solitude became as complete as any he had ever known. There was a glow sprung from the love of Zethos, and that kindling of his being he associated with the conception of new thought because he was voyaging to Origen. Otherwise there was nothing but the nature of the ship intrepid as a tree in a tempering gale, and a lassitude impervious to all buffetings.

Herod's ruinous mole provided little protection from the stormy sea when the boat was steered into harbourless Caesarea, and when he stood up he had to support himself by the mast, binding his cloak about it, with a glance at Odysseus and the Sirens' song. The coast of Samaria had nothing to win his eye and he perceived the town was decaying with its artificial haven. The long white wall before him was provided with a row of arches which made him think of the doors of beehives, and one of the mariners told him the seamen and fishers of the place dwelt in these hollow caves tunnelled in the side of the mole. He paid his passage-money, disembarked and began to walk up from the quay in the blank white light of a sunless sea morning. Palm-trees in semi-circles, gardens with green lawns and flowery thickets were foistered by runnels of fresh water channelled through the town in paved beds between ornamental footpaths. The public buildings essential to a Roman city were designed with such care Plotinus halted more than once to take pleasure in their architecture and uncumbered dignity. The sense of being unreal, a wanderer for a day on the broad-wayed earth, which was habitual to him, was stronger than usual after his stormy voyage. Something of the infinite sea hung about Caesarea as well as about Plotinus who had newly come up from the water, his clothing clinging with salty damp and his mind still riding the waves as a floating gull.

The lively smell of hot bread reminded him of his promise to Zethos. He went into the bakehouse and chose a small loaf, one that invited him by the patterns scored in its crust by the oven. Thinking how Gordian had spoken of this, and Marcus Aurelius written of it, as a kind of unintentional breaking into beauty, a gift of the need to bake the leavened dough before one could partake of it, he asked for Origen the lecturer. The pale man, with hair and eyelashes dusted with flour siftings, smiled at once, his mouth red and moist in the mealy face.

'I know him. The young men his disciples will be coming here soon for their hot rolls. They eat them under those palms with a little cheese of goats' milk, and never cease walking and talking. I don't know what he says, not I, but you'd say from their eyes they'd fallen in love with his words, if such a thing could be. When now and again I ask they say "he gives us the living truth". But as for him, why, he eats nothing.' And the baker, rubbing his hands, looked happily at the rows of loaves on the grained board.

Plotinus soon came to the lecture-room of Origen, crossed the court of cracked and missing flags and stood by one of the pillars supporting the open side of the hall. Something made him look back and clear between the buildings he saw the blue noon-bright Mediterranean. Then he recognised Origen's voice and brought together all the powers of his mind to listen to the end of the lecture. The master was speaking of the nature of prayer and of how the substance of it became the settled condition of minds illuminated by the divine revelation, so that they were constantly disposed to approach God and speak in his presence, as to one who watched over them and was present. 'He who prays to obtain the word of knowledge and the word of wisdom will always fittingly pray for these things, for he will always go on receiving more and more intuitions of wisdom and knowledge as his prayers are continually heard; and he will know in part as much as he is able to receive in this present life . . . until the mind without sense perception comes in contact with spiritual realities.'

Hearing the desired voice he could hardly bear to look at the figure so bowed and emaciated in black serge, it was as though there were but habit and voice, and radiance of being; the quintessence of the Alexandrian mind before him on the Asian shore of the Mediterranean. Would he, if he stayed in the dominion of Origenes Adamantius, where for him so headily Greek philosophy and Hebrew religion intermingled their lights and shades, would he lose his integrity, his intellectual, or was it Egyptian, hauteur? There could be no answer to this question because for him the time had passed when he could dwell in another man's kingdom. But this clash of living thought, the Spirit fleetingly embodied in two men of equal intensity in one age of mankind, were it but for a day, might well startle sparks to send fiery trails through centuries to come.

The voice had ceased and Origen with a flutter of his black robe, was in a single swoop standing by Plotinus on that seaward-facing loggia. Their eyes met and the students quailed at the lightning-flash.

'You know,' Origen said sadly, 'this will not do, for me.' And he turned his head aside.

Next instant, as though he had not let his tongue betray that reaction, he caught Plotinus' hands and kissed him on both cheeks exclaiming, though lowly, 'I love you so dearly!' Then immediately stepping back and addressing the young men: 'Here, my friends, you look upon a rarity, the perfect philosopher. No man will again so transmute thought into spirit or explore the metaphysics of the cosmos.'

The students, awed by the presence of those two as if they were gods, and wild at finding their own stronghold of thought stormed by the rare appearance of a stranger, dropped from Olympus on their coasts, clamoured for a public dialogue to be held between them there and then, between the sky-holding pillars and the sea of innumerable twinkling waves. With quiet authority Origen reminded them they had been dismissed, and added a quick plea to those nearest him: 'I give you all in our talks, now for once in this man at my side there is a charism of puissance and significance beyond our reckoning.'

At that the lecture-room was swiftly deserted; and still they did not look or speak for long after the shuffle of sandals and echoing tones had left them the liberty of silence.

'My dear son, you have been lost to me of late; while you were in Alexandria and with Ammonius word would come to me now and then, but for the last two or three years – nothing. Now . . .'

'Now,' Plotinus said, 'I have come hither from Antioch before travelling to Rome, for it was in my heart I must see you once more, that for us both it would be well to say hail and farewell, or as we Greeks do, *Chaire*, which is indeed all.'

'You did well to come first to Palestine, we can speak freely here. This is more my ground than yours, though indeed I think you need none.'

'Substance is not uninfluenced by earth while we are in the body, but although Plato tells us the soul should bid good-bye to it, to the utmost of its power rejecting communion with it, aim at what is, I now, man beloved in the spirit, break this bread between us, knowing you will not deny that we should eat together.'

It was strange, the power of that new bread in their hungry mouths. Walking and eating they talked freely: of the death of Gordian, the outbreaks of persecution – always a matter near to the heart of Origen – and of Origenes and other friends in Alexandria.

At last Plotinus said: 'We have tired the sun with talking and sent him down the sky.'

And Origen, stumbling and giving a cry, said he had forgotten the hour of his lecture.

'Do not dart back as a black-winged bird to the hall; for one day, for my day, it will not be harmful for those venerable youths to discover you can play truant. Now at the hour of lamp-lighting we can talk of what we think most, of what we know to be true, returning first to our common master and forgetting him who in this town, as I remember, was warned by another man who bound his own hands and feet with a girdle.'

Origen smiled at the younger man, his features hollow and haggard in that gray light which gives birth in man's soul to the awareness of eternal mystery. 'No one has won to the height and depth of knowledge possible to a man on earth who does not acknowledge mystery.' Then following his customary intuition Plotinus added: 'Shall we go down to the sea-shore?'

137

'Let us do that. You know, when I began to teach in the Catechetical School I sold and gave away all my classical books, even the works of Plato.'

'And then?'

'Then there came to the School men with minds of perfect clarity who had offered all the life that was in them to study and to the knowledge of the divine in the soul. I stood before them to speak and my spirit was humbled. I understood this humility was necessary for a Christian philosopher who sought to tell of the will and works of God, as they are given to man in the Septuagint and in the Gospels. I was granted a revelation in the light of which I have since lived and guided my teachings: this was that all wisdom is sacred and is given to man by the grace of God; and that it was my work to devote myself to the Scriptures, to study and examine them in this light, that the unity of God is manifest to man in the wisdom of all ages and of all people on the earth.

'With gladness I began to collect again the works of the poets and philosophers that I might show the power of the Greek reason side by side with the spirit of the Hebrews and so speak freely to these scholars and lovers of wisdom, of the unsearchable riches of Christ. At the same time I gave over to Heraclas, who is now bishop, the teaching of those who desired to enter into the new religion and examine the teaching of it and find there the way of thinking and living; for religion is what makes the life of men who have no hope but to pray, with heart and mind turned to God, that they may do what is right.'

'There is no way for the Greek but the discovery of intellect by which he knows both thought – the thinking power in itself – and the thoughts which are truth.'

Very gently Origen answered: 'Christ in God is present, not only with those who cleave to Him, but also everywhere with those who know Him not.'

'How do you know Him?' Plotinus asked with equal softness and looking at the man with love.

'Friends know not by obscure hints or by mere knowledge of sounds and words, symbols and types, but by a real awareness through which they attain to the nature of the intelligible world, and to the beauty of truth.'

'For this I came to you, for in this intuition of friendship the centre of both circles meet, meet in the centre of the One. From this time it is given us to know one another in the fullness of being in which each man is most alone. For intellectual perception is simultaneous with existence. But since for man, who is not born divine, this real awareness you speak of is, as it might be said, the unconscious consciousness of soul and that by which he lives; and because you and I are forced by consciousness energising to speak to others of that which is the first of things, and in the way of understanding this our human minds are apart, so we two go apart.'

'But this,' and in the intensity of thought movement ceased and they stood still on the shore of the sounding sea as though their bodies were invisible pure spirit, 'is essential for men who come after us, whether it is given them to see it or not, that for every mind, whatever its own endeavour, Truth is One.'

'The Unison is,' Origen said after a silence in the sound of the waves, 'but now the moment has passed will you tell me how you see the difference in what we teach – for this is our destiny – of God?'

'I say,' Plotinus answered, looking away from his companion to the night horizon of the sea, 'nothing is present without the Good.'

They spoke no more after that but continued together in an equal communion of silence neither would experience again. For once they knew peace.

CHAPTER IX

Earth is Heaven

The return voyage from the coast of Palestine to Antioch, where he had left Jeremy sick, was outwardly an even more shadowy experience than usual for Plotinus. Gordian was his companion when he re-crossed the desert; now as he sailed north, in preparation for making his way to Europe, it was Origen whose nature was active in his own; no outward vision of the man but that real awareness of which he had spoken, and which for Plotinus became a creative relation between his own intuition and the intuition of the Christian philosopher. And this organic interaction of conceptual thinking brought him, in the course of that voyage, to as full a recognition of the life of man the Gnostics described as hylic, or completely involved in matter, as he could attain to. That exclamation 'Cut everything away!' was essential to his own mystical detachment from earth, to the sheer translucency of his thought, but in a fulguration he acknowledged that not to do that made Origen's position, in relation to this world, both more difficult and more human than his own.

This reflection he let go. What remained, lit by the flash of insight, was that the complete living form, the unity of this living universe, was known by Origen as it was by himself, with none of the false cosmology and fairy-tale elements, as they seemed to be to him, of the Gnostics. But the task Origen set himself, or was set by his daemon, of making men aware of the One God of the Hebrews through a mediator rejected by them but acceptable to the Greeks because of their traditional recognition that the gods assumed human form was, he declared to himself, an impossible one. His own philosophy, the form into which his thought was ever more powerfully developing itself, which hitherto he had regarded as an interpretation of Plato for a later age, and a restatement of Platonic thought as it was understood among the philosophers of Alexandria, presented itself to him now as a bridge, balanced and symmetrical, between the paganism of the Greeks and the monotheism of the Jews. And this bridge must be built in men's minds, its tensions tested, by what Origen had called the real awareness of one human

140

being by another. What he recognised also, and confessed, was that in Origen his daemon encountered a spirit of power at least equal to its own. His daemon wrought only for thinkers, Origen's for all mankind.

Religion takes into account the baseness of man, philosophy dwelling always in the divine aspect of soul is transcendent. But the soul in man has fallen. Can it restore itself? To answer this was to be the work of his teaching in Rome for whatever remained to him of life; and the answer that came to him through his seaborne contemplation was that there was always an aspect of the soul, however obscured by the part fallen, which remained above.

What remained with him from the Caesarean interlude was a realisation of the infinite possibilities of Providence; and an assurance, after encountering the singular communion between Origen and his disciples, that he also must establish a school; and he smiled as he recollected the phrase used by the Alexandrian teacher for this world, this intractable Here, a *schola animarum*.

On the last stage of his journey when he was moving eastward from the sea-coast to Antioch, he felt nostalgia for Alexandria, for the sand of Egypt. Letting this wave of unexpected longing sweep on and break in a storm of brine on some distant unexplored headland of his being, he set himself to discover why it had risen and whelmed him. It was not difficult, but the explanation did not immediately reconcile him to Rome, which represented in his mind the scene of that desperate battle between the elements of dark and light that the follower of the prophet Mani had described to him, a battle being waged in the earthly bodies of men as well as in their souls and spirit-wrought minds. Rome stood for time, for the labours necessity imposed on man, which must endlessly be repeated and defeated, from which no one was exempt. In Egypt he could dwell with eternity before the heavens came into being. Alexandria was the city of philosophers and the mother of the sciences; there, all ways of thought were open, were being explored by minds that stimulated one the other without strife.

That was the art of dialectic. The energy ensouled in the living man was limited, exhausted itself in outbursts of strife. Yet even so some dynamism not understood brought about a restoration of this invisible perceptible force. The energy not physically expended, by some communion or interplay with intellect in its passive aspect, gave awareness in consciousness of that highest activity of mind which was concentration in the Divine. That is Being at its intensest,

141

the point where it is 'put in travail with multiplicity'. In Rome the travail with multiplicity was most manifest in the passionate living forms of men's bodies and the work of their hands. All he had heard from men in Alexandria, and in the army of Gordian, had told him this, until it became inwoven with him. The intensity of his own vision must be proved where thinking was densest now, not where it was at its rarest and most exalted. For the last time he was facing east. But he had no desire to go further than Antioch, the Christian Alexandria. There indeed he would willingly have ended his days near river and mountain and sacred groves of Daphne. There the poetry his heart craved was living to his gaze in the Asiatic abandon of buildings and statues; in the choruses of boys and girls mingled with the singing rills his vision kindled in the soul – Aphrodite. He went through the streets with a new pliancy that mocked the marmoreal gait of the sage. This, he remembered Pindar, was a rest with light feet; feet, that is, about to bear him elsewhere.

★ ★ ★

Plotinus had made his farewells and embarked, with Jeremy and his impediments, on an evening of haunted twilight, on what he believed would be his last voyage over the sea, with its hidden fish and proud dolphins. The outward-bound vessel gliding towards the mouth of that smooth-flowing river passed close by an incoming one driven with oars against the current in the unruffled nightfall. Voyagers and crew alike stared at one another with a sense of fellowship. Plotinus' eyes unraised met, as motion opposite ways carried the ships onwards, a naked foot on the planks of the other deck. Then indeed his head was drawn up, his eyes drank other dark pools in angular hollows. Across the water ruffled in the narrow space between twin keels the voice called clear and bodiless as a bird's: ' "Soul is Spirit in process of redemption." '

At those words the soul of Plotinus, which had endured the leave-taking of the city Antioch and of those he loved there, utterly dissolved, not into spirit but into an ultramarine desolation where all his philosophy became naught.

The ingrained conflict in the nature of his being, that made his life a strenuous attempt to bind together the fibres of his mind that knew itself one with the organic whole of the universe, threatened Aphrodite which for him was the life of the soul in contemplation. And a line from Empedocles' poem *On Nature*, which he had copied in the library of Alexandria, washed through his mind with the sound of the streams of Ocean against his boat: 'Severed by cruel Strife they wander each alone by the breakers of Life's sea.' With that he perceived what it was that had cast down his mind. It was the final word of Origen, redemption. All the implications the word had, and would have, in the minds of men for whom thinking was the intensest form of living pelted like a hailstorm the philosophy of Plotinus. It was that which severed them. But immediately came recollection of his certainty that the cosmos was a single interrelated whole.

'All things have wisdom and a share of thought', that word 'share' seemed to show all those flashing facets of men's minds whose brilliance dazzled themselves. His own thought was a share but where it was in pure contemplation of intellect it was one with spirit. And strife which is life in the body, that is – the form necessity takes in matter so that soul in the agony of being rent learns prayer. The ship was tossing, he felt the planks straining with every heave and plunge and he exulted in the power in which all created things have a share, this share the creator in them. He forgot that 'philosophy is the highest music' and gave his soul free, in an Homeric and elemental abandon, to nature in the waves and in the wood of the swift ship. Of what use a steersman with no living vessel to guide?

The roughness of man and nature from which he often caught himself shrinking on land became on sea no less glorious than the death of heroes clad in bronze. At the same time all that the coldness of his wisdom had caused him to turn from he received with a surge of tenderness he never forgot. With his head on the breast of his nurse, where alone it had found rest, he wept as he had not since he left his boyhood in that skiff among the papyrus stalks of the Nile. He mourned his mother's death, and sent an irradiance of love for his sister over the waves until they were more fiery than the storm-clouds of Zeus.

The gods to whom he prayed for the gentle poetic head the same breasts had fed, were not unmindful of him. They sent a great wave which caught athwart the tempest-tried boat and casting a very wall of water on Plotinus laid him on deck and rolled him down a deadly slant. His heart yielding cried within, better to die with love, king; cried it through the pain which was like a sharp sword. The ship became level and was lifted with the smoothness of a floating bird over the crest of the next billow. With his hands on the slithery boards and his feet locked against something that kept him steady

143

he had a curious inward experience of realising the nature of matter, which in his philosophy of the universe was without substance. Because he had just been rolled helpless and the Platonic circles in his head were disordered he had this vision of matter as motion, motion at different and immeasurable speeds; intrinsic motion, the unseen energy or act of the One, not the apparent movements of things in relation to each other. At the same time he became aware of the virtue of the wood passing into his hands, a sense of communion between the delicate skin of his palms and the life of wind-tempered timber dormant in the beams of the ship. And with that impulse of the Greeks when they set foot on their native land he bent down and kissed the life-saving wood.

He stood upright again, found something to support himself by while he learnt to ride this sea-charger, which was itself riding the waves, and listened to the ejaculations of the sailors, their brief prayers to Poseidon, or to others of the deities beloved and invoked by men on board ship. He looked up at the stars shining far distant one from another among scared clouds, their bright remote souls always for him a benign influence because there is no Lethe for the stars. That river does not utterly obliterate traces of remembrance. Prayers, nervous pluckings at the strings men believe to be taut throughout the well-tuned Harmony of the Whole. The stars mark them but change not, but by his cry the man who prays may find in himself a new image come uppermost, a new skill visiting his busy hands. Well. And that inclining of the whole soul in silence, the prayer the Stoic philosophers speak of, in that, as it approaches, the soul finds a new life.

He could stand no longer, the little ship was a rough cradle for thought and shook up, as he sought a niche where he might be supported and not doused or soused either, a recollection of those warnings against seafaring of the poet Hesiod; and of Horace after him:

> 'To live wisely shun
> the deep sea; on the other hand
> straining to dodge the storm don't run
> too close into the jagged land.'

His mind of its own accord composed a response to the prudent advisers of the chersonese: though I may never again sail the sea on a swift ship it is my fate always to steer over deep waters and to run in as close as I dare to those jagged rocks, the acutest thoughts of other men which threaten to wreck mine. For that is what it is to live by my philosophy.

Until that storm was past, and a halcyon-calm spread over the waves as a waning moon rose, his mind dwelt on the vision of the two vermilion-prowed Homeric ships as they passed, cutting the deep opposite ways, and turned away for the last time from the mind of Origen.

★ ★ ★

The long voyage up the west coast of Italy ended one nightfall when the vessel, with its cargo of treasures from the east, entered the sandy mouth of Tiber tossing on a sea roused by a south-west wind. Plotinus had seen the lights appearing in the villas lining the coast, the dance of fires, but it was not until the prow turned towards the east and the signal of the lighthouse-tower of Portus, on the north bank of the river, began to come and go in his vision that he recognised the ship was near harbour. The intermittent beam of this beacon reflecting as it were in that portion of consciousness dedicated to Alexandria distressed him with a curious pseudo-sense of homecoming. While lights in the storeyed buildings of Ostia twinkled evermore impertinently to his right, and the lights of the ships at anchor in the exposed haven were as so many *ignes fatui*, it was the pharos showing the entrance to the newer harbour that conveyed to him the significance of his Italian landfall.

Wearily he began to gather together all his past life that had fulfilled itself, that no longer had value for him, or his philosophy, all he believed he had proved vain. Nothing, at the threshold of old age, which was represented for him here by the flat coast and the lamp-lit windows behind which men busied themselves, must interfere with this final stage of the life the god had prepared for him. To be exciting a philosophy must be lived and experienced to the limit, but it must never become something to be hoarded for oneself alone; now, if time were given, he must hand on the torch of his vision. If this indeed were the will of the daemon there would be men to receive it. Everything that could obscure the rays must be cut away. But while he prepared, at the bidding of the shadowy shore and the admonitory light-tower, to re-dedicate himself to the old masters by teaching their wisdom as it had recreated itself in the urgency of his own inward passion, for he recognised in a flash at that point of his destiny, which was at once farewell and hail, that contemplation and creation were the poles of reality, he knew

145

that what he must not seek to cast, with the rest of the bundle of mental apparel, into the mingled waters of Father Tiber and Tyrrhenum Mare was his poetry, the wings of his intuition.

The look of the waterfront next morning, the reception in his mind of what his perceiving sense did to concrete walls and facades divided into squares by designs of inset bricks and cold-eyed windows, told him, as he stared across the sullenly lapping river, his spirit would swiftly sink without those air-cleaving swallow wings. Alexandria never forgot it was outlined by a Greek on the sea-coast of an antique land; Ostia with its frowning granaries and toiling dockyards threw him with this first glance into the ordered tedium of modern commerce. Behind the port was Rome. Through this silty grain-swallowing river-mouth he was approaching the imperial city as an 'intermediary between the Divine and the material world'.

While he was searching for the names of those grain importers, who had been friends of his father, and which had been given him by his mother with a stern command to visit these men if he ever went to Italy, Plotinus was thinking of Virgil who had by a mysterious power given Homer's lyre Latin strings. And at the vision of the poet leaving his shadow on the paved streets, on the forbidding fronts of the warehouses, he rose from before his inlaid chest, signed to Jeremy to give a cloak not stained by brine, and prepared to disembark.

Walking, with a sense of disequilibrium after his voyage, on the steady stones of the quay, in the shadow of the balconies that grew out towards air and sea from the first floor of these prosperous houses, his mind as ever indwelling, Plotinus heard a snatch of song and at the same moment something fell softly about his head.

> ' "Where have you gone from me
> Maidenhead, Maidenhead?
> Never again shall I come to you, darling,
> Never again . . . " '

He put up his hand and took what he saw was a bridal fillet of white wool. Holding it lightly he stepped back until he could see the diagonal rails of the little gallery which were twined with grape-vines. The saffron marriage veil of the girl floated over them and her grave face, still with triple ringlets framing cheeks sad as rain-washed petals, was bent over it upon him. The involuntary meeting of the eyes was for them both a vision of Eros, a discovery and

146

instant loss of soul. In surprise of eternity there could be no speech or turning away.

The calls of boatmen sounded again. With the weight of his forty years on his head Plotinus moved it aside and raising his hand said the only word his lips would shape: *Talassio*. These syllables of ineffable meaning, cried when the bride was carried over the threshold, were probably still vibrant in the place from the shouts of the previous night. She was catching from the wind her saffrony sash when he looked up again to say, after Pindar: 'There are immortal days for us although the body die.'

Aware then of the eye-beams of bystanders he tossed the fillet over the rails saying at random the first name he remembered. To his surprise the girl's face flushed and she answered:

'It is my father you seek.'

'Will you tell me then the way to the house you quitted at the shining of Hesperus?'

She explained with quick gestures of her hands and assenting ringlets which she suddenly held back exclaiming: 'My hair must be braided now.'

'Aphrodite brings her gifts and the Graces theirs,' Plotinus said in farewell, as he went the way her hand waved.

The small white arms and cloud-like veil stayed with him as he crossed an immense courtyard with warehouses on every side and walking south-east, between the Capitolium and the Forum, saw before him the portico, as she had told him, of the temple of Cybele. Beyond lay the south gate of the city and the Via Severiana. This highway, which ran along the coast, was bordered with many houses of the wealthy who had business interests in Ostia, and here was her father's home. But he had also a city lodging in the precincts of the temple of the earth-goddess with one of her branch-bearing priests. In the paved square, planted with the almond-trees of Attis, with a fountain and a pair of carved and couchant lions, Plotinus came to a stand. Fish with gold and silver scales and red-ringed eyes of unobserving glassiness wavered round and round in a porphyry basin. He was at that moment overpowered by the structures in abstract patterns his intellect was building up beyond the symbolic images that were causing various distorting ripples in his consciousness.

The luminousness of the sky filled the court with a shadowless radiance, which must have something to do with the place being sacred to the Great Mother of the gods, and into that translucent heaven entered loud-clamouring sea-gulls, swooping and turning, cleaving with clear-cut wings, thrown as wildly apart as though all the winds blew though the air was breathless. Why was it, he began to ask, with a lift of his spirit as the birds whirled over the temple of the goddess of all wild creatures and swung away towards the sea, this spontaneous exultation caught him while the frenzied acts of her eunuch priests, their lashings and yellings, were to his mind a desecration of the Logos? And he recognised his delaying in the court was not only to allow his soul to return to that limpidity in which it knew itself, but also because he shunned the presence of that fellow dedicated to the cult of Cybele.

The door in an angle of the wall was opened by an African slave who regarded Plotinus with the expressionless softness of his murky eyes, and then lowered them as if to avoid a pair of shooting stars aimed at his inmost being. The philosopher spoke the name of his father's friend. The servant bowed assent and carefully closing the door behind them without looking up, brought the visitor to an arch in the north corner of the peristyle. Standing by a pillar immobile as the solemn stone, which yet had a lucent grace as of light reserved in the granular texture, he saw a figure in loose gown and turban followed by a whelp cross the shadows. Given leave to enter, he had the impression of a room empty of man, containing but books, couch, beautiful skins and fleeces. With a more than ordinarily haunting sense of unreality he went towards the opposite arch and there met an aged man coming from the garden with a striped shawl over his shoulders.

They faced each other with a sense of liking, and of recognition and understanding.

'That is a very garden of Zeus,' Plotinus said, looking beyond the statue of Nestor.

'My sole company now my child has gone, the only one of my old age, dear son. Would you had come sooner. You have not made haste to claim your heritage.' Seeing the surprise of his visitor, he added: 'Didn't your father tell you? Well, he may not have had time. He left a sum of money with me so long ago – "for the children". It has greatly increased. You will find you have ample for a simple life when I reckon with you the sesterces. But first, let us talk.'

They strolled with many pauses among the statuary and trees, the little old man nimble and hobbling, Plotinus with his deliberate tread, oblivious and sure, as of a somnambulist. Gratian, finding his guest had arrived in Ostia so lately, began giving a glancing account of the state of Rome, touching on one thing after another until the city and its business and government became for Plotinus like a mosaic on the surface of his mind, part shadowed part highly illuminated. This narrative was interlaid with shrewd questions and edged with regret for the loss of his daughter. Why had he let her go, the old man mourned. Then halting by the statue of Socrates he asked with an air of authority, as being the guardian of his fortune and friend of his father, what Plotinus intended in Rome, how he would devote whatever might remain to him of life. The philosopher with his eyes on the sculpture, that pug-nosed face with lowered eyes and hands absently clutching the garment that covered him below the paps, answered:

'To teach.'

'Rome is plagued with schools and lecturers, teachers and preachers,' grumbled Gratian.

'So I am aware,' responded Plotinus, unwontedly humble-mouthed. 'Most men who think at all in this our uneasy age have their own philosophy or form of worship. But I have reached now the end of the course which my masters, the sages, the wise of old, guided me on. The time left is for me to live by philosophy, which I can only do by proving it upon life, that is to say, on the intellects of living men who think of these things. The more schools and gods there are in Rome the better will my reasoning be tempered. For this, with the money you speak of, I will buy a house; I will have open doors and free entry for anyone who would hear me, or speak to me.'

'What gods do you worship?' the old man asked.

' "God an instantaneous presence everywhere." '

'How do you know the one you speak of?'

' "By that way of prayer that is always within our power – leaning in soul towards him by aspiration." '

'Perhaps that is not what others mean by religion.'

'The outward approaches men feel the need for, ritual, discipline, lacerations of the flesh, after *that* kind teaching will be for me the religion of the highest mind, which is never caught.' Plotinus felt with his fingers a fold of Socrates' drapery.

The old man was Tithonus now, diminishing and graying, his face wizened: 'You would give up all men value and for the sake of an unattainable God?'

'All.'

149

'That must include, as indeed it must, what is most precious to you; until now, if I understand you, you have chosen from living masters and the writings of the dead.'

'That is fair. I do not live by and for this as I did in the past. Inwardly I wait for the vision in the silence and radiance of being. If my philosophy has meaning men will come to hear me, and what I say to them may, I think, be reckoned as my offering to the One.'

'This is madness, the sacrifice of a strong-limbed human life to a vision of the soul. You are inexorable as Hades.' The old man's voice quavered.

'Sacrifice is inescapable for life here,' Plotinus answered gently. 'But I will have nothing to do with it as a display for the commonalty. Shows of gladiators; men thrown for sport to beasts; the acts of these priests of Cybele, with whom you lodge, who lash and gash themselves into a fury; men mutilating and unmanning themselves for a joy for their gods. Sacrifice must be realised in the soul. I breathe and hold my ground here in no unseemly orgies but by knowing that in myself, in all men, which participates in the Supreme, which does not give and passes on but gives for ever.'

'How can it give for ever?'

'Because the power given out constantly returns to the source.'

'How did you come to choose this life of the intellect?' And the old man laid a hand on Plotinus' shoulder.

'I did not choose. It is the will of the god in me.' At those words the hand fell away.

They moved in silence from the ambit of Socrates. Plotinus began to speak of his sister, and asked Gratian whether he could enable him to send half the money entrusted to him to Alexandria for Marcus to convey to Deborah. A girl's voice rang through the grove just then, musical and winged with desire as a flute, and the two men, startled in their gravity and absence of mind, believed a nymph had risen from her fountain to rebuke them for their blindness, their dryness of soul in this garden of the Hesperides.

'No, father, I am not a dryad, though many of them are here,' and she touched the leaves of a tree, the bark of another. 'I have come, you remember – do you remember? – as I promised with my bridal chorus, to sing for you.'

'I remember, of course, I remember, dear child. You thought of my loneliness. Behold, the gods also were not unmindful. No sooner were you gone from me than they led hither a son in your stead. One whose father I knew in time far gone by. Do you with your shining eyes see the nymphs of the trees? Tell us.' And he glanced at Plotinus.

'I see not them but their handiwork. You see – don't you? – how all here is with grace, a disorder become adornment. That broken branch an arch to lead the eyes through to a pattern of flowers. This dead one a stag's antlers tearing the moss. Sticks fallen across and across a notation. Over there a pine wrenched asunder for Attis. Yet the very torn fibres are beautiful, the flakes of bark.'

Her swift looks, movements of head and hands as she spoke, her longing for response mingled with shyness made the air radiant round her. Nothing could have been less in keeping with Plotinus' mood than a dance-song; the pain in his midriff that was caused by his purposeful fasting, that was more often than not starving, was like a wolf's tooth, and his heart was a cold hearth-stone at sight of the girl. Not that she did anything but hold her father's hand as the flute began. She did not even look at him. But the whole of the Tower of Saturn was falling in fragments as the song and chorus of girls danced among the garden trees. They wore girdles that shone with the singing, the swinging and bending of the dancers, who moved now as one to the wind-words of the flute-player, now swayed apart, their long hair tossing as corn under the ripple of the west wind.

> ' "Not now
> When they have seen nectar from my springs
> However they thirst to another stream
> Where the water is bitter
> Let those two go" '

The chorus moved back fluttering into the shadows of the grave trees, the leader with white veil, yellow breast-knot and black trailing hem stepped stately, billowing over the grasses, swan of the choric lyric, singing:

> ' "I pray to the daughter of heaven silver-robed
> Memory and to her children
> For gifts of grace and skill
> Blind are men's minds
> Whosoever without the Muses of Helicon
> Would seek the way through the deeps
> Of those who came thither by wisdom
> To me they have handed on this immortal toil" '

151

The chorus, with filmy chitons as plumy clouds, floated forward on an exquisite rhythm of bare feet in the grass, to encircle the singing swan, repeating: 'To me, to me the immortal toil is given.' Plotinus unbreathing as feathery robes stroked him saw in among the airy feet a tortoise. The creature's scaly head was obstinately ajut and it made no attempt to advance in accord with the pattern of the dance, as he had a feeling it could easily have done had it chosen, so that one foot lighted on top of the painted shell, another all but overturned it. The girls with little laughing cries re-captured their measure while the intruder pressed against Gratian with unmistakable cold-blooded love.

Fearing he might be lost in the rhythm of this dance of the elementals, as he considered it, be unheedful of the music of the spheres, Plotinus went away down one of the alleys, pausing by one statue or another until the chorus was ended. All the girls began chattering at once till the tree dryads shook their foliage and Gratian demanded silence in which to praise them. And when he had spoken there came the desired voice and Plotinus stopped eating mulberries and returned to where the old man was resting on a stone seat with the tortoise close by, head and feet wholly indrawn under the handsome dome. Muffled in his striped cloth, which resembled an Arab haik and was evidently of eastern origin, the old fellow tapped softly on the shell with an ebony staff while his daughter stood before him with folded hands in an attitude of submission. Involuntarily Plotinus' eyes and hers met, she moistened her lips and he at once guessed his were red with mulberry juice.

'Gemina, my child,' the dry chirrup continued, 'you have filled my sorrowful grove with shining, the philosophers themselves are ravished on their pedestals, but you must stay here no longer. Her father's side is not the place for a bride of yesterday. Gather your chorus, do not leave one of these dancers behind near me, and return to your husband's house.'

'Papa, here is Marcellus Orontius, who came for my marriage, he said he would come and bid you farewell before returning to Rome.'

With cricket agility Gratian hopped towards his distinguished guest while Gemina told the flutist to pipe the girls together. Plotinus stood by her as they came up in small groups, making the air lustrous and tense with youth and grace, drawing in jingling girdles, some still barefoot, one wearing one sandal with the other swinging glittering from her wrist. Glancing at her father, she said:

152

'You will find Marcellus good company, I believe, sir, for he is an amateur wise man.'

'Perhaps then I could travel with him to Rome?'

'Perfect!' she exclaimed with subdued merry laughter. 'All the way you could talk uninterrupted philosophy!'

As she was going their hands met and held. Then it was with all the radiance of Gemina and her maiden-chorus coursing through him that Plotinus found himself close to Tithonus. In fact those nerve-strung ligaments in the back of his skull, that, as he believed, bound his mortal life to the divine intellect, were so tautened it was as if the fingers he'd felt had drawn them tight and tuned them to vibrate to another music.

Night overshadowed the three in Gratian's garden still talking; they had tired the sun with talking and sent him down the sky; even the tortoise had deserted unobserved and was mowing a row of lettuce seedlings. The road to Rome was forgotten. The white statuary grew wraith-like, unsubstantial as the airy draperies of the chorus. Marcellus spell-bound by the assurance of the philosopher, who led him by the hand into the 'meadow of truth', paced up and down the grassy glade which had been the dancing floor of the nymphs, while Gratian delightedly whetted his scepticism on the asceticism of Plotinus.

'My children, we must go in, you will have dinner with me and postpone your journey till the morning, is it not so? Then we shall all be happy.' The words fluttered about them as dry leaves, and the old man rose and tapped his companions with his wand on their flanks, commanding they be disenchanted.

'But the garden is now most like that of Epicurus. Why go away? Besides,' Marcellus halted in front of Plotinus, 'this passion we have been talking of, I cannot get my mind clear on it, and I don't think you can either.'

'Passion as a power is good in itself, positive and giving life to intellect; power used inwardly and not become the means of violence and loosed on others or on the nature of the world . . .'

'You said the soul of the philosopher confronting misfortune is passionless and imperturbable.'

'I believe it can be so, but only through suffering, experiencing the power of passion. Calm coming through the potency of these, not from apathy. As we are, men in society, citizens of no mean city, we must act in the world, I do not deny that . . .'

'Virtue? That quality most praised of Romans and Stoics?'

Plotinus smiled. 'Dull. Leading to self-satisfaction. I prefer passion.'

The silence of the garden fell upon them. No one moved till a rustling small wind slipped in among the leaves, then they knew it was the hour when the dryads would restore their chosen careless rhythm of sticks and leaves and cast-off petals, feathers and butterfly wings; mend bent grass blades; caress the plants that grow by moonlight.

Gratian retired soon after the meal, and after some business talk with Plotinus. As in Homeric times, beds were spread for the two guests on the portico and Marcellus had them drawn together so that the talk he found so delightful could be quietly prolonged. That time of meditation most perfectly known at the threshold of sleep was forgone by Plotinus without a word, although indeed he felt it as a tide in the sea-deeps pulling another way from the surface currents and moony ripples; and the dolphin leaps of thought seeking a new element.

'In this cool dismissal of virtue you do not agree with the man you name your master, Plato.'

'Don't we all rebel against our masters, except indeed those fellows in the Socratic dialogues, Marcellus? If ever I founded a city on the model of the *Republic* there would be no ban on poets.'

'For fear you yourself should be excluded? But I want you to keep to virtue, if you will.'

'You, a reader of Plato, know as I do he has two orders of this debatable quality of the soul, and one he calls civic. It may be inevitable for a poet-philosopher to look on this as necessary but dull.'

Marcellus laughed gently.

'Well, leave this virtue and its kindred gravity . . . Divine is without states. In my philosophy one can transcend all these, while recognising that the ones that appear most good in a human sense are the most binding. A man abiding in passionless gravity may believe he has attained all. This is fatal to Intellection.'

'Why then Rome?'

'Because he who has seen a beautiful vision has not attained it by his own striving. While a man is on earth, is Here, he must live this vision in life present, and this is most intense in other souls, their very existence a trace of the One. Architects go among noble buildings to learn, in the power of others who have built, the strength of their own vision; so I would go among those souls which also by thought, and self-discipline, have taken light.'

'Not by his own striving . . . I think you were going to say more about this. Do we approach here a certain difficulty in what we have been discussing? Earlier you said something of the alone to the Alone . . . if I remember. If what is most precious, the soul, the "we", does not strive but in its essence *knows in stillness*, whether we as men on earth are aware of this or not in consciousness, why philosophise at all? Can it be a way of using the passions we disown? Leaving aside men who are rich, and men who fulfil their lives in practising the "civic virtues" of Plato, why would you say a sage, a mystic, an initiate who by understanding the mysteries has become divine, is closer to the Supreme than a water-carrier . . . if this is what you would say? A man bearing a pitcher of water, is he not as close to the source of life? God is present unperceived to all. The water bearer may well endure the blows of fate that light on his head, that is undefended, as heroically as the wise man who because of his wisdom or his pride of intellect, is determined to be unshaken by them.'

Plotinus was thinking of how he and Marcus talked long ago in Lycopolis sitting up in their two cots they'd pulled close together. He recalled the look of his cousin's dark head outlined against the night sky, and remembered wondering how many stars he could not see because of that skull containing the mystery of man's mind. Because man is mortal, because his body will rot, he is more exciting than the gods that are for ever, whose proud heads do not darken the stars. His very endeavour to become as the gods gives him glory, for this strife of the deity in gross flesh is an intense experiencing of reality that the cosmos must not be without.

By the way the tide was surging seaward in the depths while the surface became glassy under the moon, Plotinus knew he was alone and he prayed Somnus hold his companion in the other bed safe in sweet sleep. He thought of Odysseus, the constant wanderer, who left behind not only isles and sorceries but his longed-for native land, that to the end he might voyage. The more a man is alone the more he recognises the solitariness of all beings and their ineffable association with the One.

For all that, dawn called him to the garden to look at the gray printless lawn, overarched with glooming trees, which had been the stage of the *parthenia*, to remember how it was when the girl had drawn her fingers through his.

Plotinus beside Marcellus in the beautiful silver-plated carriage, drawn by a pair of white horses, felt a deep unwillingness at being carried away from Ostia. Not a word the Roman was saying entered his head, he did not admire the smoothness of the well-flagged road or notice the tomb-mounds between which the horses, shaking the yoke upon their necks, drew the four-wheeled travelling chariot. Philosophy, or his life dedicated to study of it, took on for him in the course of that drive the form of a harsh necessity, an irrevocable command, something from outside instead of an inward conse-cration and concentration of his being. He had a clear vision of his back as though he were following himself through a street where men walked, his shoulders a trifle bowed under the philosopher's mantle, his head uncovered, with flakes of half-curling graying hair over the broad skull, irradiant with suffering. Some of the bypassers not absorbed in their own business and startled by his magnetic quality shunned this figure most solitary in the crowd, twitching away their cloaks; others as he saw sought contact and brushed his sides. But this eidolon of himself kept his deliberate pace oblivious of all the wayfarers, inviolable. This back was turned, he well understood, to the sea; with his face towards Rome his outward Odyssey was accomplished – even if he returned to the coast; to stand on the sea-shore with no purpose of embarking on a swift ship was not the same adventure as it had been in the past. On the other hand the life of the intellect, self-chosen or chosen because for him there could be no other, was the only one in which a man would not weary of himself and of his fellow travellers on earth. Soul immortal could not tire whereas water-carriers and even those occupied with a craft or demanding skill, would grow out of patience with their task, weary of body, mind rejecting repetition. Besides, though he did not give his companion this answer, it is in all earth-toil the presence of soul that gives worth and a man who knows in his soul the act of intellect knows also the essence of all the gifts of Athene. In the practice of these gifts of workmanship lies a merciful forgetfulness, in contemplation of intellectual-principle the whole act of life is ceaselessly experienced.

The carriage drew off the paved highway and came to a halt. He heard Marcellus saying something about a tomb it was his custom to salute. It had lately rained, the stones gleamed silverly as a white sunless radiance streamed earthwards between citadels of thunder-cloud. The solemn effigies shone faintly. Plotinus moving under the aegis of these mourning attitudes read some of the epigrams while he desired for himself a less bustling burial-place. They were not far from Rome now and the Via Ostiensis was thronged with carriages and riders on horseback. On the footway on either side, slippery now after the rainfall, the crowds of the poor poured on: peasants, slaves, tatterdemalions, vile rabble. One starving, who would not reach the city that night, fell and crawling away from the beating feet lay in his bunch of rags against a marble monument. No one heeded. 'Life justified in its victors and its vanquished?' 'The All one comprehensive universal living being.' The sage who seeks to make himself perfect and the masses. He turned from the man muttering by the tomb back to the relentless stream of pedestrians, and felt a hand on his arm. An alien touch, because of the sensitivity of his spiritual fibre, the tension of nervous threads, a cobweb binding body in soul, shook him throughout as a violent blow would, but imperceptibly to another. Simultaneously he recollected he had left Jeremy in Ostia with no guidance for his own departing. The eyes of the dumb slave reproached him from the patrician's excessive epitaph.

When Plotinus turned his reserved and luminous regard on the personage who had approached him, the hand still communicating a thousand unwanted vibrations, he saw a veritable Alcibiades, an outrageously good-looking head and a torrent of silken apparel glistening like water in the wild white fire consuming the last hour of day. The stranger began to speak, his melodious voice accompanied by the clink of chains as a gang of slaves passed by.

'Our friend Marcellus tells me he is about to honour the imperial city with a new philosopher. I envy him. Will you not agree to return with me to Ostia? I shall be in Rome again this time tomorrow, in the journey I can sound your philosophy: and the triumph will be mine.'

With the sound of the sea in his ears, and the wind through the trees in a garden with a crying girl, Plotinus answered with all the grace the gods had given him: 'I dare not return to the sea-coast, and I would not desert our friend who has brought me so far. I believe for myself this avenue of sepulchres is as the way to Hades, the way of no return. But if you were willing you could aid me in the matter of a well-loved slave.' As they went back to the two carriages Plotinus explained Jeremy's predicament, with his eyes on the tossed stormy manes of the white horses.

As the three men stood together planning a future meeting, for the handsome Graeco-Roman seemed to take all in good part, Plotinus drawing closer round him his simple garment against the wind, found his dread of the city gone. He even felt a faint flow of anticipation as he mounted the car. It was to be here after all, if he understood the daemon aright, that his arduous philosophy would flower and cast, it might be, some grains of golden dust upon other minds.

The presence of the city – columned buildings shining on the dark hills, air and light bent by buildings, distressed by sharp angles and geometries; the influence of hewn stone on which the weight of light had fallen for centuries from heavenly distances, mysterious life of an organic thing of creation and growth – was a power on his spirit now, established as something beyond the purposes and control of its human designers. They had crossed the last bridge in a flourish of silver-gilt sunlight; now the shadows of a tempest-burdened nightfall held dominion over city and champaign. Yes, just at that moment of twilight it was for him as though all who had known god-given life on the earth had gone down to the shadowy realm of Persephone; nature herself, loved in the life of beasts and trees, leaves and radiant flowers, gone as well; the only landmark where nothing breathed, no eyes beheld the light of the sun, the city.

He was answering Marcellus, wheeled vehicles were passing, the patient-footed masses burdened with food and fuel streamed on towards the looming gate-towers of the Via Ostiensis, when Plotinus remembered the Emperor Gordian. The presence of the young man visited him in as lively a way as it had in the days of wandering that had followed his murder. With that endearing leader of men touching his shoulder Rome was again the metropolis of imperial rule and the heart of the Empire and . . . the dwelling of Philip the Arabian. By entering the city, Plotinus confessed to himself, he was acknowledging the usurper emperor. Through his converse with Marcellus he was carrying on a more intimate dialogue with Gordian who conveyed to him that what mattered was not who ruled the Empire but that the philosopher should fulfil the purpose for which he came hither, and not suffer his teaching of spirit, intellect and soul to be deflected or weakened by the multitude of ephemeral doctrines and deities he would meet with. And Plotinus responded with a singular inward warmth of his own being, their hands clasped at the hearth of reality.

Love too is vision and in this inward shining he entered the city. Carriages were banned from the streets, but, although this was a law highly dishonoured, they climbed out of theirs in the broad courtyard surrounded by mews in the hour of lamp-lighting. Slaves shouldered their baggage and the white horses were led away, taking with them for Plotinus that other vision of the waves of the sea. The corridors between the tenements stank, garbage washed down by rain-water lay together like wrack on the strand. For the first time in his life he could have wept at the vanity of philosophy, and he knew henceforth to live in the Tower of Saturn would demand all the power of his daemon. Whether he could stand, while he uttered his wisdom to these builders in concrete who ruled the world, did not receive the usual answer, affirmative throughout his being. As at Antioch the strain of intensity, the relentless binding of all energies to intellection and inward prayer, was unsolemnised by children.

They were running round the pillars, darting diagonally from side to side of the open court, laughing, screaming, clapping, jumping, splashing in puddles. Now one caught a torch a slave was carrying and raced with fiery trail, shouting: 'I'm a comet! I bode evil!' weaving with the flaming thing in and out of the peristyle. A little boy with curly head fled from him and ran against Plotinus. Their father checked them all with raised voice. Each child stood where he was, the youngest one kept his head hid in the folds of the strange tunic that had a smell he never forgot.

Plotinus hid his finger-tips in the cowslip clusters and lightly scratched the scalp with nails like bird's claws, while the father called up his young one by one and presented them by name to his guest from Egypt and the east. 'He is a Greek God,' whispered Julius to his brother, 'one of those who come disguised among men.' But Alethia, who had a white dove on her shoulder and a net of silver meshes fastening her hair, said: 'No, I think he is Odysseus, he smells of the sea and his eyes look as if they were always gazing over the waves further than anyone can see.' 'He is like him in the illuminated Homer,' Julius agreed with her; and Adrian pulled away to see if this was the truth. The dove yawned and Marcellus told his daughter to restore her to her wicker cage and spread the cloth over it against the light.

Alethia went musingly down that dim-lit vista of pillars with her cheek against the breast of the bird and holding up her frock which was torn in the romps. The boys, who hung round Plotinus till he came to his room, were dismissed also and he was left alone.

He came to know well the children and the other beautiful things

159

in that house, for Marcellus would not let him go until he had re-discovered friends from Alexandria and certain men of Gordian's army who had heard his lectures; until he had found a house for himself.

CHAPTER X

Sunousiai

Marcellus Orontius indeed kept open house and the constant coming and going, talk and exchange of news, would have wearied Plotinus if he had not looked on it as a preparation for the life which he had decided to make for himself in Rome. He responded to all while at the same time his inward contemplation grew more free of consciousness, growing in power as a child grows in stature without endeavour. But he did exempt himself from the long drawn-out banquets, keeping to his lifelong habits of asceticism, and most often giving this time to the children. With these sensitive beings he could occupy a complete present where there was no flow of time. When he read aloud to them they moved as simply into the world of Homer's heroes as they did into the streets of the city. Everything which caught their attention by its radiancy was immediately present, near and now.

Imagination, the kingdom of youthful poetry, midway between sensation and reasoning, Plotinus and the children entered as princes as he read to them from the noble illuminated volumes whose pictures were keys even in the hands of the youngest, keys with magic guards ready to open door after door as the words became living in their souls. He felt their eyes upon him or downcast. That intensity of mind, in which it becomes one with pure spirit, was what he sought to make a reality to them; before the necessary conventions demanded their power of concentration for life in the world. To every question he gave a clear answer, always a light to them whether they understood or not. And these sessions of poetry would have outlasted the feasts were it not for nurses and sleep. When Adrian felt he could attend no longer he climbed onto Plotinus' knees with an instinct that by contact with the speaker he would absorb something of the power which acted as a spell on the children, not to bind but to free their imaginations.

Sometimes, after the philosopher had gone away from his father's house, the little boy went alone into the room, as if a trace would be found there of the gramarye in the shapes of the objects that had

161

also been present when he spoke. The furniture of citron-wood, the inlaid floor and bronze reliefs, they must have a way of remembering, or of being reminded, otherwise they could not be a means of himself hearing again those unfamiliar haunting lines. Staring at the wall-painting in its cunningly moulded recess, Adrian heard quite distinctly: 'We drink of Lethe and forget, truth does not. This truth, knowledge of all, is within us all. You have this in your sister's name, do you know, this word with its grace of sound you call again and again. Without forgetfulness. Truth.' Alethia had understood, the child was aware of this; well, when he was older . . .

Plotinus, when his conferences were well-known, and attended by many, always said the particular mode of these *sunousiai* was initiated in his evenings with the children of Marcellus.

One morning when he had been speaking for a considerable time and answering questions through a disintegrating pain in his midriff he was aware of a man among his hearers of mutual sensitivity, with that interacting of mind-substance underlying winged words. He had not experienced this equal tension since he himself had attended the lectures of Ammonius; and others, aware of it, had called them the double-lion. Continuing to speak, and speculating as he did so on the nature of voice and his thoughts invisibly embodied to take flight through the air and become the vision of another soul, he addressed himself entirely to this newcomer, ending his discourse by seeking to confound those who believed that by understanding what he had said they were in possession of a tangible thing: 'We must let the hearings of sense go by, save for sheer necessity, and keep the soul's perception bright and quick to the sounds from above.'

Then that man who had come in through an open and empty vestibule, drawn by the voice of an unknown speaker, repeated the words he first heard when he became part of the company: ' "Cut everything away." This you say we must do if we are to attain the highest vision given to man on earth, unity with the One. Why then these lectures, abstract definitions of abstract qualities, attempts by the energies of mind to attain to the intellectual-principle, by consciously seeking to sever soul from body by wisdom and words?'

'The soul once fallen,' Plotinus said, bending his countenance for the first time fully on the stranger, 'cannot without labour be restored to intellect. Once here, on earth, we can only know the highest, as living beings, through life. That is, throughout whatever

162

measure of life in the body is allotted to us, and through life itself, the power of the present god.'

'Yet Plato has said: "All who rightly touch philosophy study nothing else than to die and to be dead." '

'Which may be another way of saying – may it not? – cut everything away. But suggests also that to do this study is necessary. It is not easy to cut everything away, even with the certainty that it will be done, soon or late, by death. We have to know the vision is worth our utmost effort. The philosopher tries to do this, to receive sure knowledge in his life here, by contemplation of all that the sensitive principle, which is our soul, recognises as of intellect by the light which is intellect.'

'A man does not, I believe, choose that bent of mind which makes him a philosopher; and it is not everyone who calls himself a lover of wisdom who would seek for himself the vision of the Supreme, in the desire for which he must, as our master here has said, "cut everything away". Yet men who speculate in these high matters find their thoughts lit and fired by the transcendent vision by which they reason, which is as daylight to the eyes of the body. I speak from my own experience; I have visited schools of philosophy in Athens and Alexandria as well as in this city; and I can listen now only to a thinker who allows nothing to darken his ultimate vision of the truth. Whether he has attained to it or not, it is in the power of this vision that he can show us reality.'

'The light on a sudden being enkindled in the soul will then nourish itself, as Plato records in one of his letters; and this light compels a man to speak, and to live the life of intellect.' Plotinus looked again at the one who had entered his house that morning for the first time and continued: 'And this life itself, of inward concentration pursued with faithfulness, will in the end sever itself from the life of the senses and physical desires.'

'Among men there will always be few indeed who devote themselves to this unseen god.'

'So there is the greater necessity for those who can know the god not only to wait for his rising, dayspring of soul, but to speak to any who can recognise the divinity, imparted to all, but known by few. All existence is energy, but the most powerful energy is the quiet of intellect withdrawing itself from other things.'

The words were as a barrier to thought, holding it in a depth of silence throughout the shadowy hall, as roots supine of dragon mould hold back the black spring water in a pool where reflection and shadow and lost light are blended. Each man had a sense of the alone because the speaker with whom they had been in communion was no longer there. At length someone began, breaking the stillness.

'This, it seems to me, is the ultimate sorrow, for anyone of sensibility and vivid response to beauty, to turn from the loves and nymphs, nature and children, all the rush of feelings that come upon us from earth and stars and the ardours of mortal life.'

'All these are known not less but more by the turning away that intensifies inward being. "To know without image is to be." The ultimate sorrow is no longer sorrow as suffering here, but becomes one with the intensity of the life-principle. That which exists eternally.' He added looking away from them: 'In the sharpness of sorrow a man may know reality in his varied life. If grief, for it may be the death of a child beloved, throws into utter confusion and bewilderment that harmony of soul by which the father ordered his way of life and robs him of all satisfaction in his business and pleasure; then liberated from the passions of matter he may learn that the life of the soul is other than he thought. Established in quiet he will take his bearings from the divine harmony.'

Plotinus at that time could say no more as he remembered the death of Alethia.

Afterwards the man who had come that morning for the first time found Plotinus alone. He introduced himself as Amelius and said he was returning to his estate in Tuscany from Athens where he had been attending the school of Lysimachus. 'Now I have heard you I am not going to look for another master. May I stay near you?'

'Remember,' Plotinus said gently, 'all things flow. Do not bind yourself to any other man's philosophy. Since I have come to Rome I have sensed a certain crystallising of my thoughts inevitable, I suppose, from trying to present them to other minds; but I do not altogether like it. Though I do what I can to keep my lectures colourless as water.'

'That is good. Water has weight and gives life, is of the essence of life. It reflects and imperceptibly transforms images – the ideas of other men's minds. Itself the symbol of the eternal flow, we find ourselves fulfilled and at rest in its presence as in no other. And there are the still pools with unknown deeps.'

'Words are a breaking-away from intellect and correspond to the seperateness of individuals. While I speak I face constantly the one-ness of the ideas within the intellectual-principle.'

Amelius looked at him doubtfully, saying: 'Surely the ideas also are seperate, as our minds are.'

'Were they so, which indeed is unthinkable, how should we communicate one with the other?'

Amelius, unconvinced, left this topic and asked: 'What makes you give these lectures which people talk of in Rome as though something new, a reproachful incomprehensible luminary, had come among them?'

Plotinus smiled. 'Because I must, from inward necessity, as a cloud charged with lightning; even, if you prefer, as a volcano that sears what was fair before, a sunny champaign. There comes a time when much study stifles and chokes thought, diminishes the power of insight into the nature of the divine. Arts, skills, music, crafts, while we are here, must have their freedom in existence; philosophy also needs to be shared as do the other imitative arts which are our guides to the nature of reality.

'Part of the force is from the intensity of being of those who have lived before us.

'Then again in Rome, and that I believe is why I was led here – not a little rebellious – there is a desert of the spirit. This barrenness tries to fill itself with violence and destruction, exotic voices and those intellectual quibblings that remind us of the sophists. Every-thing is degraded, falling into the state of matter which is the denial of all freedom. Because I am aware of spiritual emptiness I have to speak into it. Any who hear my voice go away again to their own problems and way of life on the earth – whatever that may be. But they may also have learnt from my words it is possible to live in contemplation of the highest, that there is a light transcendent.'

'This complete austerity of life,' Amelius said, 'seeking as it were always to be beyond the limits of body, is this essential? In Athens those in the schools led also an easy life of intercourse with all men, of companionship and parties. Here in Rome, it seems to me, there is no balance. Men who live at all a conscious life energise to the limit in one direction; serving the state in politics or as soldiers, as priests or thinkers, with a kind of desperate fury of concentration. Or, in our sense, they let everything go, the charioteer flung down, existence a voluptuous orgy.'

Plotinus looked tenderly at the little thin Italian with his sparkling eyes and ruffled garments, a bird-soul caught in the frailest of human trappings with a power of devotion to thought that gave him an enviable intensity of purpose.

'Rome is the centre of the vortex where all extremes are possible. The source of the energy that, whirled outwards, reaches the breached walls of the Empire. I believe more discoveries may be made in less strained provincial cities, especially Alexandria which has a youthful vigour on the edge of the ancientest land; the best combination for advances into the unknown of mind and universe. There I spent much time with the astronomers. Aged Athens will always be a star for philosophers, but her energy for creating intellects that change the nature of thought is spent. She is now a nurse and preserver of what already is, and as with the other great cities of the Empire, she draws on the radiance of Rome.'

They were in the Forum now with columniated temples of the gods closing every quarter, a terrible weight of sacred matter generating eternal energy. Yet men moved indifferent about their affairs, accustomed to the speechless influences of Corinthian pillars and concrete domes. After Athens the man-oriented architecture oppressed Amelius. The Greek temples faced the light of heaven, the Latin the market-place. But, he saw how among those hustling crowds one head and another would lift as to meet the light; and he also halted to watch Plotinus who in his usual abstraction walked on unaware his companion had left his side.

When Amelius rejoined him he was climbing the Clivus Capitolinus and continued what he was saying: 'Athens is living now in the past. Here the tradition-bound ground is being dug up and men wanton among the bones and ruins of forgotten shrines. Past cults are shamed, and they make the fig at present. In a time of image-breaking, and the throwing-down from their high places of the once deified emperors, philosophy alone is untroubled; the principle of all things must be exempt from all things here. If your nature does not, with Plato's, "study to die" shall we say it is the business of philosophy to make us intellect?'

'Contemplative intellect, which we learn to dwell in by active intelligence?'

'The double light of the soul. But sense is not the test of reality. You can, if I may say so, be most aware of knowledge without consciousness.'

They halted next on the plinth of the temple of Saturn, which was also the city-treasury. 'Let us go in and see this oldest of the

166

gods. All teems with symbols and the worship of Saturn above all; pure intellect and the Golden Age when men were free from toil.'

'It is, I suppose, in homage to intellect that they perform his rites with heads uncovered. But his feast, *optimus dierum*, is the wildest of all. That does not go with the austerity of your spiritual life.' And Amelius looked at his companion.

'Philosophers can sometimes enter into simple merry-making with an abandon difficult for customarily grave citizens; just because life Here is not their concern. They feel happier among fools and jesters than among – Gnostics, shall we say?'

'You may,' Amelius agreed doubtfully. 'But why, in especial, Gnostics?'

'Because they try to make the reality I seek a fairy-tale and fill the kingdom of pure thought with sprites and images. No nonsense of that kind among the sports of the Saturnalia, all is Here, all is done in the name of fun. Horse-play, you see? Wasn't it this old fellow who turned himself into a stallion and tossing his mane over his right shoulder galloped over the hills after a girl?'

They were standing now in front of the statue of the god older than time, and Plotinus pointed to the woollen bands fettering his feet: 'You see,' he added gently, 'they don't trust him while *gravitas* rules in the city. Only in the one week of the Saturnalia, as you know, are the god's feet freed.'

The two men were often together in the years that followed. Amelius, for all Plotinus' warning about not binding his own way of thinking to the philosophy of a single other man, merely repeated back to Plotinus what he had said of Ammonius – 'This is the man I've been looking for.' Nevertheless Amelius constantly observed all the ceremonies and feasts connected with the gods and sages of old, and saluted the new moon, according to the custom of the Romans. One evening when they were returning from a visit to the country in an open two-wheeled car the crescent was low in the west. Plotinus held his face towards it, perfectly satisfied with the beauty and grace given the sky as dusk fell about them, silent and as though alone with the unfolding into light and shining forth of the young moon.

'You find her so fair,' Amelius could not help saying, when dark clouds with open lion-like jaws were swallowing the fugitive keel. 'Why do you not make obeisance and offerings, approaching the gods with what is their due from men?'

No other word was spoken until they were inside the walls. Then Plotinus said: 'The gods come to whoever is ready to receive them, waiting in stillness. Their influences are always about us, and within, not only in shrines and temples but in all places. Pursued they may turn away, wearied by our efforts and desires. It is rather ourselves we please by magic rites than the deities in things. Prayer is intensity of being ceaselessly remembering that aspect of soul which has not descended, and so is interwoven with our physical nature.'

Some powerful emanation agitated the air about the philosopher as he said this and Amelius noticed those brushing past in the street making gestures to avert the evil eye.

'It is easier to do that,' Plotinus said contemptuously, 'to stream on with the crowds after some image slung on an ass, to perform a routine ceremony in the temple, than to be conversant with being. Shall we visit Marcellus? Something has alarmed the citizens, and we may as well learn what has caused the hubbub.'

Amelius perceived then the throbbing and roar as of surf on a reef, that he had not heeded before, coming from the quarter of the senate-house, and realised most of those who skirted them with phallic finger-signals were hastening in that direction. Still he could not help adding as a conclusion to what it had been in his mind to say ever since he had known Plotinus, and had not known how to until they were together in the mysterious presence of the crescent.

'Life manifest must have its meed of honour.'

They halted where torches blazed by the entrance of an old-fashioned house.

'It will never lack that, if you mean offerings in the form of inanimate fragments of the world we see, *sigillaria;* or sacrifices, human and grass-eating. But, my friend, it behoves each man to honour the Highest, call it Providence or what you will, with soul at its most intense, which for some is in its devotion of itself to Intellect.'

Marcellus had not returned and the boys were ready to devour Plotinus, bringing books and questions, drawing him into hidden recesses to see their treasures and tame creatures. Amelius, prepared to be bored or impatient, found himself absorbed into the actual world of the young where everything was accepted as given and at the same time needing to be discovered, explored, transformed. Hand in hand Plotinus and Adrian were talking about feeling and consciousness in plants. 'Is this violet the same when I'm not here?'

168

the child asked, bending down and gently parting the leaves to show the flower.

'It is not the same. You do something to it by looking at it, as it does to you.'

'That is why the white doves are not the same, since Alethia died. She does not look at them any more, they don't sit on her shoulder.'

'The whole world is one living thing like that plane-tree in the middle of the garden,' Plotinus said, 'but each time you look both you and the tree are different. That is why each moment is precious, it will never be again, just like this.'

'And yet it is!' Adrian cried, delighted. He clapped his hands. 'But when people die?'

'Their being is carried on in all that is.'

'There's father!'

Two men were walking over the grass of the courtyard which was mildly lit by lamps hanging between the pillars. Adrian ran, Plotinus and Amelius followed him. Marcellus and his companion the senator Rogatianus were disturbed; the children were sent away with the slave who looked after them while Amelius said: 'We are from the country, what is this news?'

Marcellus, who had become more of a philosopher and less of a politician since his daughter's death, looked affectionately at Plotinus. 'What you've been expecting all these years has come about. The army has grown weary of Philip.'

'You come from the senate-house, we heard an uproar,' Amelius said, watching Plotinus whose expression was just as it was when the little bright-eyed boy uncovered the violet for him.

'Marinus was chosen emperor by the army. Philip in alarm summoned the senate. He spoke briefly, then at once Decius rose up and made a speech, worthy of Achilles, declaring Marinus the usurper would be done to death before a single thread of purple touched his shoulders. This speech, wildly acclaimed, dinned through the city, and was caught by the soldiers. Then said these men, according to their present fashion of electing emperors, we will have none but this Decius. The building of the senate was stormed to the discord of their cries: Decius, death or purple! Jupiter, he had no choice! Philip, who thought his touch was sure on the army's pulse, has fled the city, to join, they say, his troops in the north, whose loyalty he believes will hold to himself.'

'If that is so the two emperors will do battle. Nothing else will disperse the soldiers' madness.'

169

'This is very madness, when we cannot keep out the barbarians, to fall afighting in a fortress besieged.' As he spoke the stout senator Rogatianus looked at the unmoved face of Plotinus. 'Will the philosopher dine with us?' he asked Marcellus.

'That is not his custom. He will go home or else pass the time with my sons.'

'These ugly passions ruin blameless and peaceable lives,' Amelius said. 'How necessary is destructive force for the creation of new things?'

'Violence is an attempt of unreason, to eject evil, the evil inherent in matter; in that sense it is a miscalculating effort towards Intelligence. Those peaceable lives would soon become a drowsing, or a comfortable slumber, without stresses and conflicts to stir them to think. In the utmost intensity of being are we aware of the universe as one living organism. The one source of life flows in excess unendurable to the lesser creatures, it breaks from them in passions and lust. The stillness of the One is all powers held in perfect balance. The philosopher wields his passions with reason; their force becomes intolerable, bursts forth in the aimless energy of the populace. Their rages spent they are ready to receive anew the good which those who by *askesis* of soul seek constantly bring into the world from the Divine Transcendence. The god in each of us is one and the same. This we know by direct intuition, not through dialectic and the systems of philosophy we set ourselves to piece together. These are but our temples in time which we build rather as workmen construct sacred edifices for the deities. They raise them up again and again on foundations of others that have fallen, been destroyed by violence or flames, as we work with the thoughts wrought by men's minds in former days. The buildings of philosophy, aiming at the Tower of Saturn, are not without their influence even on those, who do not, or could not, enter them; as the influences of beautiful buildings, the temples of Jupiter and Castor and Pollux and the rest, compose the lives of citizens oblivious as they hurry past, intent on their business.'

The others, as Plotinus abruptly became silent and unaware of them, moved away talking among themselves of the character of Decius. For a time he walked in the courtyard until a freedman of Marcellus came near with food in small quantity and choice set in dishes of glass and silver. Recalled by this gesture, made as if of offerings to a god, Plotinus, shaking his head, and bending a look of kindness on the servant almost as if they two shared a conspiracy

170

of not-eating apart from the lordly diners, left the house of Marcellus.

He went to the Tiber, and resumed his meditation walking by the bank of the river. That slow-flowing god, after a thunderstorm in the hills, was a tumultuous comrade that night, roaring, with an angry crested wave arching and foaming into light above the tawny torrent. Long quivering flashes played over those hills, showing their profiles, opening suddenly as a many-petalled flower in the clouds. His body vibrant to these emanations, reflections on earth of perfect beauty, set free his soul from the clamour of flesh. He thought: It is of the essence of things that each gives of its being to another, and this giving is a transforming into light. Lightning and the stars are so fair because they show us this in the purest form our senses can suffer. And here is another light, more earth-bound, kindling the heart with heat as well, stained with the hues of soil. The watchman's fire blazed up as he threw on odd angles of wood, sawn-off ends of planks, and let his hands linger over the warmth. The look of this old fellow's features lit from below, his tattered clothes, his bulbous shadow suggesting a mime, reminded Plotinus also of his time with the army. Small odds to this ancient, the death of emperors. The crackling and bright burning of the fire, the air dizzy over the flames and the smell of smoke mingled with churned water kept him chained there while his mind went over the news of Philip the senators had brought. He kept seeing the man's swarthy face and dark sparkless eye as he played on the soldiers until they slew Gordian. A brand whizzed past him and hissed as it hit the water. He saw a band of roughs laying waste the old man's cherished hearth and grabbing his spare fuel.

Plotinus took two strides and stood above the desecrated fire. In his usual voice he said: 'Hands off. All fire is the god Hephaestus. All the old and beggars are watched over by Zeus.'

Startled, at first they checked, then in anger urged each other against him, reaching to tear his cloak from his shoulders, raising a billet. Before their hands touched him they fell back. His eyes flashed, and his tongue whipped them, until they dropped the wood and vanished in the night as suddenly as they had come. The old man was crouching aside, his eyes hid in his bent arm. Plotinus was about to go on when his mood changed. He gathered together the smouldering remnants, built round them with fresh chips until the fire revived, began to lick with sharp yellow tongues. Then he laid

171

a coin by the rugged club the old fellow had not dared handle and went along the riverbank towards the Fabrician bridge.

The majesty of those two vast arches spanning the Tiber under a sky of small stars grew into his consciousness as he approached, so that he walked more slowly but would not stand still, as though motion maintained thought and bridge in balance. This kind of alliance between mind and nature and the most harmonious works of man gave him almost the highest satisfaction he could experience; soul at one with body instead of severed and sent on its arduous course alone. A bridge, he thought, as his feet carried him onto it, is one of the most perfect structures imposed by art on matter, offering itself as a symbol, a symmetrical and visible power existing in this world; as most minds must preserve their equilibrium, by supports and stresses and tensions tangible but unobserved. The populace appoint an emperor, among other reasons, to represent for them, to keep before them at its loftiest, human dignity. He cannot stand the exaltation. They loose their tempers, scourge and throw down their self-chosen hero.

★ ★ ★

Plotinus gave no lectures for some time after the two Emperors had left Rome; everyone was on edge and waiting for news of the battle, and he used this space to organise his household, to visit Gratian who was then in the city, and to prepare in his mind the subjects of further discourses. Each night he made his way to the Fabrician bridge, and it was there Amelius came to him with the first account of the victory of Decius and the death of Philip. For days after this rumours reached the city, among them one that Philip had fled from the field of battle and had been murdered in Verona. On hearing this the praetorian guard slew in cold blood the son of Philip, who was his associate in the Empire. This murder in Rome itself perturbed Plotinus more than he would acknowledge, for he had had some intercourse with this young man; philosophy must be schooled by violence and bloodshed as well as by ascesis of the soul.

It was while he was standing on the bridge in half light, sun gone, night unbegun, unwontedly oppressed by the woes of men on the earth, his mind strained with the concept, two-edged, of time and eternity on which he had been preparing to speak, suspended between sky and river, that he experienced a vision of reality, a contact, as he thought of it afterwards to himself, of gold with gold alone. In the indefinable quiet of soul, in which suffering is

172

transmuted into intellect and there, by the ceaseless act of creativity, given back to the world in what we know as life, Plotinus was without consciousness in that timelessness of spirit unbroken. As he returned to his body, by way of a diffused sense of happiness in the beauty of the evening, to take his part again in the city in turmoil, he had the vivid experience of the god within, excellent in the power of vision, streaming forth from his veins and nerves, his single organism, into the dishevelled organism of Rome. Men in the wearisome aftermath of rebellion were assuming again the heavy inescapable burden of order.

Next morning, when a high wind was surging through the streets and bursting in almost visible whirls into storm-darkened squares, tearing in strands between the temple pillars, throwing down tiles and cornices, and further confusing men's minds by its buffetings, several of his circle of friends came to Plotinus begging him to speak. Among them was the senator Rogatianus, corpulent, stiff-jointed and in pain, who said in the gnat-like voice some big men have: 'Here is a man who will remind us of eternal things and so give us steady judgment in violent times.'

And because they had come to him for the healing of astringent words, as for bitter medicine from a physician, he began to give them the thought of his dry mind until they forgot the gales outside.

'Time is that aspect of intellect we know as creativity being constantly broken up and reunited. By the unity it possesses in continuity of succession we recognise it is established in eternity. Motion is the desire of that unquiet portion of the soul, that all things should flow and change, fulfilling itself visibly here; but it is only over against the eternal in the soul that we can be aware of this motion, which is as it were the necessity of beings in time; for time is a dimension of extension, as space is. It is of the nature of each thing to have its own particular time by which it relates itself to eternity. For a general measure we choose that which is obvious to all, inwoven with the rhythm of our bodies, the passage of earth into its own shadow from the light of the sun. But that which measures does not subsist externally, nor is it seperate, it is simply what we accept as the other half of the tally.

'Between dawn and sunrise, and in the twilight of evening there is an instant when time stumbles on the threshold of eternity; when day new-born might fall back into night, or earth weary with light not tilt into the therapy of dark and sleep. In the recovery of balance

173

we know that first nature which has no reaching into futurity; and immediately the soul leans again upon time, feeling for the succession of nows, eternity carried piecemeal in time.

'Again we may look on time as a gift of Providence, not an enemy hurrying us through life and down into Hades, but as something guiding the soul here and bestowing a pattern in each one's limited days that connects them with the principle of life manifest both in the past and the future. Not only are the minds of older time akin to our own but also the ways of thought of those to come, inherited through us, would not be wholly alien or incomprehensible. And body and soul in time have their seasons and flowering with the rest of the children of the grain-bearing earth. Birth and death put a stress on us to live to the utmost while we are here; they force us to observe the boundaries because we are in the body, and to look to intellect if we would know life infinite.'

After saying this Plotinus fell silent, for it was not his custom to speak at length but to begin with one approach and move to another according to what others said; to consider what they said among themselves; and to let the energy of his soul abide in the All-Soul.

'For a man engaged in the work of the state, who would keep the *pax Romana* always before him, and win it anew out of every fray and slaughter and shipwreck of government; out of all, in short, that destroys the tranquillity of the farmer and the divine leisure of the philosopher: how would you define intellect?' The senator Rogatianus asked this, standing and leaning forward with both his gouty hands on the head of his stick of cherry-wood, cut by himself on his estate one smoky autumn evening.

A great fly droned through the air above their bent attentive heads, unheard by most but carrying nevertheless a message of sleepy warmth and idleness.

'For this man intellect is that power in the soul by which he himself knows the idea of peace; and in the confidence of this power, in which his virtues abide, he can speak to all who have influence in the state of the course to be steered. Intellect is known also in that it gives will, will as intensity of purpose in the direction of the highest. No one can do more than be present to this inward intensity; then he will be true to his genius and play Here the part destined for him by Providence. We all make wrong decisions, yield to the partibility of our bodies, but this power of the soul does not absent itself.'

'Might one say, this energy of Intellect is pure, receives neither

174

good nor evil; in this world, the one quality or the other according to man's act?'

'The energy is creating the perfect forms which the soul desiring to bring into actuality contemplates, or receives as reflections in its heavenward side. Reflected again into matter their light is dimmed, their beauty and harmony confused. But the soul most unremitting in contemplation has the power of showing truth to others which have not this vision of eternity.'

★ ★ ★

It was the last day of the festival of Saturn, the day of the fair when the whole city kept uproarous holiday. Plotinus had given all his servants and personal slaves the customary presents and sent them forth to the merry-making. Jeremy, who lay sick, was the only one left in the house; he always lived within and because of his closeness and faithful attendance Plotinus would not allow him to be carried to the slaves' quarters when he fell ill. The cries of *io Saturnalia* which had rung from wall to wall for the past week were less frequent now as the noisiest citizens had made their way to the fair-ground. The doors of the empty lecture-room stood wide open, scraps of papyrus and brown leaves, blown in from the courtyard trees, rested in vague designs on the unswept floor. The voiceless groanings of the mute distressed his master so that he went out to the little wintry court where the bare boughs, wet with the night's rain, gleamed in transient sunshine and pleased his meditations. He walked slowly, his feet pressing the coarse grass and small heaps of worm castings, soon lost so that he did not hear the light step of Zethos or his inquiring call as the physician crossed the hall and then seeing him halted by the little stand where Amelius, with his simple loyalty to the cult of the gods, had arranged candles and clay models of slightly grotesque human shape, the *sigillaria* friends exchanged at the feast of the old god. The philosopher, never long unaware of the influences of another living presence, moved towards him while the Arabian in his turn was attentive to another thing. He was listening.

Plotinus said quietly: 'That is Jeremy, he would not go, and is indeed too sick for any amusements.'

'Why did you not send for me, then?'

'Does one send for the most sought-after doctor in Rome to medicine a slave? Take advantage of a dear friendship?'

Zethos made an impatient movement. 'I wish you had. It is no

175

use now. Among your detached considerations it may have escaped you that the plague is rife in the city. Smouldering for some time it is now flaming up in all quarters at once, among poor and rich. Five hundred plague-dead were burned and buried yesterday.' As he moved forward his sallow pale skin caught a silvery reflection. 'This is only the beginning.'

A flight of pigeons passed over the small interior garden and a darkness followed as if the sun would shine no more that December day. Zethos, although he had quickly become renowned in Rome as a healer and wealth had been heaped on him by his patients, lived and dressed plainly and gave his leisure to philosophy. Without his friendship with Plotinus he would have given himself no space at all for study and lectures, and his visits to the *sunousiai* were rare; but he came, as now, when he thought the master would be alone. These two found a balance and simplicity in the relationship begun under the trees of Daphne. Especially from Zethos Plotinus learnt to accept that men are 'beings whose nature implies a task'. That task once seen must be fulfilled in acts and thoughts; but it is possible in certain fortunate intercourse, that the experience of the highest power one man has attained in his single concentration is a freedom also for another. The intellectual labours of Plotinus were a reward to the physician, a flowering for which he had not toiled. And through the practice of this friend Plotinus came to value and observe the workmanship of the body in which he had been ashamed to find himself. ' "All that is done in the light of sound reason is Soul's work," ' he agreed, when the doctor refused to yield the claims of healing to those of philosophy.

Standing together by the unconscious Jeremy they recognised this sinister outbreak of disease, of which the present darkness seemed to cast a measureless shadow ahead, would still further limit their actual physical nearness on which a certain enlargement of mutual sensitivity depended. 'Forget the rest of the sick for this day, when all do as they choose,' Plotinus said, when they had given Jeremy what care they could. 'Let us spend it together.'

★ ★ ★

After four years when the plague had spread throughout the Empire, and was above all devastating Alexandria, where the daily death-toll nearly equalled that of Rome, men had learnt to live with it as with a foul taste in the mouth, inescapable but to be disregarded as far as possible. They gave up consulting oracles, speculating as to who among them would be struck next, or paying attention to the funeral processions which night and day were passing through the streets. At this time Plotinus' household, which had been untouched after Jeremy's death, as if this faithful one had been accepted as a sacrifice for the well-being of the rest, was suddenly attacked. One after another the few slaves he maintained were struck down. Amelius was away in his home in Tuscany. Alone among sick and dying Plotinus was aware of corruption in himself: the poison especially centered in his throat so that he constantly swallowed it. The pain and acute soreness caused him to become as incapable of speech as the devoted Jeremy had been. A great negro, who haunted the dwelling as a stray dog might for thrown-out food and above all for a chance contact with the master's hand which would make his formless existence not utterly destitute, for an uncertain time brought cups of water and morsels of bread to Plotinus and the two who still breathed with him in his mortuary halls. Then he came no more.

Obedient to his tutelary spirit Plotinus lay in the room he had chosen from the first for his own, making no movement. He could still breathe clean air which came to him in soft waftings from the garden court. He heard bird-song and now and then a whirr of wings. The season was spring. He had seen enough of the plague to believe his own sickness was of another order and one from which he would recover. The recurrent misery of swallowing with a throat that felt cut became something he left to nature, seeking to impose nothing by will on her working. His soul thus relieved entirely from the charge of body drew itself together in a state of self-consciousness to which it cleaved as to life itself. Now indeed it would be possible to act in accordance with the oracle: Know Thyself. But this, Plotinus conceded, was not to cut everything away. Thinking and knowing were themselves forms of imperfection, ways of approach, not consummation. Consciousness as an act of intellect is not consciousness of the Highest, which has no need of this. The soul aware of being illuminated by moving towards the Soul above it is not yet one with the source of Light.

When his mind roused again, unwilling to be recalled to parched mouth and cracking throat, it was also to the sense that a living being had been near, had hovered above his head as dream presences did in Homer giving clear counsel or solace. Presently he was convinced one of his hands had been moved and that an aromatic smell came from some wood kindled on the hearth. The next time he opened his eyes they focused with pain, that came from blinding stabs of light, on a face young and concerned, and a lime dripped on his dry lips that slid into his mouth with a sharpness and refreshment that was agonising. Plotinus recognised Julius, read the alarm and grief, underlying the care, that he had found his god fallen, and smiled, slightly pulling with one hand a fold of the toga which he then saw the youth wearing for the first time. For some reason this caused a gust of fury; Julius struggled with the garment of elaborate folds and overlappings until he was free in short close-fitting tunic. The mass of woven white wool with purple borders he bunched up and flung at the open door where it caught and was caught by an entering Libyan servant of Marcellus. The fellow's expression caused the two inside to exchange a glance of delight.

Although Plotinus' eyes closed again at once and did not reopen, Julius was completely satisfied that the god still burnt in the gaunt frame draggled and foul with sickness; and he took full charge of the deranged dwelling-place. He sent the Libyan to summon Zethos or any other doctor he could lay hold of. A freedman of his father was asked to go to the market and buy new slaves and arrange that the dead were buried. The negro, who had probably saved the philosopher's life, was found in the well-house. He was still breathing and Julius dragged him into the dry air and light and tried to revive him with wine. In youth and eagerness Marcellus' son forgot nothing. The place was swept, washed and fumigated, the new slaves were installed, supplies of corn, meal and oil were brought in, as well as the fruit grateful to the sick. He sent for, from his own house, that scarce wood whose acrid scent was said to cleanse the air and promote health. In all these things the boy had a sense of the closest companionship and guidance, although he scarcely admitted this, even to his own thoughts. His counsellor was Alethia who had roused him in the first place to go to the house of Plotinus.

Late in the day, when the sun had withdrawn all his rays from the small court which gave light and air to the old-fashioned rooms opening into it, and the yellow-green of the leaves of the fig-trees had stealthily receded, leaving them colourless to the touch of coming night, Julius revisited the philosopher. And the content that had spread over his weariness fell from him. He thought his friend was dead; the Libyan who came near at the same time said no doctor had paid attention to his appeal. Together they satisfied themselves the man lying motionless in the angular little cell was

178

breathing; in vain they tried to give him water. Then Julius told the dark-skinned servant to go away and eat and rest and himself sat down on a stool, the only other piece of furniture in the room.

Into his state of being heart-broken, childishly because there was no one to admire all he had done, and in a more complex way because this was the first grief of manhood and so with it there was a certain pride at knowing the bitterness of adult woe, came a smoothness resembling sleep. From the *sunousiai* he had attended with his father, and from conversations between the two men he had heard at a time when he heeded them little, in Marcellus' house, Julius had absorbed much of the doctrine of Plotinus, and now in the calm, which he began to think emanated from the unconscious presence of the philosopher, this teaching represented itself to his mind in a different manner. For he did not associate it any more with the need of most men for a guide in their life of action, and for sustainment under the blows of fate, encounters with private and public fatality; the philosophy of Plotinus became for him as he crouched with rounded spine, his brows and cheek-bones pressing on his paired hands, the living content of his being. Present at the centre of himself he neither tried to understand nor did his heart cry any more; his mind was quiet, entirely unmindful of the flow of divine energy. Presently this living content revealed itself to him in a phrase he must have heard and forgotten: 'The respiration of the still life of the divine.' Thus all breathing passionate living had its reality.

Someone had lighted the lamp which was suspended by chains above the bed, so that when he held up his head it was mildly illuminated. Without surprise he saw a man in the doorway leaning on a stick. Then, knowing a stranger, and fearing any disturbances where silence was precious, he asked in a low voice: 'Who are you?'

The bent man replied in the same tone: 'I am . . .' But even before the stranger had spoken his name Julius had had that sense of realisation which is sometimes born of the meeting of two previously unknown to one another, soul naked to soul before all the inevitable or necessary human elaborations intervene. Intensity of the instant, the encounter of gods, enemies on the battlefield, wayfarers in a crowd at once and for ever severed again, an experience of high-wrought suffering that does away with the common exchange. Once he understood Eustochius of Alexandria was a physician the boy began talking quietly of Plotinus and the symptoms of his illness.

'Partly I came to Rome to find him again,' Eustochius said,

agreeing with Julius' unspoken worship. 'I knew him only slightly when he walked Alexandria ablaze with hidden fire, inscrutable as an Egyptian sculpture. My studies of medicine have been a kind of earth in which the root philosophy can take hold; lest ideas in air should be scattered by alien winds. Word of his *sunousiai* has come to the city of his old master Ammonius.' Then looking at the slight youth instinct with passion and devotion, Eustochius said: 'My son, go now to your own home. You have done your part here. Leave me with our friend and I will do all I can for him. There is need for his wisdom among us, and I believe he will live.'

Julius obeyed at once; all that day he had prayed for a physician, and now one had come who was more, who had experience of the essential reality. He stood a moment by the bed, and half smiling at himself bid as he turned away Alethia to stay.

CHAPTER XI

The Essence of Things

Plotinus in his slow recovery was aware of a change in himself. As he talked with Eustochius, who came to him day by day, while he lay on his couch under the fig-trees looking at their broad leaves and the chinks of blue sky between, his spirit returning from the deeps brought to him a new sense of the urgency of the present generation, of the life-principle entangled in his contempories. Unwontedly enslaved by the 'bile and bitterness of the body' he watched the huge negro in his clumsy tendance of the grass and plants, and observed, too faint for intense labours of intellect, the unprepossessing servants who had been found to do the work of his house. He no longer resented or forbade their aimless intermittent talk among themselves, sensing in this as in their presence a therapy that restored his torn fibres. Why is the living ugly more attractive than the sculptured handsome? he asked himself, and knew at once the answer: Because there is soul there, some glow of the light of the Good. So when Marcellus began to tell him of children who were orphaned by the plague, which had taken their parents and all of their kinsfolk, he asked to have them brought to him and made room for them, allowing them the whole of the house for a playground; clear voices echoed through the court, and sometimes like wind-spirits with long thin limbs and streaming hair they fled through the lecture-hall.

Besides giving the hour of lamp-lighting to teaching these young inmates, by letting them tell him whatever they would of their thoughts and desires, Plotinus brought himself to begin something he had often been urged to do by Amelius and the rest: to write his philosophy. So high-wrought and concentrated a way of life and thought, they kept suggesting to him, needed both to be preserved for those who come after and to be freed from the intrusions and diversions that were unavoidable in his manner of dialectic. Often his teachings were phrased as questions and all who chose could interrupt with theirs, and although in his reply he always returned to his own reasoning under another guise there was diffusion and loss of fire. His own master, Ammonius Saccas, wrote nothing,

Plotinus would remind them; and those who had attended his school had made a compact not to betray the inmost secrets he had revealed by lips alone. Now, since the arrival in Rome of Eustochius, he understood from him that others who had heard Ammonius had spoken freely of the man's wisdom, his reconciliation of the cosmology of Plato and Aristotle; the absorption of his thought with oriental metaphysics; and the passage of the soul between intellect and consciousness. Would you deny the life-principle, finding its existence in the generations to come, the entering into it of your individual soul which speaks to us from its own experience of the transcendent God?

In the end it was the appearance at one of his lectures of another who had learnt his philosophy in the school of Ammonius that brought the daemon of Plotinus to suffer the particular discipline of consciousness in writing on cold parchment the thoughts so readily kindled in his mind in contact with others, so mysteriously iridescent in solitude. He was speaking at the golden end of a summer day, when although every door and aperture was open wide there was not the least motion to suggest the presence of air, when someone quietly entered but not unobserved by the nervous being of Plotinus, always alert to the magnetic currents caused by the play of other minds, and stood aloof from the rest behind a pillar. With a sense of loss of tension in the invisible web of words and ideas, he became silent. Origenes perceiving the reason moved forward. Plotinus' cheeks burned. The others gathered there begged him to continue, but he answered while he went up to the newcomer to salute him: 'The fire dies down when the speaker feels that his hearers have nothing to learn from him.'

As he talked to the man he had not seen for so many years, and afterwards while Origenes was moving from one to another of the circle, the sound of the sea, the waves, the influence of the beach and the Egyptian coasts where he had walked at midnight rose to memory, returning his mind clear with vision to the lit hut, the boy dreaming over his song, the man's bent studying head; the smell of salt, the feel of the fishing-net curtaining the cot; the nights when they had launched a little boat and pushed out from the shore to drift and talk between sea and stars. All this was so overpoweringly present to Plotinus, as in a single realised experience that all Origenes was now saying in so uncommitted a manner of the doctrine of Ammonius, which to him it had not seemed right to make public to all whether they could by any means entertain it or not, was a kind of forgetfulness of soul; for all that we have forgotten is not lost, although it may be transmuted by Lethe. Only, as he invited Origenes to stay with him, as a slight return, he emphasised smiling, for his Alexandrian hospitality, he felt a total release from his guarded loyalty to the porter. If Origenes had learnt from Ammonius in so different a way, he was keeping silent about his own intuition, not that of his master. He felt the pen now between his fingers, and felt a passion for the prepared papyrus leaves, waiting for the clear principles intellect had imparted to his soul. Had not the heaven-fed river nourished them both?

The children in the house missed their conference that night. Plotinus recollecting when they were all asleep, took the tiny flame burning faithfully as a votive-lamp outside their rooms and carried it in. He stood a moment by each bed until the sleeping face of the child had communicated to him the soul which wakes when the body rests and causes the features intent in slumber to become transparent to the spirit. He perceived how it would be when the characters being so intangibly moulded in his house came to their season of flowering.

The brief darkness of June he and Origenes let pass over them in the little garden, so lost in their shared meditation even Plotinus did not record the turning constellations. Nevertheless the zodiacal light drew him from the deeps of consciousness to look at the sky, and at once the intimate interchange ceased, the two minds were again enclosed by bone, irrevocably separated one from the other by something more mysterious than the skull of man, namely his personality. We shall not easily come together again on the common ground we have inherited with our manner of reasoning, Plotinus thought, and for his spirit-beings I do not care one hair. At this his ear caught a light and loved foot and he went forward to meet Julius who came to him with his face whiter than the dawn. They stood silent together until the young man had received from the nearness of the philosopher renewal of life.

'Dear child, you have come,' he said, wondering whether that alabaster countenance were reflecting light or giving the young sky a whiteness of the spirit. A motion of contact was rare with him even towards his dearest friends, but he touched for a moment the youth's shoulder now, with a half-smile, as if to reassure himself this was not one of the insubstantial beings of Origenes. 'Whence?'

'From those who are persecuted by Decius.'

'Those people are reaching towards a new way of life. They

worship suffering, and indeed seek what they call witnesses to it, to draw men away from this world of which they deny the beauty.'

'Perhaps that is why in their art they show something which has no place here, features on the shadowy walls that have looked through suffering into glory, Orpheus with another face bent on dog and goat, a bare tree at his side with a pair of doves. There are three young men with backs turned on a sculptured emperor. They are set alight. That is what I have seen tonight.'

'Symbol and reality.'

'Everywhere they stand in attitudes of prayer, with lifted hands, not pleading, exaltation in humility; forgive me, this talk does not please you. Yet I ask, will you go with me one day to see this new mode of art which is, I believe, transparent to intellect.'

'Why do you want to see me in the catacombs?' Plotinus responded with an amused note. 'Is it so that you can compare the cranium of a philosopher with that of a – saint?'

Julius was flushed now as the eastern sky. He spoke under stress but looking clear into the eyes of the master: 'There is something among these people I cannot understand without you. When I am with them I know a strange happiness, but it is not as when I am with you. There is this element of torture never forgotten. They celebrate agony joyfully. Perhaps that is why they attract to themselves the torments they endure fearlessly. Yet no one in the city succours as they do the plague-stricken . . . Yes, indeed, there is a head in one of their caves which if I could see yours beside it might make me hope the misery of our time is giving birth to a power of the spirit not yet known on earth: he generates the lightning that has struck himself.'

'He who has a daemon of the nature of the celestial fires knows that every soul is a child of the Supreme; and he devotes himself to that knowledge in the way the spirit within wills. You speak well of their pictures. If you find in your harbouring with these people that virtue arising in your soul that makes God manifest, then, dear child, keep yourself among them. In these paintings you tell me of, they have revealed, I think, a new intuition into the nature of things.'

'That is true of their faces also; this fusion of Greek and Jew, of intellect and faith, has bred a new race of men on the earth; as it has a solitary philosopher who moves through the luminous way of his own personal vision.'

Origenes, who had slightly withdrawn as he recognised this

dialogue was for two, a trial of spiritually tempered minds that flashed not to wound but to make a brightness not readily brooked, saw that pair of heads as though they were actors in a cosmic drama on a sky grown pregnantly sorrowful. As if, he found himself thinking, the shining of dawn must be veiled in an interval without deity before the sun rose. The difference of a generation between them certainly counted for something, as they stood side by side while light restored colour to earth, but Origenes did not have the impression Plotinus was looking back to an old world, or the youth beside him forward to a vision that would transform living, it was that they faced in different ways the tragedy inseparable from being man. In his philosophy Plotinus transcended humanity, his way was clear but unattainable; it must be revealed by one who had the power, because pure thought is. For Julius truth must be realised in the body with all that meant of flesh and blood, filth and lust; not only his own body but all flesh and the passions of animate clay. If the master said 'cut everything away' the new religion under persecution said 'cut nothing away', all that man is will be preserved and transformed. By the death of the martyrs, by the life given for other lives? Origenes shook his head, the wings of his moment of vision were flagging. Plato spoke somewhere of there being, at long intervals, a variation in the course of the heavenly bodies, and such it seemed to him he was witnessing now, not being brought about by some misguiding of the chariot of the sun but by the contact of these two with the soul and intelligence of the living being of the world.

Origenes moved, as for reassurance, to the neighbourhood of the watchful tree that expected as men did the sun's salutation; the leaves drew in a caress over his hair and cheeks, he leaned his hand on the trunk. Then he found Plotinus was close to him, his face clear with the light of day. 'You have been in the silence of wisdom. It is your turn now to make an offering to our morning meditation.'

Origenes shook his head.

'For the sake of past days and because of those influences stars have one on the other when they draw near. It may be, after this, we shall only be aware from afar of our voyaging.'

'I had an impression of witnessing one of those variations in the course of the heavenly circles that may make our age see the beginning of a new life – *incipit vita nuova* – not, I think, in the sense that anything is done away with but because the forms of poetry, of thought, of the celestial beings have, in a spiritual sense, been so wrought as to have become a barrier which must break, or be broken through. But the growth of the new is in and with the content of the former things; their relation is changed and the spirit that is now released to be creative in the world is not yet recognised. We observe rather what is being broken. That is something of what was in my mind, Plotinus, as I watched you two, with a feeling in this dawn and primal dayspring you were both lifted into a new light that shone with past and future through broken Roman ramparts.

'I am not a seer, my heart is bound by the old as I hold by the being of this tree, not one with roots in heaven as that traveller to Egypt would have it, but firm in the life-giving earth.'

'The tree is the best of all symbols.'

'Why not a tree simply and nothing else?'

'Because it is not simple. In loving the tree as it gives itself to your senses you are loving a complexity.'

'Well. But love is simple: a full direct outflow of essential life upon life visible.'

'The flow is reciprocal.'

Julius was striding up and down in a passion of youth and distress. 'It is not only the barriers that are breaking, everything is. How can I know what to think, or what sin is?'

'In the midst of the waves there is a calm,' Plotinus answered, 'which is free of all commotions both of waves and words. It is sin for the soul to forget the way back. Once fallen it is meant to play a part Here with the utmost intensity of our being; and that intensity comes from ceaseless recollection of the divine source. It is in blameless contemplation of this nature is so fair. Quiet, that virtue of the soul in solitude, learns how to keep itself in tempests by observing the contemplative beauty of nature. Do not strive too hard with your reasoning intellect, the Good is known apart from all reason. Once entered upon the life of philosophy you will find you can attend to all that is of the Necessity of this sphere while your highest intellect can wait tranquilly . . . the rising of the sun.'

★   ★   ★

In the years that followed the succession of the Emperors Gallus and his son Volusianus Plotinus had a sense of his inmost integrity being deliquescent, in a way singularly unpleasing to him, as he put in practice the resolution formed in the early languid days of his recovery from diphtheria. Once it became known he was open to receive and give help to all who were at a loss, his scrupulous

186

honesty and aloofness from business affairs made him sought after as arbitrator, executor, guardian of the property and persons of the young. Besides this the demand that he should write his philosophy was, as he began to fulfil it, more exciting and passionate an experience than he had supposed; even with his long familiarity with the objects of intellect and his life conformable to them, he found writing drew more from the deepest understanding of his soul than addressing his contempories, or having discussions with the philosophers who were his friends, or with the young men who came to him on the brink of despair because they reckoned they were born into a dying world. The excitement reminded him of his earliest studies of Plato in Lycopolis; the thing that was born in him then was now desiring to be brought to birth in other minds, not only those with which he could have immediate and present communion, but those also who in aftertime followed the way of philosophy. His ideas in their living truth must be expressed in a manner to be understood by men of other ages and environments strange to himself, for he had an absolute certainty that his own building of the Tower of Saturn would have value as long as anyone among men sought the way. In this passion, suffering from strained eyesight and constant distractions, he wrote execrably, but from the very nerves and sinews of his intellect, from the thought-marrow of his whole being.

The concentration on his creative writing began, as he presently discovered, to restore that intensity of soul by which he approached the Divine Mind, and which was to him the only justification for being in the body. Each treatise, once consciously planned, grew and evolved as a living organism all through the tasks of the day, so that when he came to write he could dash off the whole thing, words coming faster than hand and pen could form them. His thought on a single theme thus expressed, without the constant intrusions of other active but differently oriented minds that he always invited in his lectures, gave him a sense of both liberty and stability in the calamitous rule of Trebonianus Gallus. He wrote little indeed in these two years but enough to find confidence he would, if life lasted, be able to fulfil what had now become a demand of the daemon. The plague raged; the Persians overran Mesopotamia which, because of his own adventure, he regarded with personal interest; and the Goths, who had been bought off for some time, resumed their invasions. 'The unquiet faculty of the soul that caused it to bring the Cosmos into being by laying aside eternity and clothing itself with time' was dominant now in the senate overruled by the army, and in the waves of barbarians breaking against and flooding over the boundaries of the Empire. The constantly threatened ruin of the forces, both the spiritual and physical, which consisted of the lives of men arrayed and armed against chaos, decided him to direct all his god-given energy to the calm in the midst; not because he did not recognise that politics was essential for civilisation but because he knew the quality of intellectual contemplation was rare and, at least as it existed in himself, must be kept clear as a way for wisdom and divine virtue to enter the world of the future.

There was a brief reassurance when Aemelius conquered on the Danube, but as his army immediately proclaimed him emperor it was plain the defeat of the Goths had simply thrown back disorder into the nerve centre of Rome. The Emperor Gallus sent to his emissary in Raetia, Valerian, to bring his troops to support him; but Aemelius, whirling down from the north, encountered Gallus before his reinforcements arrived and in the battle both he and his son were murdered by their own soldiers. Plotinus witnessed the entry of Aemelius, and the exultant welcome given him and his army by the citizens, passively and as if the cold water of the spring of Memory, that has its source in Hades, were flowing over his soul. Amelius had only saluted one new moon after the arrival of his namesake the new Emperor when the city flamed again at the news Valerian had received the purple from the troops he commanded. At this the victorious army of Aemelius, who had carried him to the Capitol on their shoulders, there slew him and threw his body over the cliff. The senate accepted Valerian and everyone ran about the streets preparing for the entry of the new hero and his plague-spotted troops. Even in his fig-tree shade Plotinus was dinged by the public acclaim.

On that day Rogatianus renounced his political life, his great house and his riches, and heavy and handicapped with gout put on the plain garment of the philosopher, after he had distributed all his apparel to his slaves. Henceforth he lived among the friends of Plotinus reading in their quiet courts, and eating on alternate days only a piece of bread and some fruit.

Under the terrible irony of that hilarity – the *Vivat Valerianus*, the fanfares and street dancing; the night gaudy with fires, pyres as they seemed to the philosopher of all past princes murdered and massacred – Plotinus who, even with the attentions of the physicians of his circle, had remained unwell, found himself receiving intimations from what passes in the soul, unperceived by the senses, of the closeness of death. The arm laid along his shoulders he received without recoil, met without fear or surprise the eyes of the vision. Yet he recognised that since all things are in the soul without time the form of the event was constantly present while the hour of its fulfilment was uncertain. Under the impact of this, and the proclamation of Valerian by the citizens of Rome, he let go the last defences he had until then preserved about the alone which was now, or in a little while, to return to the Alone. He accepted the last challenge to cut everything away. For him this signified giving up silence and solitude, certain spells guarded for reading his dearest books and for the new determination of preparing treatises of his philosophy, when there must be no interruption. Never again would his doors be closed night or day, his friends denied entrance, his slaves driven off, their tasks undone, because his thought cried for silence. What good would be in his writing for men to come if these living children could not carry their griefs to him, those men ready to quit life by their own hands not at least hear his word first. To call upon drugs for the release of the Soul seems a strange way of assisting its purposes, he wrote, following his thought, for this is in some sense an attempt to numb the highest in man because it cannot endure life in the intelligible. To anticipate fate could not be a happy act; a sign rather that the progress of the soul Here was unaccomplished. With eyes darkened, because his mind was drawn together in the veritable man he looked upon the ones who now entered, as though summoned by his genius to prove his resolve to give freely of all he had to give. All, he concluded, as his consciousness accepted them and his gaze received them, that the energy of intellect by its still power causes to vibrate on the strings of my tiring lyre.

He perceived, by the slightness of their physical impact and the emanation of life singularly purified, that they came to him fasting and after celebrating some mystery. He rose and held his hands apart in a gesture of accord, and immediately, as if a pair of doors were opened, a thunder of the populace in tumult burst upon the men in that enclosure of bare walls where formless shadows wavered and the living beings caused no solidity or darkening of flesh on the air. As clap after clap of those seeking, as Plotinus said, and said smiling, to steal the thunder of Zeus, stormed against the unechoing walls of the house of philosophy, a wail arose near at hand. A little child crying paused in the entrance from the court, barefoot, holding up a white nightshirt with one hand, curly and sleepy headed. He padded over the floor and climbed onto the knees of his protector, who was seated again, scattering the papyrus leaves, and hid his face. Drawing his cloak round the shivering Potamon Plotinus returned to the two who had chosen to visit him on this night of celebration. He understood they were assured on their path and that they had been sent not to seek anything of his philosophy but perhaps to show him another way. Certainly the impression that they made on him was one he had not experienced before, one that proved they had penetrated the deeps of being and knew exaltation. They embodied a pure spirit. What then caused his own to meet it with so harsh a shivering? Two spear-points swift as lightning, glancing flash against flash, the clash of metals of totally different equally unyielding temper.

When one of them began to speak, mildly with joyous mien, he recognised it was not what they said now, or were in themselves, but what announced itself through them concerning the future that caused him to resume consciously that constant activity of unobserved consciousness, the contemplation of intellect. In his natural austerity he remained unassailable.

After the man fell silent the philosopher took up the little horn box of eye salve that stood on the table and turned it round in his fingers. The boy on his arm took it from him and pulled off the lid. Then the pleasant scent of saffron touched their nostrils and Potamon smiled. 'I could go back to bed now,' he said, 'if you were to go with me.'

'Run along and I will come soon.'

'No, not without you,' replied the child, 'I want to hear you answer these men who have come to teach you about God. Usually people come to ask you questions; these men are some of the ones I've heard Amelius talk about and call "insolent".'

' "We must allow other beings also their place in the presence of the Godhead." If that event you tell me of, that took place two hundred years ago, is made for man by the highest God it can only have true meaning if it is for all, an act in Eternity manifested, as you expound to me, in a certain time and place, but with its reality not Here, for Spirit is not in space. I have no need "to turn my philosophy into a story", and I do not think Intellect has any need of magic. It is not altogether clear to me whether you have come to instruct me or to look for instruction, but what I know is that the religion you have come to talk about will not take a place among the religions of this world unless it finds room for the wisdom of the Greeks.'

He put the box back on the table and laid his hand for a moment on Potamon's head. 'You will allow me to go away with him. I have also work before me.' And he signed to the writings tossed in confusion about the board.

'They aren't going away,' the child whispered as he crossed the court under a red sky enjoying the sense of grass between his toes at each step. 'What kind of men are they?'

'Men of a religion that has been persecuted abominably from its beginning. That is something you will always find with religions, child, when they are weak they are persecuted, when they are strong in numbers then in their turn they do the persecuting.'

'Then that is a difference between religion and philosophy,' the boy said sagely, 'but what is the difference, for you are not like them?' He rubbed his head against his friend's side, causing him to stand still on that caressing lawn. And while Plotinus answered, seriously as he always did those questions of the children in his house that had reason in them, Potamon stared up at the face with hurt hollows under the cheek-bones and the brow powerful against the sky as a rock he remembered on the sea-shore above the beat of the angry waves.

'Solitude and society: in religion men seek God in fellowship, binding themselves together by the things they do and look at, by initiations, by the acts and words of their priest who performs the rites for himself and for them. Even when they are alone they remind themselves they belong to this company, they pray in the words they hold sacred in common. This sustains them. They think the more men who believe in their god the more powerful he is to succour them. For the most part they want religion to help them in their living.

'The philosopher is one alone, who finds the utmost intensity of being in the life of thought; in the solitariness of his soul he knows the solitude of the One. All this world we see and love, my child, is something that has been broken for us, as you see reflections broken in water. The truth known in solitude has no images, no dark and shining reflections.'

'So you do not pray to the gods when you are afraid or when you want something,' Potamon said, sitting up in his cot and beginning to shiver again.

191

'Remember the One is always present, your guardian spirit tells you this. Prayer is the soul remembering its own stillness in contemplation, which is the act of God. You can surprise this in the instant of waking in the morning. An instant of happiness as of clear water, before, just before, the ripples begin, brought by the little boats launched of what you are going to do today; the thoughts darting this way and that like a flock of small birds. Have no fear. Sleep is coming to give you happiness.'

The boy was thinking hard of something to say that would be important enough to keep close to him a presence that he found considerably more potent just then that his interior tutelary spirit, while he pretended to himself at the same time that the spirit itself was suggesting he did this.

'If solitude is all, why do you have all these men come to your house, talk to them and let them ask you questions?'

'Each body is a different instrument or reflection of the One Soul, looks to this, in so far as he is a seperate human being, with unlike sight and reason. Because of this we desire, while we live, to share our vision with others and to let the light in their minds shine into the darker places of our own. The body, the shadow, is full of desires for things for itself – I want, as you children cry all day long – and it is not possible perhaps even for a man, old and sad as you see I am, to say no to desire; but he can decide to use this power, always unsatisfied Here, for one purpose, that is for approaching the Source. The intellective is part of every soul and this is what I remind everyone who comes to me, because to know this is to know truth and to go free of all earthly desires.'

Plotinus had ceased speaking to the child who had fallen asleep and was addressing some one else standing outside the room by the lamp bracket. He drew the blanket close round the gentle curve of body, human but anonymous, leaving uncovered the head seat of essence and reason. When these have taken flight with the soul, which was their shining, then the head also is covered. Julius was so evidently in distress the philosopher rallied him saying:

'You look as you did when I was ill. What is disturbing you now? Have you been talking to your friends or . . . have they gone away? It is a long time since you have been near me.'

A pair of dimly gilded lions breast to breast with prancing paws and tails curved angrily along their backs and ending in fiery tufts, adorned the shelf. Carved in low relief they glared with jaws wide and single eye not at each other but each at his own tail. Unlike the beasts between them Plotinus and Julius faced one another, the flame hovering over their tragically haggard features and the stylised averted creatures on the bracket until the terracotta vessel was replaced and the men turned away.

'That was a strange moment, a time complete, of our being mortal gods,' Julius muttered. 'Yet you say it is not possible for God to descend hither.' He stood still. 'How then do we know . . . ?'

'Every intellect is always in the intelligible world. It is enough to remember this.'

'Why is it so hard?'

'Body itself is a river of Lethe for the soul enclosing it, which forgets as it grows enamoured of beauty of visible form, and forgetting believes life to have no other dwelling.'

'And this is evil?'

'Forgetting the loved shining is itself a reflection of intellect, caused by the beam of irradiance of *nous;* through this power and nature of the soul the sensible world itself is a god and eternity shines through the forms. For this we look on them with love. But you know well, my dear child, how my thought energises.' He moved forward again. 'Were not eternity vivid to us in liberty of intellect There we could not endure the forgetting and corruption of the body.'

The ungainly negro, who had kept the philosopher alive when his household was plague-stricken, and whose amorphous appearance always brought with it a distaste in part due to a recollection of suffering, heaved up to them in a state of agitation, as they sensed by an emanation from his impenetrable darkness.

'There is some loss of intensity in our communion tonight, Julius, thoughts fall helpless and wilful as leaves in an autumn grove when the wind is absent. Perhaps it's to do with this noisy recurrent theme of emperor-worship. The commonalty set up some figure as a bastion against chaos and let loose on it their own dementia. What is it?'

'They have come here, they want to see you, they will not wait in the lecture-room, they are coming through now. You can hear.' The slave made a gesture with his arm.

'Who are they?'

'The Emperor and his son, the old and the young.'

Torches and voices made unaccustomed designs on the air of the little yard. The Nubian brought from the guard of the two lions the red lamp and held it on high a pace or two behind Plotinus.

193

The son of Marcellus Orontius, though his friend's hand forbade, moved back a step or two. The torch-bearers branched aside leaving the Caesars and the philosopher alone in the light, that drew all its rays towards them as Julius observed, while night was dense along the fringes. Was it the dyes and jewels of the apparel, or another thing, he wondered, while his heart turned craven as he saw how sick Plotinus looked and incapable of making any salutation. Yet it was he who broke the momentary rigidity with some light-winged word of welcome, and instantly the air rippled, Valerian was smiling, and Julius felt rather than saw a flash of recognition pass between Gallienus and Plotinus.

The new Emperor, aged in wars and years, was wearied by the ceremony and festivity of that day. But it was clear he wasn't going to sit on the chair being edged into the circle by his attendants. A hauteur which disdained the claims of the body, the least succumbing to comfort, smote Julius as if it were a lightning-stroke from Olympus as he stared at the heads of the two elder men. He recognised for the first time in his life, in an imperial ruler, the qualities and dedicated spirit that can make one mortal man deserving of the homage of others. Whence could this power come if not from the gods? At the same time he resented the impression burnt on his mind of this figure with bald forehead and broad hands spread now on the air, now on the purple robes, with just the gestures they must have used when Valerian was in his cradle.

'My son, who already knows you, spoke to me at the bitter end of this day of public display of the philosopher who is the true king of Rome; and my heart kindled at the thought that, after receiving so great a weight of overt honours, I might use my authority, temporary no doubt, to do something pleasing to myself. I ask you, let us talk a little while as two who have some kinship, it may be, with the Celestials, although we sojourn in a city besieged and plague-hit.' When there was no quick answer he added: 'Do not resent it.'

Julius perceived these last words recalled Plotinus to the necessary courtesies of a householder, above all of a man who was a citizen of Rome, to an acknowledged Emperor. What he did not know was that the philosopher was receiving these two men with inward unbending because, however it had come about, they were successors of Gordian, and also for the quite different reason, that their visitation defined for him the close of the second phase of his life in Rome. He suddenly ceased to regret the inevitable departure from this house, which had been suggested to him by Gratian.

The Emperor and the philosopher began to pace up and down that court, which was the heart of the house; consecrated for thought, as Gallienus said laughingly withdrawing to devote himself to the cooking which was something, he added, apt to be neglected by the thoughtful. For a time Valerian in a monologue bewailed the condition of Rome and the whole Empire, and the fate which had fallen on himself also, forcible election by the army being merely a mark of the general disruption. Then abruptly halting, looking at his companion and changing his tone he asked: 'What made you a philosopher? I came to listen not to grumble. Tell me.'

'An inward power no more to be resisted than the legionaries. Looking to the past a man finds he was least free when he most believed he was choosing for himself. The idea of choice is a lure.'

'Yet we read a man should live guiding and being guided by himself.'

'That is when he is sure he is not deceived by the guiding of his guardian spirit, which is always, however he develops his divine part by "thinking immortal thoughts" on a higher and more exalted plane than he has attained.' Plotinus hesitated before adding: 'Aristotle makes the life of the scholar come closest to the limitless bliss of God.'

'Perhaps. Plato on the other hand believed in the duty of the philosopher to the state. I do not ask you in person to fulfil any action of this kind, but you might, from your endeavour of making your own soul, let some light fall on this age of darkness. You have a guardian from the Golden Age to lead you.'

Plotinus' eye fell just then on the young man Julius who, although they were passing him, had no awareness of this. 'There is one thing certainly I would like to suggest, that you halt these unseemly persecutions of the Christians. They are a kind of philosophers, their own lives are as equally devoted. Do not add shame to your state by stamping on men who are looking out of our world; who are called, because they wrestle with something new in the life of religion, "the third race".'

Publius Valerianus shook his head: 'They do not recognise the divinity of the emperors. If they are a new race they may well be a menace to the Roman peace, without which the world where philosophers move with liberty and leisure, will end. A city beset by Goths, Persians, plague cannot suffer rebels within.'

'Is the state so unsound within that those who would let in light are considered to be evil?'

'If the Christians are destined to overturn our world they will survive the treatment we give them and arise the stronger for it. If they are not, we shall tame them. They are a subterranean force we know little of. Rome is fighting for her life.' Valerian moved forward two steps and checked again. 'This is not tyranny, it is one of the natural laws that power must use all means to maintain itself, whether it would or not. This very seeming injustice is part of the harmony of the whole.'

'Thinking is the movement of Intelligence and it must needs move Here under constraint. Men in this age look more closely into the soul, looking for a god who fills it, not one showing himself to the eyes. He who finds himself a philosopher gathers all his energy for the most perfect Act which is Intellection. For it is of the essence of things that each gives of its being to another. That is what those who call themselves Christians proclaim by their myths. Their faith breaks into a slumber and so they see the world with new eyes. The more they come into the open and show their revelation to the world the less intense it will become. Heraclitus has said the invisible harmony, the Logos, is more powerful than the visible.'

'It must needs be,' the Emperor said with a certain gesture of helplessness, 'if it is to sustain the visible disharmony which I am called to cement as a barrier against chaos. It is of import for us both that I came to your house tonight, here I can experience that irradiance.' Halting again he looked into the face of the philosopher, still with a light other than the flickering torches.

'The law is that the Soul may never succumb entire, by the very fact of its being; in my philosophy the creative power, of intellect if you will, is in all things but limited by their essential forms, the forms imposed on matter by soul. Even in those most dead, even in a stone, the supernatural essence of soul is present. Soul remains within itself a whole, the distribution into parts is the passion of bodies. This passion is the tension of life, desiring at once to be broken and separate and to be in the fullness of reality.'

'You would persuade me to throw off the purple and assume the plain dress of a philosopher!'

'The soldiers will not allow it, nor will your son who will never give up being emperor.'

'That is true,' Valerian responded, with a flash of the eye, 'so why should I not hand the power over to him at once?'

196

'Because the good judgment, for which the army elected you, will not allow you. You know that. The true dialectic, the revelation of soul to itself, continues silently with the utmost concentration through the storms and wars.'

The two talking and pacing would have forgotten all else, absorbed as they were in their intercourse, if the food provided under the direction of Gallienus had not been spread before them with a rising up of savours the little court was unused to.

'You don't, you know, have to give up the purple to enjoy the society of thinkers, papa, any more than you have to eat nothing but bread as they, or rather he, choose to do! Let us feast and do honour to his austerity. I assure you he loves me dearly, and you also for my sake.' And the young man laughed.

Plotinus and Valerian exchanged a glance and the philosopher returned to his writing, content that his guest could have a meal without formality in his house. The lamp beamed freshly trimmed on the table where all had been prepared with affection for the labour of writing; sharp quills, stylus, papyri in a neat pile to hand. He was checked by the intimate timeless attitudes of the patient materials; they waited, as it seemed to him just then, a little apart from the flow of all things, conscious they were his means of transmitting the nature of the Act which was his life of contemplation.

In the pause he was aware he and they were not alone. The energies for writing and composing prose were drawn another way. 'I think you had more to say to me. Where are you Julius?'

'I so meant to go away,' the brother of Alethia came up to the other side of the table.

'Well if you did not it is right for us to be together a little longer, to renew a compact.'

'What can I do?'

Plotinus studied him for some moments in silence. 'Shall I give you a thing to do for me?'

The young man's face became alight.

'That is better. No one will know you are doing it for me. You will forget yourself. I appoint you as guide to the Emperor. I will offer you to him as a secretary, but you will soon find he talks to you of our philosophy. Do you understand? The life of a man in the purple is brief in our age. And he has need of a friend who watches for him his political friends and enemies; and one with whom he can approach the pure energy, that is Intellect.'

'Is it right for me to do this?' Julius asked, the lines returning.

197

'You may have heard among your friends of the underground springtime, Julius, of a love that gives itself, that is to say gives all. I believe it is right, as you call it, for you to have some experience of living, to go with Valerian wherever war calls him. It is not wise for a man of your age to be too religious. Give philosophy free wings first.'

'Have I made you understand the Christians have not the same philosophy as the Gnostics you keep attacking?'

'You have. I have even spoken to the Emperor about halting the persecutions; he won't of course: nor shall I cease to show the weakness of the Gnostic philosophy which makes life here meaningless.'

'The real mystery,' Julius muttered, 'is how so many different people one has high regard for can think in different ways, and all be so sure they are right.'

'Most of us, Plato says, lack measure and grace. The only way to come at these is to live among men of principles and gods that seem strange. I know it is hard but the passion of thought in your soul, which is now clamorous as your whole body of physical desire, must never make you rough to another or, which may be a thing that escapes your notice, to yourself. The intelligible world, which you cannot see, will in no way suffer if for a season you serve visibly another man. We live, and indeed while we are in the body think also, with the whole of our physical being. The divine in us knows that.'

Julius thought he could never look his fill on the face of the man before him, the weariness of flesh translucent to the tranquil luminousness of soul was as a revelation to him of a kind of beauty he had not until that moment perceived. How does one do these things, he asked quietly of himself within, convinced that he must go away without any more speech, without a gesture of love. If he did not go now he would have failed at the outset. Yet he did not move. It was indeed a long time before he realised he was alone.

CHAPTER XII

Anapaulai en Chronois

'The regions beyond these places are either difficult of access because of their excessive winters and great cold, or else cannot be sought out because of some divine influence of the gods.'

Potamon read out the passage in a clear voice of approval, closed his book and went to find Plotinus. He went whistling between the statuary brought from the garden at Ostia indifferent to these cold sages and the poets staring upon nothing. Suddenly he saw him at the end of the vista and ran, sandals clapping the marble.

'Father mine, I wish we'd never had to come to this great house of halls and columns and uncomfortable grandeur. It is not fitting for study or love, which is to say for you or for me.'

Plotinus smoothed back the curls from the boy's brow and looked into his face, the shallow brilliance caused him a sense of misgiving which he translated into words: 'Sleeping and waking in the spring dawn I hear the singing of many birds, soon arise the storms of wind and rain. How many flowers are scattered on the ground.'

Potamon looked delighted: 'I don't care if you are prophesying an early death for me, for the gods love me. Tomorrow is the Fontanalia festival, did you remember? Let me go, with the other changelings of your house, to the country to find flowers to fill all the fountains. We will have a pleroma of flowers.'

'Go and ask Gemina, with her leave you may order the carriage and take as many children as are old enough to be reasonable, and who want to go.'

'O,' Potamon's elated mood sank. 'Don't you want to come? It's so long since we've been into the country. Come! Come!'

'You call like Pan-pipes!'

'All the Romans who come here are so stern and O, hefty! They come and say how wise you are and go away and are just the same as if you hadn't shone on them.'

Plotinus smiled a little, wishing himself he had not sent away Julius. Full consciousness Here is a crown of thorns, he had said, this bringing of the subject of thought from the intelligible world.

199

It is the bringing over from oneself the separate knowing; for there can be no conflicting in truth.

'Shall we go to Zethos then?'

Potamon's delight fell into regret: 'But then, for his farm is far, we should miss the festival altogether.'

'Thus you see, you cannot escape necessity. Choose, child. You either go a small journey to the autumn fields and return for the fair and fill the fountains with flowers, or we go, all of us together, to the house in Campania.'

While the boy considered, a pigeon flew in and alighting on a sculptured brow began its amorous crooning. 'I know what I should like,' he leaned his head against his friend: 'To go to Zethos alone, just you and me.'

'The others must have their amusement also. We shall all be happy to go away from the city, there have been too many processions and visitations to the temples and thanksgivings to the deities to mark the end of the plague. You cannot remember when the plague was not in Rome, can you? It wasted the Empire for fifteen years.'

He isn't remembering me either, the boy told himself, and throwing a backward glance both at the philosopher and the sports and dances at the conduits he left the arcade of Gemina's house to look for her in the kitchen. Child though he was he halted at the living beauty he saw through the archway, both in the room and beyond where morning sunshine warmed the herb garden. The laughter of the little girls carrying bunches, gray-leaved plants on the table, scrubbed and sleek to the touch, the woman with her high-piled hair and daffodil dress held him as though he looked at a picture and his previous life were but a preparation for this instant, which would never be again. It's after being with him I see things in this way, and not only see but live them with all of me. His moodiness fell from him like a shabby garment as he thought the proper purpose of remembering is not recollecting but reminding oneself only the instant is.

Suddenly he realised Plotinus was near and the children falling upon him; Gemina was laughing and Potamon, wondering how long he'd been ensorcelled, saw the slaves carrying wicker baskets to pack provisions for their journey.

When Gemina's husband died of the plague and her old father found her unwilling to return to his home in Ostia, he had suggested in his dry way the philosopher and his orphan family move into her huge half-empty palace: you are all in need of proper care and direction, he had said, with a gesture that included Plotinus, the children and the slaves, and when there is want of a grandfather I will come and stay there. Another widow and her young daughter joined the household, and to his surprise Plotinus found all was well; his energy of intellect was not diminished by the demands they made on his influence, and he was thankful for the happiness of these young whom he was bent on bringing up to be philosophers. In fact 'the thinking house', as Marcellus called it, became so popular because of the liveliness of the environment in which men were guided through the principles of the philosopher who said the subject was comprised in the words 'study to die and to be dead'.

'Of course,' Marcellus had said, 'you need a full flood-tide of young unthinking life round you to recognise the importance of that phrase. More people come than ever before, and from all quarters of the city, to listen to Plotinus now they will see also a pair of fair women and a circle of light-hearted youth.'

'But' Amelius had countered, 'there is no lack of houses in Rome inhabited by beautiful women and children graceful as olives and palms in their first and tender growth, yet I do not think our friends go to them when they are in need of those "pauses in the present" which are both the solace of the soul and the means of attaining for it a higher intellectual being.'

'What I am going to ask him next time he is addressing us,' Zoticus the poet attached himself to them, 'is what is the meaning and purpose of that vision or union of which he speaks, which he advises us to wait upon as we wait for the sun to rise. It seems to me to resemble annulment rather than fulfilment, or, if you will, experience of the pleroma. To desire anything at all, even at the level of pure intellect, if one can speak in this way, is a contradiction of the Stoic elements in his teaching.'

'It is not, I think, to be compared to a conscious desire to obtain this thing or the other as a good for oneself. Rather it is the nature of soul to be one with its source. All our other desires are a kind of substitute for this reality; the series of relative satisfactions which lure us into living in the contemporary world, as well as into forget-fulness of truth.' Amelius paused.

'The soul once awakened, whether by initiation or by contact with the living presence of a man who is vision to himself, cannot choose; otherwise we would go to the banquets where they wear garlands and rose wreaths instead of attending the lectures of

Plotinus, who calls us to endure thorns of thought.' Marcellus Orontius spoke with a tinge of regret in his voice.

'Or you might say the habit of intellectual strenuousness once formed cannot be disowned. All else becomes pithless.'

'The value of the vision of reality for men given to dialectic and argument, as most philosophers are,' and the poet smiled, 'is that it is a liberation from the tyranny of words. We can, I believe, mistake these symbols and the vivid patterns we learn to form with them for a singular revelation. Silence is closer to the contemplation of the Whole. Words are children of the brain, the body may be disdained, or we behave as if it were not, while we are speaking. Now I believe contemplation which, as he tells us, is the Act of Intellect before it was broken in souls, demands the attention of all that a man alive on the earth, and beholding the light of the sun, is. He may not need to exercise his body after the manner of the athletes but I think the philosopher must not sever his power of mind from the physical nature that sustains it.'

'And, if one is not careful, engrosses it.'

'There are always for me two distinct mysteries which however much of a philosopher one reckons oneself to be, or comes to be regarded as by one's equals in intellectual discipline,' and Marcellus smiled at them as though he were overrating himself, 'are never really dealt with. The first: that however "high" one contrives to lift thought by strenuous concentration there is always something uninvolved and observing beyond. The second: and perhaps this is not really so separate, the essential nature, character, destiny in an inward sense, or call it what you will, that makes us seem so unlike, even in what we might describe as parallel approaches to the One.'

'As poet and critic,' Zoticus responded, 'I have a shameless interest in the difference of essences and take a delight in discovering them. My observer is passionately involved, and this passion which is my being as poet is what makes contemplation living.'

'Living contemplation could not be better and gives us, as well as words may, the answer to your question at the beginning concerning union. This living contemplation is Intellect itself, and we receive in this Vision an abundance of new life which, when we are again in the mode of reasoning mind, gives us power and awareness for our intellectual commerce. If I may put it in clumsy terms – an impulse of energy for all minds Here from what is beyond intellect.'

★ ★ ★

202

Plotinus, watching the children let loose from the carriage to run in the fields and explore the wilds of the ample domain of Zethos, knew that for himself also this visit to the country was life-giving. 'I have caught the infection from the Romans, who are all true farmers at heart,' the Arabian said in welcoming him. 'The earth is a mute patient, suffering and rewarding our attention. What I cannot grow accustomed to is the sickness of animals; the way they are in decrepitude and blindness; when they are overworked. I cannot say what it is, my dear. Men, and the meanest of slaves, I can succour by means of my training; be untroubled; let them die without regret when I've done my part. It is all very well for Virgil to say we shouldn't pity old age; banish the old horse out of sight. But I do pity. I cannot say why. They are a feebler creation than we are, closer to nature and the earth-mother. Yet in affliction they have a dignity that is greater than ours.'

'Is it because they give their all unceasingly to Providence with no calculation for a separate self which, although it may be an illusion in us, can be something we hold between ourselves and the matter of bodies. The idea that you as a farmer can put things to rights again when they have been ruined by weather is, whether true or not, a strength of the soul which they have not. These creatures close to us look to us as if we were gods who could help them, if we would . . .'

'And instead of that we abuse them; offer them as sacrifices for an evil in ourselves they know nothing of; treat them as shows . . . but you have come to the country to find health and sanity which do not belong to the capital of a decadent Empire. Let us walk about the fields, and discover again some grove of felicitous trees. You remember Daphne? Whenever I fell the oaks or plane-trees I must have for timber, or when I am clearing more ground for the plough, I always leave here and there a cluster or a solitary fine trunk for Artemis.'

Zethos fell silent content now to walk with this friend to those parts of his farm he loved best, calling attention neither to the country nor to the works of men, knowing what was pleasing would influence both their minds best by quiet; as the water flowing in small streams scarcely heeded makes thought itself musical. And for Plotinus it was Virgil who made living this unusual communion with landscape; the art of the poet of the *Georgics* gently interlaying his meditation. Near the end of the day when his soul was filled with golden light as with a god they came to a field in an arc of shadowy woodland where stubble was burning. The play of flames dancing, red racing over the ridges, the hissing and crackling of those fiery tabernacles of straw swiftly fallen in blackness at his feet caught him anew with the splendour of something beyond all material bodies, the devourer surging upwards, the subtlest element. Then running over the hill came the younger children, leaping the rows of colour carrying leafy brooms which took light and blazed as they fled with the wind and the flames.

'Your boys and girls do not grow old as ours for you are always taking new ones,' Zethos said, when their shrilling voices had torn their silence.

'But they do not take to philosophy either as I had hoped. The girls think of marriage; Potamon, the first, who is unwilling to leave me, kindles to other fires, he is frail and will burn out as the straw does.'

'The children of your living intellect will shine through the ages of man so that even the unhappy learn the shining of that transforming gold.'

'It interests me,' Plotinus responded, 'that it is always the physicians who readily enter into the mind of the highest music, as Plato calls our philosophy. Those, that is, who look most constantly and steadfastly into the world of the senses when it is distressed by loss of harmony, and the beauty we all find in flesh is stained and foul; withdrawn altogether. They labour for the harmony of health which at its best is so perfect we are unaware of it.'

Zethos did not speak again until they were standing near his house which Plotinus had paused to admire; to let, as he thought to himself, the original design of the architect, without the stones, re-form itself in his mind. One light appeared as a small star in the shadowy facade.

'It is because, intent upon living men, we are most conscious of the mysterious power that reaches through all existence to the lowest limit. However weak, as you say, the contemplation of nature is, it will have its own way. It is only by discovering this in ourselves we can learn to be healers. There must be a One that holds all together and yet that, because it is infinite, remains unhurt by what we see as the ceaseless irrevocable breaking up of the finite.'

He had the sense of being alone well-known to the friends of Plotinus, and fell silent. The lamp had gone. Night with the first star . . .

'Perhaps that was our prayer to Silent Night,' Plotinus said at last when the evening sounds returned, voices of herdsmen and bleatings, a slave passing with a tray of living embers. The children coming also were unusually quiet, holding in their hands whatever it had pleased them to gather from the country. After the random troop of young, walking with downcast heads, the two men followed, as if all were attending on the country muse. Only Plotinus staying to pick up a flower a child had dropped collected a little dust as if to sprinkle on the dead, waited until each one had gone in and then went after them into a room bright with lights and hearth-fire: here the spell was broken with laughter, each looking to recognise the other as after an indefinite separation. The children were no sooner assembled then they scattered again through the shadowy halls and half-lit arcades; and Zethos disappeared with them thinking it well to leave Plotinus alone with his wife, whom he had known in Alexandria where her father Theodosius had been a friend of Ammonius. Theodosius had been one of the numberless plague-stricken and his daughter, named after him Theodosia, had re-found Plotinus in Rome and thrown in her lot with Zethos. Impatient with the city she remained in the country and watched over the farm while Zethos moved between his rural and urban patients, never denying the gifts of Aesculapius; for that is my contemplation, he was used to answer Plotinus, who feared for the physician's own health and *eudaimonia*, spent in giving life.

Langour came upon them both as they stood there at the hearth thinking of the sleepless light and remembering earlier days when love of wisdom burnt as a high passion in the soul. Plotinus had a visionary sense of Odysseus placing himself, with his unerring instinct for what is becoming with women, at the feet of Arete among the ashes. Virtue, reality, one approaches them at the last not with words or the prayer of a supplicant but with a laying-by of the weal of body. 'Memory' he said smiling, speaking scarcely in a whisper, 'is a grace of the soul. You can fancy her as a butterfly with folded wings at rest under a green leaf; woken by some gesture from the past to flutter again in forgotten sunlight.'

'The radiance of being we caught in Alexandria is with us tonight, an all but intolerable lightning along the nerves.'

When dinner was over, a simple meal not prolonged in the house of Zethos, and only the older ones were left by the fire of fragrant wood, Plotinus read aloud passages from the *Odyssey* until all their hearts were kindled by the poetry and perils of the adventurer. Last of all he read how Athene with a golden lamp went before Odysseus and his son through the hall lighting all with celestial radiance: 'And Telemachus said to his father: I marvel at what appears to my eyes. The walls of the house, and the beautiful spaces between the rafters, the beams of fir and the pillars are exalted in radiance, as in an unconsuming fire. Surely a god from broad heaven is with us. And wise Odysseus answered him: Silence, quieten your thought and do not speak aloud. For this is the way of the gods who hold Olympus.'

If Theodosia had allowed it the two friends would have walked and talked all night in the interior court of the house, but she came at midnight and summoned Zethos to bed as firmly as she had the children earlier that evening. A slave following her extinguished the lights and prepared, with a lamp in his hand, to lead Plotinus to his room. When Zethos wanted to do this she said smiling that, if he did, she would not see him again that night. They submitted and parted. As soon as the elderly house-servant had bestowed the guest and the polished lamp in a remote chamber, chosen for its seclusiveness and silence, Plotinus prepared to lie down, deciding this would be the most natural posture to continue his thoughts on the soul of the All.

The first moments of solitude after being with companions, and especially those who were dear to his heart, brought him always the sense of being left on a bare strand unvisited by any other mortal, with the sound of waves that had never borne hollow ships. This, he told himself, is how intellect is both at rest and in motion. Tonight, however, the great rhythms of Homer's poetry would not be gainsaid, and he yielded to the vision in which the poetry was All, a pure unheard music of the whole drama; sea and suffering, gods and the counsels of crafty Odysseus realised indivisibly . . . 'at night in the darkness . . . sight without act'.

A stone on the edge of a gleaming pool was the centre of this passive seeing, small, dark, parti-coloured in the sense that a vibrant silver line rimmed rock and reflection, and that the cap of it was white like a closed eyelid. Invisible sunlight revealed serene objects laid on the floor of the pool by the guardian nymph and obliterated the silver line. At that point consciousness swung on the surge of the sea into no-consciousness that was, when he afterwards sought to re-experience the vision, only to be spoken of as intelligible light.

Weariness caught him as a net knotted with restlessness and that curious-faced dog, some friend of Zethos had imported from the island of Britain and given him as a rare present, began barking and howling near his window. He opened the door that led onto a loggia and called the animal. Rather to his surprise it ran into the room and bounded on his bed. Making a place for himself beside it and with the pressure of warm weight against his thigh he instantly fell into a sound sleep.

He woke with a sense of physical gratitude, intimate with the delicacies of youthful perceptions, his mind tirelessly sleeping, his heart still suffused with the glow of the god. At the scratching of his bedfellow he rose, and the dog rolled into the hollow he left carefully curling himself. Plotinus heard a snuffling groan of reposeful ease as, with all the Greek alert in his blood, he faced the dawn.

Without looking up he knew the presence of the last stars astray among thin vapours; the dew washed his feet and ankles. The beauty of earth surprised by light becoming was akin to that of the soul. Distressed by matter's indefiniteness it hastens to impose form upon it. So at this hour he sensed the vagueness about him tranquilly recollecting the manner of its partaking of infinite beauty. The groups of trees assumed their accustomed symmetries with shyness as though wearing them for the first time. He felt as if upon a transparent globe, clear as the diamond spheres the cobwebs cradled, where light eternal was unobstructed, the contours simply a means of condensing the vision. Earth for him was the breathing of reality, nothing could be lovelier than the things he saw, while they attended the rising of the sun.

* * *

On his return to Rome, after another of his infrequent visits to the country home of Zethos and Theodosia, he found Julius unexpectedly returned from the army in the east. His own household reflected the dejected emotional state of the city; the women were silent and listless as though for once their numberless domestic cares for the well-being and overseeing of the inmates did not satisfy them, or keep them from grieving. Julius was so aged Plotinus almost failed to recognise him; they met in silence, and it was clear, whatever had been the younger man's condition when he joined the Emperor, his experiences on the Euphrates and at the rape of Antioch had destroyed the unity of a sensitive organism.

After a day or two, when the main features of the total ignominy of the Roman army under the hands of Sapor had been swallowed, rejected and swallowed again perforce by the citizens, so that they went about the streets as though they had drunk poison, Julius

207

began to tell in short sentences like a child what he had seen. And the philosopher, who was accustomed to continue his private thinking whatever was being said or performed near him, gave his full attention, releasing as it were for the support of his friend the energy usually directed to his intellectual speculations. It was indeed only because of the gentleness of his master, communicated without words, that he could speak at all; for, as he explained, he felt himself to be no more than Valerian, a skin stuffed with straw.

'We crossed the Euphrates, encamped over against the Persians; I was with the Emperor as he went, with bold words, but bowed by age and his life as a leader of men, through the host. The soldiers were as those who have already suffered a defeat, you would have said they had never borne the name of Romans. When he returned to his tent Valerian wept. "I always looked for my own death at their hands," he said, "but not this." There was a half-hearted battle near Edessa. He was taken prisoner. The men beaten without fighting shouted the Emperor had betrayed them to Sapor. They laid down their arms. I am no warrior but I declare that was the most shameful act I have seen.

'Then the praetorian prefect, who was the real betrayer, offered a sum of money beyond naming to the Persian to let these, naked of weapons and manhood, retreat. Sapor laughed at him. "It is no place for the disgraced to bargain." I think he was well pleased to have these incarnations of the ruined Empire beside him as he marched on Antioch. The army, so called, deserved that, but not Valerian.' Julius paused. 'Your Gordian had a clean end compared to his. In the purple with chains on his neck, waist and limbs, with filth poured on him, he made sport day by day for Sapor and his nobles. He was old and weak, reviled by deed and by tongue beyond what anyone who saw and heard not, could imagine.'

'Day by day I was near him. When he fell from pure exhaustion, not from shame, they let me hold him up. They must have him supported that their mockeries could go on. Not one chain was lifted from him at night. No water was allowed for cleansing blood or sores. How many times I thought him dead and saw him smitten back for their delight I cannot say. At the last his eyes, long lost to me, gave a clear look I understood.'

'I knew my father was a mortal. Since he seems to have acted as a brave man I am quite satisfied at what I learn of his end.'

How long Gallienus had been present listening to the narration was not clear to Plotinus as he turned from the haggard face of

Julius to the Emperor, whose attitude of dignified affliction was so overpoweringly contradicted by the glow of his inward triumphing. The atmosphere suddenly arid perhaps affected him for he inquired in the same satisfied tone how this intimate of his father had escaped the Persians and achieved his swift journey to the capital.

For a moment Plotinus wondered how his loved pupil would reply to the son devoid of feeling. At once he was reassured. In witnessing and intimately sharing the mock of Valerian Julius had found his manhood. His manner in replying to the imperial question was beyond reproach, his speech correct and respectful, while his whole being, as the philosopher sensed, was centred on the spirit of the father unflinching before the cruelties of his captors.

'Sapor took a runaway debauchee from the sack of Antioch and had him presented to the disarmed army of Rome. The men cheered him to the brazen heaven. And this caused, you may be sure an extreme degree of pleasure to the soldiers of Oriens. To this successor of your father I applied for leave to bear the news to yourself. Eager that you should know you had been supplanted in the hearts of the legionaries he obtained my release from the Persian tyrant, and I was given priority with the post.'

'And after all that you left me to hear the news of our defeat from the common errand-men?'

'When I entered the city I could speak to no one. I came blindly to this house and waited till a measure of strength was given me. Then involuntarily I began to tell what I had seen to the man who has taught us both many things.'

'That is true, that is allowed,' Gallienus responded gaily. 'It is thanks to this I am as unmoved by my father's fate as a wise stoic philosopher should be. I know he will admire and praise me for this, as do all those in my court. It is indeed the part of a brave son to accept with indifference his father's destiny. As to that shameless usurper, when my soldiers recover their weapons it will be no time before they dispatch him. I'm sure of that. And I've no doubt Sapor, satisfied with the ruin of Antioch and laying waste our Empire in the east, will soon take himself back across the Euphrates. It's all a long way from Rome, isn't it?'

'Is it not your intention to lead an army to the east to avenge your father and to restore order?'

'I don't see the advantage of that. No troops can be spared from the fighting on the western and northern marches. Besides, there is so much for us to do in Rome; not least to attend the lectures of

209

our philosopher.' And Gallienus cast on Plotinus a look full of benevolence.

'The soul has an action of conscious attention within itself. Dwelling in this effortlessly while the storms of passion toss and heave it allows the principle of reason to restore order. The penitent senses are quietened.' Julius knew this slow speech was addressed to himself, and knew also the speaker was withdrawn from the two men, as if he were lifting their essences with his own apart from the flux. Something even in the mere difference between his own response and that of the Emperor to the degradation and death of Valerian gave his mind more stability. His own horror and the unfeeling coldness of Gallienus, the very sufferings he had so closely shared, were no longer obdurate iron spikes driven into the nature of his being. The evil in them fell away. He ceased re-experiencing his own hurts and condemning the carelessness of the other's attitude. 'The suffering is in the communion of soul with body.' As Plotinus began to speak again Julius realised he had been looking all the time into his eyes. 'This is the nexus, by this tension, all but endurable as our awareness of it increases, we live. Body strained to the utmost by being in soul partakes of a more abundant life, and desiring to restore this to God recognises the freedom it attains is not Here only. In this freedom the soul is constantly in the divine life. This sharing in the pain and suffering of another, a thing so intense and bitter we shrink helpless before it, proves our indwelling in the one soul of the cosmos. "In the souls within ourselves there is true knowing." Evil itself can bring us nearer to this, can rouse a power for prayer and for looking to God.'

A further realisation of what it is to be man was experienced by Julius in the silence following those words spoken to him alone, as to one who understood. The silence itself was one of those pauses in time, of a peace apart from thought and consciousness and high-wrought nerves and senses. Indeed the whole interval had not existed, he perceived, for Gallienus, who was resuming his talk with the philosopher. Just in the same way, Julius observed to himself, there are forms of life and intellect around me of which I have no inkling, and I darken what I could have by too much anguish and ardour. He recognised, with something that would once have been jealousy, that Plotinus was as interested in the Emperor, and his plans for enjoying his sole possession of power, as in himself. The philosopher knows all men are as they are because, in a sense, they do not belong to themselves; he listens and speaks as to dreamers, but with hope we may awaken.

Plotinus in his apparent attention to the imperial discourse was aware of a certain recovery and restoration in the troubled nature of Julius; as when the herbs and grasses are trampled in a woodland where no path is. Pausing the wanderer is taken by faint sounds that declare themselves in the curve of his ear. He looks down and observes delicate jerky readjustments as the resilient stalks and blades take up their rhythms. Presently new growth will be urgent above the bruised and broken.

CHAPTER XIII

Porphyry

'Energy is immortality for the Greeks. In our own we know the freedom of timeless life; in the work of those who are before us, those happy ones akin to the gods, we have a part even more intense according as their creation is, while there are men on earth, eternal in our mind.'

'Do we need "on earth"? I believe a blessed soul must have no body,' Porphyry interposed.

'I am speaking for those who have, or who once were known in that way. This is the feast day of Socrates who was present on earth, I believe, as a mortal man, however he may be now with us.'

'Let Amelius show us his theory of the first virtue of the Greeks.'

'Poetry: Homer, war and wanderings; Pindar, athletic contests. I think you will agree with me none of us can listen to these poets, or read them in silence, without himself finding his soul, though it be in the body, winged with their power. I say the same for the writers of tragedy. Suffering, reproach, ruin of all we honour, these themes transmuted by the highest poetry win us the discovery of the dynamism at work in the being of man. Those who take their way self-doomed to Hades prove this, as well as those who prophesy and foretell, and the characters who are fearless.

'The energy of the Greek philosophers, Plato and the rest, there is no need to speak of in this company, for this is the structure of our lives. And I think I will not praise the energy we know best of all, the contemplative energy of our master.'

'Do we know this energy to the full?'

'Each of us as far as his own being allows. I believe we acknowledge it by some subtlety of our essence when we approach it in another man; if he be a stranger, by the texture of his physical body moistened with the potentiality we speak of as a net with water: whether, when we meet his eyes, he is vision in relation to himself.'

'The vision by which we know every soul is of the Father.'

'I,' said Porphyry, 'have begun to write on the Return of the Soul. But what is of first importance is that our master should write.

I as a newcomer to this circle am aware of a loss in not having heard his lectures.'

'You can have what I've already done in that direction,' Plotinus said smiling, 'and I intend to continue while I may. You will find my notes rough and uncorrected; I write, I find, in a certain passion that suffers no delay. Compared to writing speaking is a reflective activity, a division into parts. Writing is a direct encounter with intellect unbroken: this must be thrown off by halting reason into whatever words it can snatch.'

'That is the mode of inspired poetry. Afterwards one can return and recast.'

'I cannot do that. I can only write on, though no doubt I philosophise with a certain repetition. The cosmos repeats patterns with variations, yet it never returns upon its course.'

Amelius responded: 'I should like to read a passage from Parmenides, our earliest instructor in the ways of thought; it has I think the nature of a promise, one indeed that may never be wholly fulfilled as regards the reasoning principle of men, certainly not the men of this time. Nevertheless because it has been uttered we receive the grace of a bountiful promise, and experience a liberty of spirit, a sense that all things are possible. He tells us the goddess spoke these words: "And thou shalt know the substance of the sky and all the signs in the sky and the resplendent works of the glowing sun's pure torch, and whence they arose. And thou shalt learn likewise of the wandering deeds of the round-faced moon, and of her substance. Thou shalt know too the heavens that surround us, whence they arose, and how Necessity took them and bound them to keep the limits of the stars . . . how the earth and the sun and the moon and the sky that is common to all, and the Milky Way, and the outermost Olympus and the burning might of the stars arose." '

'I have lately been studying the Book of Genesis,' Porphyry spoke first in the silence which followed the reading of Amelius, 'and I find a fine contrast here between the Hebrew exposition of the creation and the promise of Parmenides. Both have their poetry, both acknowledge the inevitable, which we name Necessity. The Hebrews are satisfied with an account of the preparation, by the spirit of Almighty God, of the visible universe, which is sacred because it has been created once for all. But their main concern is with the way of life and the means of life of the men made by God on the intractable land. Once their sojourn in Paradise, the Golden

Age, is over, their concern is to live as best they may, avoiding the wrath of Jehovah by keeping his law when they remember, returning to it when, because of rebellion, things get too bad for them. Live out your days on earth, accumulate wealth, obey the Law: there is here in our sense no adventure of mind, to bend our highest energies to not transgressing the law would be the death of us philosophers of the schools of Athens and Alexandria. Yet I declare to you the sense of power and dignity, and the very mystery of this remote God who yet can, in manifest contradiction, walk the earth and converse with his friends, is something no one can believe who has not kept company with these patriarchs of Genesis and let himself be absorbed with the business of sheep and cattle and camels.'
Porphyry shuddered.

'Of pure thought I find nothing among them. I have come to conclude my task as a thinker is to keep minds free of the shackles of the law, which I think is working among us now in a more dangerous form than that of the practice of the Jews. That is, in the sect that calls itself Christian.'

'The Greeks accepted the law of Necessity because it is the only way to be free to explore the universe, stellar and intellectual. And the law of Necessity is reshaped by each generation, by its thinking and living in wisdom. Another difference between Greeks and those who are at work making the law of the Hebrews life-giving is that they make man the centre of the universe.'

'Each of us in true growth generates wisdom while he recognises it,' Plotinus said. 'And since this is his feast day let us all pour libations to the spirit of him who said: "Life unexamined cannot be lived by man." '

'To explore life by every means *is* the living of philosophers, whatever gods may be.'

'I think Porphyry will have to be careful in his self-chosen work of guarding the liberties of Greek reasoning and logic that he does not bind himself too closely to the gods prayed to of old. Do not let them assume in your mind the power of the God of Abraham, Isaac and Jacob.' Plotinus smiled at the man lately introduced to his circle, but he spoke with gravity. 'That which exists eternally is set in no region or place or support. God is omnipresent in Intellect alone.'

'No one, I think, can gainsay that, who learns to approach his own intellect with the energy our master communicates. He speaks with authority and his energy is constantly renewed. Many men disperse theirs in dispute, thinking, it may be, to increase their powers by the sense of triumph that comes to them from overturning another man's arguments.'

'There are inexorable laws by which our reason operates just as our body has its tangible bounds within which it may grow soft or else as strenuous as an athlete's; sicken or be restored from sickness by diet and moderation, as our friend Rogatianus recovered from his gout. The mind because it is, so to say, closer to soul, to immortal being, is a more delicate instrument. There are few men who can rest in the life of intellect and at the same time reason with lucidity for the guidance of other minds, as Plotinus does. We who know him best know also how it is in his presence alone we can keep our own thought centred upon the principle of Intellect. As soon as his influence leaves us there is loss of concentration. But this is a difficulty. If a man does not stand on his own feet in the realm of thought, he does not give his share of living energy to the highest intellect.'

'They talk of a way of life held with unshaken conviction and consistency; with our master it is a way of thought. Or should I say *the* way?'

'The way is right. But for some it must be given adornments, for others human form, or support. Truth is One and central to all, demands all, which he would say is ceaseless remembering even without consciousness. Thence is pure knowledge, by which we learn to live Here.'

* * *

Plotinus gone the men's talk lost at once its virtue for Porphyry; just as Amelius had said. He had only lately come to Rome from Greece with Antonius of Rhodes, and Amelius, whom he had known in the schools of Athens, had brought him to the philosopher believing they would understand one another. He was so far right that he began to consider retreating to his home in Tuscany and leaving the guardianship of Plotinus and his work to a younger and more skilled man than himself, who in all his eighteen years of attendance on the lectures and person of the philosopher had written nothing except notes. His devotion had not diminished but he doubted his calling as a sage, and began to meditate a life of rural evenness free from the rigours of thought.

When Amelius at a later time, and alone with the master to whom he had become as a shadow, said something of this, Plotinus agreed readily. 'After so close a companionship we shall not feel apart, the reflection in the soul being always present to look to.'

'What do you think of Porphyry, as man and philosopher?' Amelius inquired. 'Since we have always spoken freely.'

Plotinus smiled: 'I think he is necessary and has come at the call of my daemon. He has more confidence in his powers of analysing than you have. The precise sense of ordering and organising he has shown already is always of value Here. But it has dangers also. He will have a tendency to introduce celestial beings into intellectual-principle. I would say he recognises pure metaphysical thought when he is with us, and in what he has seen of my writings, but I believe afterwards his energy may fall from the Supreme. He may please himself with a kind of marshalling of spirit-beings akin to that of the Gnostics he is so stern in attacking.'

'I would like to ask you,' Amelius said, with a silent acknowledge-ment of understanding, 'what your own feeling is, in heart perhaps as much as in soul or reason, about the gods in things, and the divinities.'

'Dear Amelius, I know how you love these and give them honour and praise. In this, fulfilling your nature, you do well. All the intelligible gods are generated by intellect, and the beauty of ideas; and I say we should remember that the highest praise we can offer to these deities, who are of the earth even as men are in the form we know them Here, is pure thought. By the shining of the god into our soul we can perceive the glory, shall we say of war? The dryad, as the branches overshadow us, gives clear vision of the tree's reality. I declare that Intellect should look always to the one God, in doing this it gathers the vision vouchsafed by the gods of earth; the grace of these gods we hope to prepare ourselves to receive by our worship and attendance at the shrines, and the sacred groves, and wherever especially we discern the presence of the god.

'Beauty unfailingly disposes us to contemplation, as do the arts. And you may compare, if you will, the differences between Greek and Roman by the objects in which they are most aware of the supernatural essence, or indwelling sense of the numinous. With the Greeks the cosmos, and nature visible to our senses, have first place; weapons and instruments of craft and toil follow. With the Romans I think it is the household gods, the objects of daily use and handling; which are not less divine for being man-made and ministering to his well-being. Something in the heart of the Greek answers first of all to the wild gods.'

Watching Plotinus as he spoke, seeing his face narrowed and carved with hollows below the might of his brow, Amelius questioned what it was that made him decide he would soon have to go away, to let go the constant intercourse which had coloured his whole being. Was it that the man's talk was as a spell to which he could listen and assent for ever, and imagine because he understood, he himself was thinking and expressing the truth of the soul?

The philosopher answered with his usual gentleness all that the Tuscan had not spoken aloud: 'Be sure, my dear, if you must leave our circle it is by the will of the gods we have been talking about; as well as in obedience to your own guardian spirit, who may be directing you for reasons at present beyond our comprehension. All that is precious in our relationship is constant.' Seeing Amelius still distressed he went on: 'It is not enough to satiate ourselves with the thought of those who are wiser. That is a way of training and preparation, which must be completed by the nature and living growth of the separate intellect. Philosophy is not scholarship, it is the liberty of the individual mind moulded by those men of former days who have found in contemplation the *eudaimonia* of spirit.'

Slaves passed with silence of naked feet; soft strokes of one sweeping soothed the nerves. How patient they were and unquerulous, the instrument on which the taut strings of thought sounded. Something of the radiance of the master extended to the servants in Gemina's house, Amelius thought, watching them in an unexpected weariness of words. He imagined himself on a sudden burning up all those volumes of notes he had made of the lectures; what value had they now Plotinus was writing? They would be dead reading although he had made them in the heat of dialectical and sometimes dithyrambic discourses that had been his life's breath. He faced simply that he was not a philosopher, but he knew at the same time it was not beyond him to live out the rest of his life in a way worthy of a Roman. Henceforth he would forget the soul; it would be enough to remember the One is present to all things.

* * *

Although he continued his *sunousiai* and wrote now almost daily and with incredible speed and sureness, Plotinus was aware in himself of being further removed from the friends who kept the atmosphere of the thinking house swirling with talk of politics, and the controversies and discoveries of men all over the Empire. This closer approach to the solitariness of the One made him appear more

217

present to those who sought him; for he found while he was reading to the children and preparing lessons for them and sharing their difficulties, when Gemina was consulting him over some domestic problem, even when Gallienus crossed the threshold with a flourish of talk and of courtiers, carefully chosen however for their enjoyment of philosophy and literary discussion, the wording of his next treatise, which would actually be written with the high-wrought passion of a poet, was being prepared in all tranquillity in some part of his intellect inaccessible to distractions.

Apart from Porphyry, who was thirty years old when he came to Rome, none of the younger men joined themselves now to Plotinus. His unwholesome body offended them, but the distaste he himself had always felt for it was less of a trouble under these ugly traces of mortality. However, he allowed the physicians to do what they could for his health. One of the ideas that did preoccupy him at this time, and for which he won the enthusiasm of the Emperor, was the founding of a model city to be governed and regulated entirely according to the laws of Plato.

Almost the last excursion on horseback he made was to the ruinous site of a legendary city of philosophers in Campania, which, while the whim lasted, Gallienus was delighted to bestow on Plotinus together with the means for rebuilding it. They rode side by side and as the Emperor was in his poetic vein lines of startling unoriginality fluttered in the sunshine. Plotinus' way of responding was to repeat some favourite theme of his own from Pindar or Virgil, according to whether Greek or Latin was required. This being always taken as a compliment left him free to experience beauty resting upon this expanse of level landscape; as though a lustre of gold overspread the earthiness, shone through the fallow land and sparkled on the tiny fountains jetting from hollow stalks in those fields already reaped. The thud of hoofs; the ring of voices under boundless heaven, the utterances barely glancing downwards, knowing themselves winged for an infinite voyaging; above all the fierce torrent of heat as the August sun went up the sky, reminded him of his venture to Oriens.

The city itself, when at last they came to it in a wilderness of rankly aromatic shrubs, after deciding more than once to relinquish their search, pleased him so well in its formless ruin, he felt an unspoken reluctance to disturb the genius of the uninhabited place once the abode of men. Severing himself from Gallienus he went along flowering alleys where lizards' light toes scratched the rocks and entered at random a crumbling cell. This dwelling had been one on the wall; from among the fallen rubble and mortar he looked to the open country with a lift of spirit altogether youthful, as if four of his six decades had suddenly left him. Whoever had owned the little room had left there a perpetual sweetness.

Here Plotinus remembered Deborah and felt his heart cleave to her. The women who loved him and praised his philosophy and were infinitely and often self-effacingly solicitous for him, even Gemina herself, had for him no power of Aphrodite. For a little while he allowed himself a story of their living together in this house on the city wall, sharing their brief life under the sun and the stars with poetry and reading. The ancient writers of tragedy knew what they were about; the passion when after long parting brother and sister found one another, and came together in an ecstasy that had something both of the unexplored and the confidence of a flawlessly knit relationship about it, came over his soul; and he knew at the same time with his customary clairvoyance this city would never be Platonopolis.

Determined to recover his concentration on the universal consonance he raised his tired hands from the mouldering embrasure, but without the instinctive motion of rubbing away the dust after such a contact, and took his way from that unexpected refuge, which had offered a human pause to his stricken exalted mortality.

By what had once been the well of the deserted city he came on Porphyry sitting on some tumbled stones and scraping with his feet in the hot dust. Nearby was a broken plough, the pole lying on the ground, the handle snapped off where it had joined the tree. Old earth was caked hard on the once shining ploughshare. The man appeared so moody, Plotinus, who usually disregarded signs of ill-humour in his friends, asked after his health.

'I heard them saying, over there where they are feasting *al fresco* on the Emperor's cates, there was no money to spare in the treasuries to rebuild a tumbledown town for the idle tribe of the philosophers to come and live in. So there goes the last hope of trying to run a city under the laws of Plato.'

'I knew it would be like this. The wars take all and more than all. We would not have Gallienus add further taxes to the peasants, overloaded as they are, for us to experiment. From afar I saw good in the thought, Porphyry, but now I am here I feel reverence for this place exactly as it stands, or lies. I would even prefer it remained desolate.'

While he was speaking, and looking down on the implement of labour, a narrow green snake passed from under Porphyry's seat, gliding as a thread of water over the dust and vanishing in a crack in the rim of the well.

'The tax money doesn't go to defend the Empire, you know that. It pays for his fancies.'

'Something else is disturbing you and you are putting it down to this,' Plotinus answered. 'Do not distress the shades here who have shed their cares and are not without a sunny awareness in these streets of sand and walls that need no watchmen.'

'I should know it is vain to conceal anything from you. Well, it is Olympius; you remember he also for a short while was in the company of those who studied under Ammonius, and made sport of him because he was a Christian turned pagan – he said one couldn't be uninitiated from any religion; which might mean you learnt more from your master than you knew.' Porphyry glanced up askance from his dejected attitude. 'Now this Olympius is matching his name, and deciding he out-tops all the philosophers, since he arrived in Rome from Alexandria.'

'And, I gather from your tone, you withheld your homage to the high Olympian.'

'I was more foolish than that. I said you excelled.'

'And now?' Plotinus inquired, as they made a move to rejoin the Emperor's party.

'He is threatening to work evil on me by magic means.'

'As I am the cause, as it appears, of his malice, get him to transfer his attack to me,' suggested the philosopher, 'and we will see then what happens.'

Nothing further was exchanged about Olympius of Alexandria between them until a certain winter afternoon when the statues and marble paving in the arcade were exuding an unpleasing clamminess, and the children in total rebellion against the theology of philosophy were playing a noisy touch-last round the plinths of the chilling statuary, when Porphyry came among them carrying some leaves of his work on the Return of the Soul. At the same time Plotinus entered the colonnade from the opposite end, and perceived his self-appointed editor was in a state of elation. The children, who had quietened at the advent of Porphyry, now flew to Plotinus, the youngest of them holding out both arms; while an elder one said in explanation to the guest that Plotinus had been sick.

'What was it?' Porphyry asked when the joy abated.

'It was, I believe, our friend Olympius.'

'It was, it surely was. For last time I saw him he said he was suffering so unbearably in his attempts to bring a star-stroke on you he was giving up.'

'I believe,' said Plotinus 'the reciprocity of my daemon with the souls of the stars is too close to let them launch such a malignant ray upon me. But I knew what he was up to for I felt that my limbs were squeezed together and my body felt like a money-bag pulled tight.' He looked amused. 'Poor Olympius, he came here once when you were absent and we had a discussion on contemplation. I quoted to him from my best defence of our traditional philosophy, which I shall soon have ready for you: "No contemplation no God!" '

'I don't think that would trouble him.'

'For us,' Plotinus answered in his usual quiet manner, and with his hand on one of those curly heads, 'in the beginning is the One, from this all else is. We approach by thought, in so far as, because we are Here, we employ our human reason; but this very thought unthought by our conscious mind is in God.'

'You do not, I know, hold with magic or theurgy either, although they call you the "god-taught".'

'That is a title of my master, Ammonius. It seems to me, Porphyry, there is a difference between a man regarding himself as taught or inspired by God and his trying to use a god to achieve ends he desires Here. Magic, and the practices of natural magic, are not of interest to a thinker because he has no fleeting desires to which he would be prepared to direct the energies he inclines to the intellectual-principle alone. Because the nature of all is mixed it is possible for things to be used to influence others. Nothing is outside the All, which we may see in this discussion as unity comprising variety, so that everything within it is not without effect on all other beings and presences; and the magician by concentrating his experience of the patterns of power may seem to bring some longed for reward to the reasonless soul. Or, on the other hand, to work harm on a thing so susceptible to fear. We are all acquainted with the power of fascination. And with panic terror. What we look to draws us magically if we consent to be deflected from the highest God.

'Contemplation alone stands untouched by magic.'

'If it has nothing in philosophers, what of the people?'

' "Their entire life is a bewitchment." Most concentrated this at certain times: birth, marriage, death, religious rites. The power of

221

priests is concerned with this universal concentration; it is their business to see to it the potent belief in magic is wisely directed, that through it the plebs approach the Good.'

'So you would have worship of the gods in the way of popular religion to be an act of magic?'

' "There is no magic when actions recognised as good are performed with the recollection that the veritable good is elsewhere." '

The echoing voices of the children had ceased long ago, there was the chill of the end of a winter day, shadows were presences and the statues drifted past them as they moved like the processions of mist up a mountain valley. Gemina with a lamp appeared between the pillars scattering the eeriness, but Plotinus knew at once she was anxious, and went to meet her.

'The child you call Fauna is in a fever, we cannot quiet her or make her rest. Will you come?'

'Our friend Porphyry is himself a library,' Plotinus said, assenting, 'No scholar could desire better stocked shelves, when he is with us I never open a book but simply call on him. Perhaps for all that he will not mind waiting in mine?'

'Not if you let me have the treatise you were speaking of.'

The room with a fire dancing and parchments and codices lying in uninviting confusion, a bust of Homer on a pedestal and a single spray of yellow flowers, had such an air of secret withdrawal as they halted in the doorway, and Gemina raised the light, that they neither spoke nor entered. At length Porphyry said, moving forward with a dedicatory gesture: 'I did not know I was so handsome.'

'As if we did not know there was such a room in the house, as often in dreams, and opening a door discovered this for the first time.'

But Plotinus went straight to the hearth.

'Is that a dog?' Porphyry asked, seeing a brown tangle.

A flushed face was turned upwards at the word and at once buried again in the bearskin rug. They could not tell whether she was shaking with temper, tears or fever. 'I didn't know she'd come here!' Gemina exclaimed. 'She's been running wild from room to room and will be so cold.'

At her voice a storm of passion passed through the little creature in the smock and her bare feet raged. With a sign to Porphyry the philosopher caught up two corners of the skin, the four were quickly brought together. Gemina led the way to the little chamber reserved

222

for the sick, and the two men carried the hammock rocking with fury within. When the other two had closed the door firmly and gone away Plotinus unrolled the bundle on the floor. The child stood up with difficulty and remained with her white feet among the dense dark hairs of the pelt and her hands pressing her head through the mass of elf-locks. Her look made him wonder if she were delirious, but he decided it was her mind that made her sick and that to touch her or to take her to the prepared and open cot would only make her violent anew.

He began walking the few paces this way and that the narrow space allowed, withdrawn in meditation; but the grief of Fauna found its way into his serenity, her tempest and torn heart identified themselves with his inward experience until his life of devotion to philosophy, his deepest intuition of reality, the intellectual-principle his king to be attained, even attained, by self-mastery, were nothing. Truth can know no conflict. Plotinus' heart and the heart of the child suffered together in the quiet of that rarely visited cellule until the air grew rigid as granite and there was no more life.

When the lamp Gemina had left for them began to drink again and raised a fraction of yellowish flame that wavered hopelessly over the boat-shaped vessel as though about to die, Plotinus felt something ice-cold on his instep and knew the child had come close to him. They were both trembling, and their nerves numbed by the extremity of suffering allowed none of the liberties and privileges of living beings. Only presently Plotinus found he could lift his hand and rest it on the thin skull, feeling the nature of it through crisp tangly hair.

Lamp and man and child recovered something of their customary virtue; the small foot slipped to the floor and hand in hand Plotinus and Fauna went to the narrow bed and sat side by side on the edge. Between quick catches of her breath the little girl told all her woe, ending with a confession of her terror at being banished to the sickroom. 'You are so cold now you cannot stay here,' he agreed, 'I am going to wrap you in the bearskin again and we will go back to the library; then you can grow warm and happy by the fire, and sleep, maybe listening to our good Porphyry discoursing.'

They stood up. 'But is God ever not there?' the child insisted, still shivering.

' "God does not leave off taking thought for us but we make ourselves unfit and think God is far from us who is always present equally to all." '

CHAPTER XIV

Alone

' "The uttering head that groweth not old of the whole world."
That is what they say of me in flattery, Julius, but I am old, and
those who say that, and turn aside from the foul breath that chariots
my eager speech, know it. For the uttering they are right, the
thoughts rush into the light of the sun; and with Porphyry's urging
the heap of treatises grows. He is even giving them names, I could
never do that, although each one has a unity of its own and tells
me when it is done. I cannot then add a single word, any more that
I can re-read one.'

'I can tell you another thing Porphyry has done for those who
come after, he has had a sculpture made of the uttering head.'

'He asked, and I refused to let anyone paint or carve a single line
of it.'

'He told me, but he was cunning . . .'

'Well, it is no concern of mine, the inside is all I am interested
in. It is time I was set free of this, from which indeed by nature I
have long been free.'

The two friends were walking along an avenue of trees planted
for the sake of their shade and stature and ornamental foliage. Under
the feet of the walkers many fallen leaves, arranged by the nymphs,
lay in a certain formation; the duller ones anonymously paving the
footpath, the brighter sown in the green grass. Dynamic as curled
slivers of metal, or as vermilion fish, thought Julius. And with the
thought he knew his being had taken a leap as a fish from some
element to which it would not return. The freedom from conflict,
suffering and thought confused with imagery that he looked to
experience in the company of the philosopher was unquestioned
now. He recognised it as the clarity of that aspect of his soul which
had not fallen shining full into the earthbound. This was *eudaimonia*,
taken not as the undividedness of time but the life of eternity. The
measured walk of Plotinus, which had such a singular power of
communicating to those who moved at his side, or followed him
through a busy street, the activity of his soul in pure thought,
thought without consciousness, was unaffected by the sickness of

body which was beginning to disfigure him. The silence between them was fulfilment. By the last tree they stood still looking through the spaces between the branches to light, blue sky and the drift of cloud.

'There is not greater happiness, as Homer says somewhere, than to be with one of like mind; we have an equal companionship in intellect and keep both to our deepest intuition of truth. Although, in our life Here, we may seek to show it forth in different ways. I am beginning to find it a weariness to deal with all the questions that arise in the school.'

'Yet Porphyry tells me you are more scrupulous than any other philosopher he has encountered in dealing with his.'

'I like this young man and he has an uncommon gift of scholarship,' Plotinus answered readily. Then after a pause, while an unfelt wind on high sent spinning and darting down a shoal of thin crimson fish and caused a shuddering in the pendulous foliage, he added: 'You will understand, I want to make my vision distinct to the one who has the ordering of my writing. For the sake of those who come after. There are certain periods in the life of the mind when the Divine Intellect flowers among us and the nectar may be gathered and stored. Perhaps it would be better to say, when things present, but unrecognised from the beginning, become realised through a different mode of creative thinking. You have a concentration of intellectual force which at once chooses and fashions its own instrument of expression. There may be a number and one among them supreme, as we see in Plato.

'The essential thing is to be true to one's own vision, to answer all who question seriously, in the light of that . . . for the light is itself the vision. Have no fear, Julius, if you are "swept beyond all you have held to by the very crest of the wave of intellect surging beneath". In the full light, knowledge without image . . .

'I am indeed concerned for Porphyry whose intensity of being sometimes brings him to despair. He wears himself out with studying and comparing and analysing and then suddenly finds the whole thing empty. The dangers of concentration are tempered by society, but then it has to use means to bind itself together which are a denial of free intellect.'

The next time Julius returned to Rome from one of his missions abroad he found Plotinus in the school. News had come to the master of the death of Zethos and he was speaking of the gifts of

225

this early friend who had healed him in the grove of Daphne. No one who heard was unmoved by the philosopher's praise of the life of the physician, and especially because they were made aware as he spoke of death how close he himself was to giving up the lyre, to which he compared bodily life. 'No one,' he said, 'used his more for the advantage of other men than Zethos, proving the instrument was not given him at the beginning without good reason; but the time has come for him to give it up, and it lies unregarded while he sings without the lyre. The separation of soul and body is no grievous thing to the man himself, he who has learnt to live in soul, for it is something well-known to him, not waited for but ever present. But for us who are left without the loved voice, the audible music, there is for a time discord; and our own music is mute or jangles.

'For our comfort at this time, as though indeed he had been summoned by Zethos, another physician has come to join our circle from Alexandria. He has once before visited Rome, in the early days of the plague. This time, he tells me, he will not go away again. But in his devotion to philosophy he will not forget his other skill for any of us who may need him.'

After that Plotinus did not speak in public of the Arabian healer but continued a series of lectures on the themes of the Living Being and What is Man. In this, and other discourses on the soul, he often answered indirectly the criticisms of men from the schools of Athens who said, after hearing him speak, there was nothing original in his philosophy; that it was a reshuffling of the teaching of Plato and Aristotle offered according to Numenius. Porphyry, in his anxiety to show his master's thinking was his alone, put question after question, until they complained of his interruptions. We must deal first with Porphyry's difficulties, Plotinus had answered with a teasing gravity, or my treatise will come to grief. At which Porphyry looked round excited and bright-eyed on them all and said he would ask but one more, the answer to which they would all be glad to hear: 'What is the difference between a scholar and an original thinker and how do men recognise the latter when they read him or stand in his presence?'

'Love of learning, love of wisdom.'

'That is a suggestion, but not enough, for surely both terms may belong to a scholar, who does not love wisdom less because it is that of other men living anew in him.'

'Porphyry's last question is a good one because the master tells us the soul of the All, by which we approach intellect, is upon each one of us. The vision in which we behold intelligible beauty everyone possesses, as he has said, but few use.'

'Even if it is given us to close our eyes and awake the inward sight we may have a clearer thought in that light but not one the light has never shone into before.'

'Then also there is the means of communication. How does one man find words to entrust to another something never conceived or spoken of by those of former time?'

'The thought once in the world Here finds its way from mind to mind; for there will be others able to receive it.'

'Enough!' Porphyry cried. 'Let him speak now.'

' "I sought for myself." This is Heraclitus, who began for us metaphysical thinking; the aphorism in its two-fold meaning may define the original thinker. He says also "the unrevealed harmony is more powerful than the manifest". And with this I should keep silence, which is the true response of the initiates.'

Afterwards no one could say the length of the interval during which each was with himself alone. The first to speak was Zoticus the poet whom now because of his increasing blindness they called their Homer. 'Now we have revered the god I think the second half of Porphyry's question is also answered. The cithara to which we tirelessly listen gives us the music not of a daemon but of the god who has chosen to dwell with Plotinus.'

When he was with Julius apart from the rest the philosopher said, smiling a little: 'That remark of Zoticus pleased Porphyry, who is always wanting the guardian spirit to become visible by some magic means. The Divine is in all men unseen, as Heraclitus has it, but the fitting moment for knowing it has the briefest measure; when, as Pindar sings, the Clashing Rocks stand still.'

'I think Porphyry is strained and overexcited.'

'He works arduously at his own works and mine, and too much attention to theurgy and oracles strains the fibres of being. There are more priests and proclaimers of every kind of religion in Rome than a man of his temperament can tolerate. He was better off in Athens where in our age the schools are cool. Here all is war, and the thinking houses and temples are under storm as are the frontiers of the Empire.'

'That is what you like, for it heightens the intensity of your philosophy.'

'The mind becomes a burning-glass of concentration, that is its energy. The act of contemplation attains the utmost lucidity. Some shadow of a vulture now crosses my limpid pool. I must go to Porphyry.'

'He is still here, surely?'

'He has already gone home.'

'I will walk with you,' Julius said, willing to experience again that privilege of being with him in the street.

Plotinus' intellectual power was so actively present in his motion and his perception, or imperception, of passers-by, buildings, the physical substance of the city was reflected into the senses of his companion through his own. When they came to the door of Porphyry's house Julius knew he was dismissed.

Addressing all the suppressed urgency and concern of the younger man Plotinus almost tenderly checked him: 'This is a case for my philosophy, which has nothing whatever to do with the shedding of blood; although for some this may be a necessity, and inseparable from sacrifice. The true end set before the soul is to take the light of the Supreme by a contact purely intellective, and to let this shine into the world Here. I have heard them call my philosophy bloodless. It is a thought of the Greeks that a creature without flesh and blood, as is the cicada, is akin to the gods.'

The door, which had been opened by the crippled porter, was closed again, firmly dividing them.

'Where is your master?'

'In there.' The slave pointed to an interior door with his crutch. 'He came in quickly and passed by without a word.'

'I will go and find him,' Plotinus said, reassuring the man with his voice.

He crossed the peristyle between columns of cloudy marble and opened the door with decision. The room he entered was bare except for table, stool and Grecian couch. Porphyry, who hung over the table head in hands, did not look up. Plotinus' gaze penetrated the back of that afflicted skull. He said softly as he went round to face the man:

'My dear, I believe you are doing too much work for us both. You have enough of your own. Let me take my treatises off you.'

Porphyry's eyes were glassy and unseeing, he sprang up with a kind of desperate violence saying:

'Leave me alone!'

It was a difficult thing for the philospher to bring himself to touch another full-grown human being at any time, but he put both his hands now on Porphyry's shoulders, shuddering, shrinking and yet rigid as they were. The man was furious, but the serenity of the face close to his began to engender a calm in his tempest. When he first spoke, and made as if to gather up some of the parchments, Plotinus had taken and hidden in his own garment both the razor and the phial of gold that were on the table.

'This place is holy,' he said in a voice of authority, that could not be questioned, and moving his hands down the arms, 'and there is nothing which is without a share of soul. Because of this, while we are here, we must give some care to our bodies, matter though they be. Soul dwells in and covers you.'

He brought the younger man to the couch and drew over him the purple rug he affected to match his name; he sat stiffly upright but some expression, as of wonder, was returning to his eyes.

'But you will not take your writings from me,' Porphyry said, suddenly remembering, 'although I have let passion break the harmony. How could it have been . . . ?'

He saw for the first time the marked look of sickness underlying the radiancy of his friend's face bent upon him, and he could have wept, but would not. Yet this release of emotion within began to restore the balance of his tired brain.

'I don't want to. No one will deal with them as successfully, I am sure. But you need to be steady to bring this torrent of mine into some shape, to grapple with my thinking and not let it over-master yours, which it will try to do. Let us make terms, Porphyry. You agree to go right away from this ferment, find a place of retirement among woods and fields where time is unmeasured and leisure is all about you. Then you can take what you already have on hand with you. Whatever else I may write I will forward to you. Is this a compact?'

At first Plotinus feared he'd said too much, and there would be an outburst or a falling again into despair, as the younger man made some cry of being banished from a god.

'That is nonsense,' the philosopher said in a teasing way that shot the gloom with light. 'I am very mortal as you see by the illness that besets me. On the other hand, if my daemon is too strong for yours you must go away until you recover yourself.'

'We have talked enough. It would help you to sleep. Lie down, my dear, you've only been lying up, as I call reclining, so far. When you wake you will know just where you would like best to go. The oracle will decide in sleep.'

229

Porphyry obeyed, turning his back to the room and with a gesture of misery dragging his beautiful blanket over his head. Plotinus went to the table, took up a leaf of Porphyry's work on the Return of the Soul and in spite of his poor eye-sight ran through it in a few moments. He sighed, and then supporting his head with his left hand so that his eyes were covered remained perfectly still. Porphyry kept moving uneasily and looked out more than once, as a child would, to make sure the master was still present. When he was convinced by his breathing Porphyry slept Plotinus went out, spoke a few words in passing to the doorkeeper, and left the house.

★ ★ ★

After the departure of Porphyry for Sicily the school of philosophy was even less frequented by the younger Romans; many of the older friends had died or left the city for their country-homes. Although he felt his energy for communicating his philosophy in living speech undiminished, Plotinus acquiesced with his usual temperance in this tacit withdrawal. 'I've given lectures for twenty years,' he rejoined, when Eustochius lamented the words unwinged, 'and I declare to you, my faithful friend, what you in your love for me will not doubt that I've said enough to have quite a powerful influence on whatever more stable mode of philosophy, and of theology also, emerges from this melting-pot of our times. I risk that prophecy. I will even add I think I have lived at the right time for this, when the whole Empire is imperilled and the old gods are suffering because men question all forms of worship, and doubt the potency of deity.'

'From what I can see of it here,' the physician grumbled, 'Romans and Jews are alike in reckoning the law is all. For those who must have something to behold there are rites that are best forgotten, at least for a man who claims to be a healer, if he has had the misfortune to be present at one of them.'

'Well,' Plotinus agreed, 'there may be a few in aftertime who know the life of Intellect, and that it is independent even of our consciousness. Now I have in mind to compose and scratch out a few more chapters for Porphyry, so he does not think I have abandoned him. And I am going to spend more time on the estates of the children which are in the care of slaves and feeble freedmen.'

Whenever now he entered his private room in the house he looked round upon the things there, especially those well-handled books and codices, his counsellors, from which he had been in the habit of reading aloud to give point to his lectures. Their time had passed,

230

he did not open one now except the sayings of Heraclitus which, written large for tired eyes by the hand of Julius, always lay on the table. He stood in front of Homer and looked into the level blind eyes of the sculptured head wondering at the gathering of divine gifts this man had had, and had poured into a form immortal for all mankind. Poets speak truth more vividly than philosophers. To each thing there he said hail and farewell before he turned to those crabbed accounts the stewards sent him, or to his own writing on *Eudaimonia*. Why should not intellect be active without perception?

Half stunned for the time by suffering which was increased by the sitting posture, he found a pen and wrote standing, one hand covering his eyes. 'As far as his own pains go, when they are very great, he will bear them as long as he can; when they are too much for him they will bear him off. He is not to be pitied in his pain; his light burns within like the light of a lantern when it is blowing hard outside with a great fury of wind and storm.'

At that Zoticus was led in, for he had free entry at all hours, by a young slave with hyacinthine hair, graceful as a Hermes, and doubtless, thought Plotinus, up to as many rogueries with his almost blind master. While the visitor was repeating with labour an addition to his long Atlantis poem, Plotinus continued in his mind the form of his essay on Well-being: 'Man is not the composite of body and soul, the real "we" is the activity of intellect; and the "greatest study", knowledge of God, is always ready to hand and always with him, all the more so when he is on the rack.' What did distract him was the speculative eye of the youth upon him and he suddenly decided he would leave Rome; leave that is to say the few who still came to see him, and the house of Gemina. The god within was bidding him go and with speed, while he had strength and will. Zethos was dead but there was still his country-house and Eustochius had said he would go with him anywhere.

When there was a pause he asked if he might borrow the boy to take a message for him to someone on the Capitoline hill. He wrote a few lines, the naked white foot lightly crossed the threshold; Zoticus resumed his recitation and Plotinus his treatise, the words coming faster than he could scrawl them or remember the spelling: Porphyry would see to that. The letters arriving from Lilybaeum conveyed that the moods of depression were becoming rarer: they brought an echo of waves on the shore and Theocritus.

Next morning the lawyer came whose uprightness and restrained sympathy made Plotinus liken him in his mind to the younger Pliny.

231

He was a friend of some years, and so perfect was his manner Plotinus was able to forget the foulness caused by his malady and the hoarseness that had captured his voice. All the business was carried through pleasantly, and not without an occasional pungent jest on the part of the master. What would be less easy was the farewell to Gemina who had laid out her family wealth without stint for the adopted children and for the needs of his poorer disciples. He saw her that morning of his landing at Ostia welcoming him to Italy with her yellow bridal veil. When the lawyer had gone, refusing to partake of 'a lettuce and two snails', Plotinus went to find Gemina in the room full of all her treasures and a stream of sunlight, so that that 'simplicity of colour' which had always delighted him was bright to his failing sight.

The scene, now and for ever and never again, stuffs and metals taking the light, the melodies in the voices of the women, the children practising music, or running, moving their thin arms for mere pleasure of supple bending; he stood in silence for an hour watching all this which made his soul conscious of inward beauty. No one spoke to him or even seemed to notice him, yet the children knew a certain happy excitement in their pursuits because they were within his contemplation. And Gemina attended to whatever was brought before her with a sense that everything today touched her with revivifying grace.

* * *

Alone on the porch outside the room which was always known as his in the house of Zethos, Plotinus passed an unreckoned period of nights and days, forgetting the hours and the foulness of his infirmities, oblivious of the slaves who did what could be done to help him. As long as he could he continued to write. Sometimes Theodosia would come and sit pensively looking over the country which for him was being lost in mist. He heard the quick-falling summer rain, and smelt the hot earth suddenly drenched and refreshed. There was thunder, and the surging of those trees he remembered in their Arcadian groups, sweet chestnuts, walnuts and ilex, when the stormwinds fell upon them.

One day Eustochius, who paid regular visits to the villa, said he had to make a journey to Puteoli. Plotinus willingly agreed and then as soon as the doctor had left him, knew himself to be worse. This will be my final trial, he told Theodosia who was called by the slave she had set to watch him, for I want to render to him my last word and thought before, with thankfulness, I depart. She asked whether he would like her to send a messenger after him, but he said there was no need; he has been so kind to me, I can I believe live and recollect until he comes back of his own accord.

In those last days many vivid visions surprised his inward eye. He was still 'lying-up', often with his head free of support as in the days of youthful meditation, but he could not leave the bedstead any more; not at dawn and the hour of bird-song, when the air was piercingly sweet; nor at the hour of lamp-lighting and incense of flowers. He did not eat even a crumb of bread, the Attic black *kulix* that held water from the chalybeate spring, much lauded by Zethos, was rarely brought to his lips. Yet he saw and loved the two-horse car, the charioteer holding a long whip bowed over the reins and narrow rail. Long he looked at the black steed and the white, their rear hoofs still on the dark curve of the planet's disc, their tiny forelegs already clear plying in space. 'They are racing off the earth,' he said to Theodosia. 'The light car with four-spoked wheel will soon be whirled up among the stars. You have given me a beautiful cup.'

When she was not near he returned to his skiff on the reedy Nile, gently the water rocked him while he waited for the sky to whiten with dayspring and the blazing Sirius star to narrow and withdraw his shining. Time was already no more for him; only the intermittent visions, the voice of Theodosia calling to him along the shore at Alexandria, and the cup stirred the fringe of his tranquillity. At length disturbed by some commotion of arrival in the distance he imagined Eustochius was at hand. A man stepped onto the loggia and came silently close, travel-worn with a reek of the roads about him as Plotinus' senses, acute in his dying, told him.

'Hermes come for my soul,' he said huskily; then as the man knelt: 'Julius! This is good. I have finished all my eloquence, my dear, and it comes to me now, there was far too much of it; one sentence, one word, would have done. I am as bad as Zoticus with his endless *Atlantis*. You remember that fellow in one of the Greek epigrams who had to keep himself alive for some reason or other a few extra days, his name is lost to me, he did it with the smell of new-baked bread. I'm keeping myself Here for Eustochius, and now you have come it will be easy. Better than bread. There was something I said long ago: "In sheer dread of holding to nothingness." I am beyond even that now. Alone. "He does not fear who loves to be alone." '

Plotinus did not speak again until Eustochius returned. He knew him at once and said: 'I have been a long time waiting for you. "We must try to bring back the Divine in ourselves to the Divine in the Whole." '

As he said this with his last breath a green snake came from under the bed on which he lay and disappeared into a hole in the wall.

'Once turned to God again it is
what it was.'

www.ingramcontent.com/pod-product-compliance
Lightning Source LLC
Chambersburg PA
CBHW021355090426
42742CB00009B/867